Packers Pride

Packers Pride

*Green Bay Greats Share Their
Favorite Memories*

LeROY BUTLER
and ROB REISCHEL

TRIUMPH
BOOKS

Library of Congress Cataloging-in-Publication Data

Butler, LeRoy, 1968–
    Packers pride : Green Bay greats share their favorite memories / LeRoy Butler with Rob Reischel.
        pages cm
    Summary: "For more than 90 years, the Green Bay Packers have been the model of excellence across the National Football League. Now, LeRoy Butler—a 12-year veteran and one of the most popular Packers ever to don the uniform—teams up with Rob Reischel to tell the stories of the Packers' most memorable players and coaches, including Bart Starr, Paul Hornung, Forrest Gregg, Jim Taylor, Herb Adderly, Willie Wood, James Lofton, Sterling Sharpe, Brett Favre, Aaron Rodgers, and Donald Driver to name but a few. *Packers Pride* looks at the favorite games, favorite moments, and behind-the-scenes stories of the men who played and coached for the team with 13 World Championships, more than any other team in football" — Provided by publisher.
    ISBN 978-1-60078-880-2 (hardback)
    1. Green Bay Packers (Football team)—History. 2. Green Bay Packers (Football team)—Biography. 3. Football players—Biography. I. Reischel, Rob, 1969– II. Title.
    GV956.G7B87 2013
    796.332'640977561—dc23
                                                                      2013030978

This book is available in quantity at special discounts for your group or organization. For further information, contact:

Triumph Books LLC
814 North Franklin Street
Chicago, Illinois 60610
(312) 939–3330
www.triumphbooks.com

Printed in U.S.A.
ISBN: 978-1-60078-880-2
Design by Alex Lubertozzi
Photos courtesy of AP Images

LeRoy Butler:
I want to dedicate this book to the real Packer fans,
without you there is no LeRoy Butler; my kids;
my hero, my mom; and my best friend, LeRoy Butler IV.

Rob Reischel:
For Mia and Madison—
You fill each day with laughter, merriment
and an endless stream of memories.
You're the greatest blessings I've ever received.
Love,
Dad

CONTENTS

FOREWORD

I am a Green Bay Packer.

I say that as proudly today as I did when I wore the uniform. And there is something special about this uniform and this franchise. The Green Bay Packers are more than just a football team. They're something bigger, and whether you're a player, coach, trainer, fan, owner, or anyone associated with the Green and Gold, you can't quite put it into words, but you know exactly what I'm talking about.

Being a Green Bay Packer fills you with a sense of pride.

There's a lot to be proud of, especially for a former player like me who was able to experience what it means to be a Packer firsthand. As one of football's oldest organizations, there is a rich and storied tradition that surrounds you as soon as you walk onto the field and see the names honored on the east and west sides of the stadium. There is the nostalgic wonder of the small town, the perpetual underdog and the last of its kind surviving and thriving in a big-market game. There is that winning tradition, the glory of Titletown U.S.A., exemplified by the great players and coaches through the years, including a man who not only put Green Bay on the map, but impacted the entire league and a generation.

But more than anything, what always made me feel the most proud to be a Packer was the fans, by far the finest fans in all of sports anywhere, ever. Make no mistake about it, while the Cowboys, Steelers, and even the Bears and Giants will make claims about their widespread popularity, the Green Bay Packers are America's Team—some could even argue, in the realm of American football, they are the World's Team.

A Packer fan is devotion personified. They know their team and its history and they are as proud of the uniform as the players. They eat, sleep and breathe Packer football. It is their fascination, their obsession. Week to week, regardless of who the Pack is playing, they win and lose with their team.

When I played and we lost (which didn't happen very often), fans would see us around town in the grocery stores, bars, restaurants, or on the street. They would always come up to us, ask us about the game, maybe drop a little advice and then all give us the same message, an encouraging, "You'll get 'em next time." They tried their best to hide their disappointment and show us just how much they supported us and believed in us. It got to the point that while we wanted to win for ourselves and of course, for Coach Lombardi, we wanted to win for the fans more than anything! We felt we owed them at least that for their support and devotion.

In my 10 years there and beyond, I fell in love with that city and its fans. It's amazing to me to think that I never wanted to go there in the first place.

I was traded to Green Bay from the Cleveland Browns in 1960 and I couldn't have felt worse about it. In fact, I almost quit, and I would have if a certain legendary coach hadn't called me and convinced me to give it a shot. Green Bay, back in the late '50s, had the reputation of no man's land, the Siberia of Football where players, coaches, and careers disappeared. I was disappointed about the trade because I had started to build a life in Cleveland. I knew nothing other than Green Bay was a small, cold town in northern Wisconsin (and some small towns still weren't as progressive in their tolerance of minorities back then). I was unsettled to say the least. The only thing I knew about the franchise was that they had lost consistently for a long time and while they had brought in a new coach that had showed some improvement, they were still a long ways from playing championship football...or so I thought.

I was wrong about everything. The lesson I learned in going to Green Bay was to never judge a book by its cover. That stuck with me for the rest of my life, as did many of the lessons I learned playing for Coach Lombardi. He convinced me early that we could win. The players he brought in convinced me we *would* win. And the fans convinced me that win or lose, as long as I was wearing the Green and Gold, I would have a city, a huge family, Packer nation by my side.

As I discuss in my autobiography, *Closing the Gap,* I was fortunate to find myself in Green Bay at an ideal time. Pro football was growing in popularity, slowly earning its place as the national pastime. The Packers as an organization had built a little momentum the season prior with its first winning record in years. Coach Lombardi, the fiery and inspiring motivator, was already earning his reputation as a coach that might be able to turn this franchise around (little did we all know that would be just the tip of the iceberg). Yes, I got to Green Bay in the middle of the perfect storm, and I was happy to be a part of it.

More than that, I was lucky to be a part of it. Not just because of the fans and what they taught me about acceptance, loyalty, and passion, or the players who showed me daily what dedication, guts, and a strong work ethic can achieve, but also because I had the opportunity to play for coach Vince Lombardi.

From the moment I met him, Coach Lombardi had a direct impact on how I pursued my goals and lived my life. Everything I did in football and beyond, I measured by him: what he would think, whether it would live up to his principles and expectations of me. That remains true even today. We all heard his words and we were moved by them each and every week. Those words made us champions. They weren't reserved for just his football team. Coach moved the NFL, the nation, and generations to follow. People like Coach Lombardi only come along every so often, and when they do we are all fortunate to witness what they can do. To play for him was the greatest honor of my life.

"How you play this game is a reflection of how you will live the rest of your life. Success is not a gift, it's earned."

"Winning isn't everything, it's the only thing."

"The quality of any man's life has got to be a full measure of that man's personal commitment to excellence and to victory."

I can still hear him delivering those speeches, motivating us to live up to our potential, to be the best, to be champions. Bart, Jim, Paul,

Ray, Forrest, Jerry, Dave, all of us…we all learned what it meant to be champions because of Coach Lombardi. And once we knew how to be champions, we spent the better part of a decade showing the rest of the league and the nation what it meant, how to do it right, and the pride we all felt being Green Bay Packers.

There was no greater example of this (and for me no greater Packer memory) than the 1961 NFL Championship Game. While winning the first two Super Bowls was impressive, it was that championship game that made the entire country aware of Green Bay, its players, its coach, and its fans. It was the game that built Titletown U.S.A., the greatest football city in the country.

In the 1961 NFL Championship Game we defeated the New York Giants 37–0.

We were the underdog, the small-town team on the rise going up against, well, Giants! While we were vastly improved and had even been in the championship game the year before, nobody expected us to win…except for us. We knew better. We knew what we were capable of and what we could and would do. We didn't listen to any of the pregame hype. We weren't intimidated by quarterback Y.A. Tittle and his high-powered offense or by the Giants' bruising defense. We focused, worked hard, and got ready for one thing and one thing only…winning, more specifically winning decisively.

The Giants never had a chance. By halftime, it was 24–0 and they were done. Offense and defense executed everything they wanted to with pressure and precision. As for myself, I played one of my best games ever, sacking Y.A. and putting so much pressure on the offense that Tittle told the press about me after the game, "He was always coming at you, coming all the time." It was a complete game, a perfect game. It was what we wanted, what we knew Green Bay could be. It was what Coach Lombardi expected.

"You are the greatest team in the NFL today," Coach said, and that meant everything.

We could hear stunned silence all across the country, everywhere except the state of Wisconsin and the pockets of Packer fans in other states that would start to grow from that point on. Everyone knew something special was happening here and we were just getting started. Over the next six years, we would build on that legacy and firmly establish our place in the record books and NFL lore. Through it all, because of who I played with, who I played for, and where I played, I was fortunate to earn my place as a Hall of Fame player, a champion, a defensive captain, and a better man for being a Green Bay Packer. Along the way, I would build several other great memories associated with the Packers on and off the field.

There have been so many incredible moments and memories in Packer history, many of which are remembered and celebrated in this book. There were plenty more championships and Hall of Fame performances in the reign of Coach Lombardi's team of the 1960s. There were the great rivalry games with the Bears, Vikings, Lions, and Cowboys even in the down years. There was Holmgren, Favre, and White leading the Pack back to glory and McCarthy, Rodgers, and Matthews doing it once again.

For myself, all other former players and coaches, Packer fans young and old, anyone and everyone who bleeds Green and Gold, we look to our past with pride, our present with pure devotion, and our future with excitement. We realize how lucky we are to support this team, to be a citizen of Titletown U.S.A. It's an honor that we embrace like nobody else now and always.

We are all Green Bay Packers.

—Willie Davis

INTRODUCTION

LeRoy Butler was one of the most captivating players—both on and off the field—in the history of the Green Bay Packers.

Butler was a four-time Pro Bowl player, a four-time All-Pro selection, and was one of the safeties selected to the 1990s All-Decade Team. Butler was an enormous part of Green Bay's rise to prominence in the 1990s, and helped the Packers win the 1996 Super Bowl and the 1997 NFC crown.

Butler was a dynamic player in coverage, a sensational blitzer, and a defensive leader. And when a shoulder injury ended Butler's 12-year career in 2001, he left the game with 38 interceptions and 20.5 sacks.

More than the numbers, though, Butler was always a conduit to the fans. While today's athletes have become more and more sanitized, Butler was always honest, accountable, and loquacious.

He felt the fans—those same fans that opened their wallets for anything Green and Gold—deserved answers. And no matter how bad things were, Butler faced the music.

So when I was asked to co-author a book with Butler, I jumped at the chance. And this unique project is one we hope fans will thoroughly enjoy.

Over the next 300-plus pages, you'll find several terrific stories from Butler. He shares his favorite tales about Brett Favre, Reggie White, Mike Holmgren, and several other ex-Packers teammates.

Butler tells you how he became the inventor of the Lambeau Leap, and he takes you through many of the magical games and intense rivalries he was a part of.

This book is much more than that, though.

Along the way, we interviewed roughly 70 current and former players for their favorite tales of being a Green Bay Packer. Their stories are gripping, riveting, and shared throughout.

The book is certainly unconventional. Many of the stories are told in my voice—one of a reporter who's covered the Packers since 2001. Many are in Butler's voice, which I'm sure you'll agree is descriptive, powerful and honest.

As you proceed, don't hesitate to bounce around the book. There's not a traditional starting and ending point, so to speak.

Find your favorite players and discover things about them you probably never knew. Or page toward the back and let Butler tell you how Reggie White helped Green Bay become a team, or how the Packers changed their entire defensive scheme during their 1995 playoff win in San Francisco.

In the end, though, don't miss a page. The subjects were largely chosen because they have unique stories about their Packer days, uncommon paths that took them to Green Bay, and fascinating tales of their time in Titletown.

Many of these stories were new to me. I hope you enjoy discovering them as much as I have.

—*Rob Reischel*

Packers Pride

1

THE MEN UNDER CENTER

ZEKE BRATKOWSKI

The job of backup quarterback isn't glamorous. It's never led to mega-endorsement deals, enormous publicity, or great acclaim.

But having a top-notch No. 2 quarterback is often vital to the success of a team.

Never was that more evident than the 1965 Western Conference Championship Game between Green Bay and Baltimore.

On the first play of the game, Colts linebacker Don Shinnick returned a Bill Anderson fumble 25 yards for a touchdown and Packers starter Bart Starr injured his ribs chasing Shinnick. But backup Zeke Bratkowski came on and led the Packers to a memorable 13–10 overtime win.

The next week, Starr was back and guided Green Bay past Cleveland 23–12 for the NFL championship. But it's doubtful the Packers would have ever been in that position were it not for Bratkowski.

"Bart and I never talked about No. 1 quarterbacks. We both had to be ready to go," Bratkowski said. "And we worked so close together and became such close friends. We studied together, we thought alike, and I think I made his job easier."

Bratkowski certainly made things easier for the Packers on that cold December day.

Bratkowski completed 22 of 39 passes for 248 yards. He also led Green Bay to a late Don Chandler field goal—one which Colts loyalists insist to this day sailed wide right—that forced overtime.

Green Bay won the game 13–10, when Chandler connected on a 25-yard field goal less than two minutes into OT.

Interestingly, the banged-up Colts were missing their top two quarterbacks that day, and had to turn to halfback Tom Matte. Green Bay held Matte to just five completions, and when Bratkowski got the better of the quarterback matchup, the Packers advanced to the NFL Championship Game.

"I'd like people to say, 'If we didn't have Zeke, I don't know what we would have done. He was always a guy who performed when Bart couldn't go,'" Bratkowski said. "You always knew you were just one play away from going in, and that happened a bunch of times. You just had to be ready."

Bratkowski was always that.

He played under the legendary George Halas in Chicago from 1954 to 1960, missing the 1955 and '56 seasons to fulfill a commitment to the Air Force. While many players would be bitter about losing two years in their prime, Bratkowski was anything but. In fact, he loved his time in the service and even served on the same flight team as future teammate Max McGee.

"I wouldn't trade my wings for anything," Bratkowski said. "That was an obligation I had and I'm proud I fulfilled it."

Bratkowski was Chicago's primary backup through 1960, then got a chance to start for two years with the Los Angeles Rams. But when the Rams drafted a pair of young quarterbacks in 1963, Bratkowski knew his days were numbered and shortly thereafter he was traded to Green Bay.

"I was really excited," Bratkowski said of the move. "The day before, I had gone in and won the game for us. The next day I got traded. I knew I really didn't fit in their plans."

But he was a big part of the Packers' plans. Green Bay's backup quarterback situation was in flux, but the addition of Bratkowski stabilized the position.

Over the next six years, Bratkowski started eight games when Starr was injured. And in that time, he threw for nearly 2,800 yards, 16 touchdowns, and completed 53.5 percent of his passes.

In addition to being one of the NFL's elite backup quarterbacks, Bratkowski was also Starr's trusty sidekick, his best friend, and sounding board.

"He was the best backup quarterback in the league," Starr said. "We were really blessed to have him."

What Bratkowski gave the Packers was more than just a security blanket. He also brought a level of professionalism, dedication and work ethic that rubbed off on teammates.

And his contributions went a long way toward Green Bay winning four championships during his seven years with the team (1963–68 and 1971).

Bratkowski certainly made Green Bay coach Vince Lombardi's life easier, although you wouldn't always know it. Because Bratkowski played under Halas and served in the Air Force, his skin was thicker than most players. And Lombardi was legendary for knowing who he could get on and who needed to be handled with kid gloves.

"I remember there was one year we were playing Dallas in the preseason and we scored two really quick touchdowns," Bratkowski said. "I came off the field feeling pretty good and Lombardi hollers at me, 'What the hell are you doing? You're scoring too fast. How do you expect me to get this team into shape if you're scoring that fast?' But that was Lombardi, always keeping you off balance."

Lombardi had a great affection for Bratkowski, though, and even offered him a job with Washington when he left for the Redskins in 1968. But part of the deal in Lombardi's departure was that the Packers wouldn't allow him to take anyone else from the organization.

That certainly didn't stop Bratkowski from a long and successful coaching career, though. Over the next 26 years, he worked as the offensive coordinator in Chicago, Baltimore, Indianapolis, Philadelphia, and with the New York Jets. He was also a quarterbacks coach with Cleveland and the Jets and worked two stints as a Packers assistant.

Bratkowski was Green Bay's offensive backs coach under Phil Bengtson in 1969–70, then came back to work for his old friend Starr from 1975 to 1981. Along the way, he worked with standout quarterbacks such as Randall Cunningham, Boomer Esiason, Lynn Dickey, and Jim McMahon.

"I wish I could have been a head coach," Bratkowski said. "I was just never in the right place at the right time."

But Bratkowski was certainly in the right place during the 1965 NFL Championship Game. And without his steady hand, the Packers may have gone without a title that season.

"That's a nice thing to be remembered for," Bratkowski said. "Those were great teams with terrific guys. And that championship in '65 was important, because it was the first of three straight.

"To be part of that was really neat. And to have had a hand in such a big game is pretty special."

LYNN DICKEY

Lynn Dickey was covered in sweat. He was physically and mentally exhausted.

Dickey had left everything he had on Lambeau Field. And as the Green Bay Packers quarterback looked up at the scoreboard, all he could do was shake his head.

"I walked over to [kicker] Jan [Stenerud] and I said, 'Do you believe this? We're going to lose this game. What a shame.'"

Not so fast.

Dickey's Packers led Washington 48–47 during a 1983 *Monday Night Football* game that ranks among the most exciting ever played. But the Redskins had driven into field goal range, and ace kicker Mark Moseley was set to try a 39-yard field goal on the game's final play.

"Moseley was automatic," Dickey said. "You always hope he might miss, but really, I thought we were done."

Rightfully so.

Moseley had been the NFL's MVP in 1982, when he connected on 20 of 21 field goal attempts. And with Moseley off to another terrific start in 1983, it looked like the efforts of Dickey and Green Bay's high-powered offense would be wasted.

Amazingly, though, Moseley missed this kick as time expired. And Green Bay and its sellout crowd celebrated on a chilly October 17 night.

"We kind of rushed it," Moseley said afterward. "Maybe we should have taken more time. I just missed the kick."

Moseley's miss allowed Dickey to walk off the field victorious in one of his finest moments as a Packer. Dickey threw for 387 yards and three touchdowns that night, as the Packers beat a Washington team that would go on and play in the Super Bowl three months later.

"Listening to people talk about that game today, you'd think about 250,000 people were there that night," Dickey said. "Almost everyone I talk to tells me they were there."

Dickey was just happy to be there himself.

Back in 1976, Dickey was a backup in Houston and simply wanted a chance to prove he could lead an NFL team.

Packers coach and general manager Bart Starr gave Dickey that chance when he sent washed-up quarterback John Hadl, defensive back Ken Ellis, and a pair of mid-round draft picks to the Oilers for Dickey.

"Bart's the guy who gave me a chance," Dickey said. "Bart's one of the few guys out there who believed in me."

Turns out Starr's leap of faith was a pretty wise one.

During Dickey's nine-year stint in Green Bay, he threw for 21,369 yards and 133 touchdowns. He still ranks No. 2 in Packer history for most passing yards in a season (4,458 in 1983) and most passing yards in a game (418 against Tampa Bay in 1980). He's also No. 2 in most consecutive completions (18 vs. Houston in 1983) and most consecutive 300-yard passing games (three in 1984).

"Playing in Green Bay was a great experience for me," Dickey said. "I enjoyed it immensely. I wanted to get out of Houston and get the opportunity to play and Bart had enough confidence in me to give me the chance. It was a wonderful time in my life."

Dickey led some of the most exciting offensive teams in the NFL during the early 1980s. With pass-catching targets such as James Lofton, John Jefferson, and Paul Coffman, Green Bay averaged 26.8 points per game in 1983, the most since the 1962 bunch averaged 29.6 on their way to an NFL championship.

Between 1981 and 1985, when Dickey started 63 of 73 games, the Packers averaged 23.4 points per game. Unfortunately, they also allowed 22.4 points per outing.

For the most part, that meant mediocrity, as Green Bay went 8–8 in four of those seasons. The 1982 campaign, in which the Packers went 5–3–1 and reached the second round of the playoffs, was the lone exception.

"How many years in a row did we go 8–8?" Dickey asked, knowing the answer, but electing to forget. "We had a decent team, but it was always one thing or another.

"One year, the offense would roll but the defense would give up a lot of points. Then the defense would play well and the offense wouldn't.

"Year-in and year-out, if you have a defense that can stop the run and an offense that can run the football, you're going to be one of the better teams in the league. And we didn't do well in those things."

Which meant Dickey stayed plenty busy. With a leaky defense and without a 1,000-yard rusher, Dickey and his sensational receiving targets were often asked to carry the team.

While Dickey embraced the opportunity, opposing defensive players often embraced him. Through the years, the less-than-agile Dickey suffered great punishment and would eventually have 10 different surgeries—four on a broken leg, three on his knee, two on his right shoulder, and one on a dislocated hip.

Dickey had plenty of weapons at his disposal. Lofton and Jefferson were as dangerous as almost any receiving duo in football. And while Coffman didn't possess great speed, his moves were second to none.

"I had no problem with my weapons," Dickey said. "That was a fun offense to be part of."

The crowning moment came during that Monday night game against Washington.

On that night, the two teams combined for 1,025 yards of total offense, 552 from the Redskins and 473 from Green Bay. The fourth quarter featured five lead changes, and to this day, remains the highest-scoring contest in the history of *Monday Night Football*. That's no small feat considering the 43-year show has produced nearly 700 games.

Washington entered as a five-point favorite. The Packers, on the other hand, were a mediocre team that would finish the year 8–8 in what would be Bart Starr's ninth and final season as head coach.

Before the game, the mild-mannered Starr gathered his team, turned out the lights and put on an overhead projector. Up came a quote from Redskins tight end Don Warren that read, "The game is going to be a rout."

"Bart showed us all the quote again," Dickey said. "But then he said something new. He said, '[Warren] thinks it's going to be rout. But he never said which way. Now let's go kick some ass!' Now that was cool! Bart just never said stuff like that. I'll never forget that."

The night was unforgettable on many levels, though.

Packers tight end Paul Coffman, who caught six passes for 124 yards that night, had two first-half touchdowns as Green Bay raced to a 24–20 lead at intermission.

"I remember getting home after that game and friends of mine from around the league had left messages like, 'You're going back to the Pro Bowl,'" Coffman recalled. "That was a great game."

The second half was a see-saw affair, and Washington took a 47–45 lead after Theismann threw a five-yard TD pass to running back Joe Washington. Back came the Packers, though, marching 56 yards to set up Stenerud for a 20-yard field goal with just 54 seconds left that gave Green Bay a 48–47 lead.

That drive capped an unforgettable night for Green Bay's offense. Coordinator Bob Schnelker had a terrific game plan, the Packers' skill players were outstanding, and the offensive line stymied Redskins standout defensive end Dexter Manley.

"Dexter had kind of spouted off in the papers before that game that he was going to wreak havoc," Packers left tackle Karl Swanke said. "Well, there were no disruptions with Lynn.

"And that night was a culmination for Bob Schnelker and our offense. Everything he called worked to perfection. It was an incredible night."

After the 1983 campaign, Starr was replaced by Forrest Gregg. And following two more 8–8 seasons, Gregg had pretty much cleaned house.

That meant Randy Wright was Gregg's quarterbacking choice in 1986 and Dickey was gone. Two seasons later, Gregg was gone himself.

"Bart and Forrest were like night and day," Dickey said. "Bart would work you extremely hard physically. I've never worked harder than I did under Bart. But he treated people with decency and treated you like a man.

"Forrest came in and he yelled at you and he insulted you in front of the team. Some things went on with him that would never work at any level.

"I remember our first meeting with Forrest, he was berating guys he didn't even know. He said, 'Some of you guys have been living on easy street. Like you [Larry] McCarren.' Well, Larry McCarren was probably the hardest-working guy on the team, making about $220,000 a year.

"Forrest knew his X's and O's, but he had no idea about people skills. And he brought in his own guys and they walked all over him.

"They were late for meetings and Forrest would say, 'If that happens again you'll be out of here.' Well by the 10th week of the year, it was the same idle threats. They knew they weren't going anywhere. It was a bad situation."

Dickey still watches the Packers, and the entire league for that matter, religiously.

He's a member of the Packer Hall of Fame and still attends several Packer-related functions. And he'll always reflect on his days in a Green Bay uniform with a smile.

"The fans there are like no other," Dickey said. "I always said if you're 14–0 or 0–14, the stands are going to be full and the people will support you.

"And to be honest, while I was playing I realized how lucky I was to be doing the thing that I wanted to do. How many people can say that? It was a great time."

BRETT FAVRE

Here's why there will never be another Brett Favre in the world—
ever—and I tell people this all the time. He broke the mold. I've
heard the rumors about him not studying and all that, but believe me,
that's completely untrue.

He was maybe one of the smartest quarterbacks to ever play the
game. I don't know who put those rumors out there, but I remember
a writer—a national writer—asked me about it in 1997. He said, "Is
Brett just getting by on talent?"

I said, "Dude, the guy gets there early, he stays late, and he loves
his teammates."

He knew the playbook. He knew it as well as anybody in that building. And if you know the playbook like that, do you really need to be
there 15 hours? You know your stuff, you run the same offense every
year, so what if you're not sleeping at the facility.

But here's why they'll never be another Brett Favre. When Brett
Favre got there, you had black guys playing a game of spades, white
guys playing backgammon, the younger guys playing video games,
the older guys playing hearts.

But it was different once Brett got there. Brett fit in with every
culture.

He'd go over to the brothers and listen to hip-hop. He'd go over to
the white guys and listen to country. He'd go hang out with the hunters,
he'd go hang with the young guys. There was no guy that ever did that.

Hell, I never did that.

It's nice when organically, someone can fit in with everybody else,
and Brett did that. When he came in the locker room he didn't wait

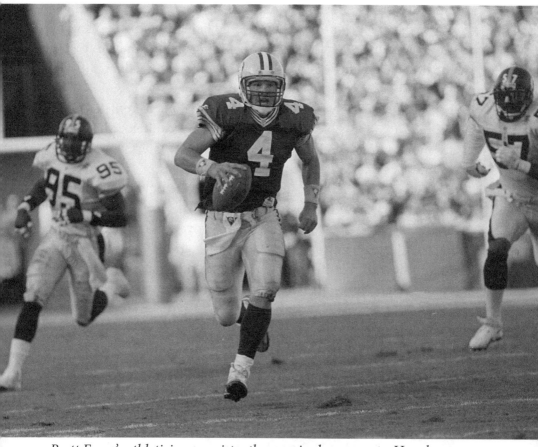

Brett Favre's athleticism consistently surprised opponents. Here he runs for a first down in a 1992 game against the Steelers.

for people to come over to him. He went over to people. And that wasn't publicized. He didn't want the publicity of that.

But he was an unbelievable teammate. I'm telling you, no quarterback has ever done that—to realize there's so many different cultures in the locker room and to fit in with all of them. It was amazing.

He knew how to do that. He got that from his dad. He was tough as nails and I don't think any other quarterback has ever done that. I've never even heard of that. Brett would crowbar his way in there, and I don't think I ever met a guy like that. He thought it was so important.

He didn't even know how to play spades, but he'd be yelling, "I got next." He didn't like hip-hop, but he would dance to it. He didn't want to get up at 4:00 in the morning to go hunting before practice at 9:00, but he did it. He didn't want to go to some of these functions with us, but he did it because he loved his teammates.

I don't think there was ever a guy that loved his teammates more than Brett. It's impossible to think that someone could love his teammates more. I don't think anybody ever put more energy into loving his teammates than Brett did.

And it bothered me after he left the Jets when guys were taking shots at him, because I knew it was bullshit. The guy I know doesn't change. Everywhere he's ever gone, people love this guy. He was the quintessential team guy.

I've always felt that if I was in a foxhole with somebody, I'd want a son of a bitch that won't put his gun down when I'm asleep, someone that will give his life for me. That's Brett Favre. I want him in my foxhole.

He used to give rookies his truck. Brand new truck to run around in and he'd say, "I can get another ride." I mean, who does that? He got along with all the races, all the cultures. They broke the mold on Brett Favre.

A lot of the negativity today is a misconception from when he went to Minnesota. That kind of stuff happens, but he'll get his due someday. Right now, his career ends with a dot, dot, dot. There's a "To be continued" until he gets in front of the camera and says what he wants to say. Until then, he has to speak through his teammates.

Ted Thompson doesn't care about that stuff from the past. He cares about what's going on now. He couldn't care less about the past, but Ron Wolf really cared about *how* players exited. And after you left, Ron still cared a lot about you. Ted could give a crap.

But Ted hates standing in the way of Brett having his jersey retired. If Brett was coming, Ted would be there clapping and smiling. But it isn't for Ted to do. That's Mark Murphy's call. Mark Murphy, by the way, was the perfect guy to replace Bob Harlan. We all loved Bob Harlan, and Murphy's been great. Murphy's the most approachable guy I've ever seen in that position. I love Mark Murphy. And as for Ted, he isn't thinking about Brett Favre. Brett might have some angst on Ted and all that, but he needs to understand something. His legacy is way bigger than that. Brett needs to think about the people and the fans. If I was talking to him right now I'd say, "Your fans are bigger than that. That 'G' on the helmet is bigger than that. And we want you to come back and have a good time."

But Brett understood what would probably happen when he went to Minnesota. He knew everybody was going to hate him. We don't like anybody with purple jerseys. Greg Jennings is going to go through the same thing now. We know it's a business. Business is business. But you're still going to get booed.

But Brett was a one-in-a-million, unbelievable dude. Like I said, they broke the mold with Brett.

MATT FLYNN

Aaron Rodgers, Brett Favre, Lynn Dickey, Don Horn, and Cecil Isbell. That was the list of Green Bay Packers quarterbacks that had thrown for five touchdowns in a single football game.

Until January 1, 2012.

That's the day Matt Flynn went from a little-known backup quarterback in Green Bay to a folk hero in one afternoon.

During the Packers' 2011 regular season finale, Flynn got just his second career start because Green Bay wanted to keep Rodgers healthy for the postseason. By the end of the day, Flynn had etched his name in Packer history.

In one of the most stunning performances in team history, Flynn set a new Packers record by throwing for six touchdowns. Flynn also completed 31 of 44 passes for a franchise record 480 yards that powered Green Bay past visiting Detroit 45–41.

"It was clearly one of the best performances I've been a part of," said Packers head coach Mike McCarthy, who's coached players like Joe Montana, Favre, and Rodgers. "No doubt about it. I can't say enough about Matt Flynn.

"The whole world got to see what we see every day. He's a talented young man. He has full control of the offense. But just the way he plays, he's very even-keeled, he had some bumps in the road, and he just stayed the course."

The Packers needed every bit of Flynn's brilliance on a day where the two offenses put up video game numbers. Fortunately for Green Bay, Flynn made every throw imaginable on a chilly day with wind gusts that exceeded 20 miles per hour.

"We told you all all week that Matt was a gamer and we had 100 percent confidence in Matt," Packers wideout James Jones said. "He just showed the world what Matt Flynn can do and he can do it really well.

"You can't say he's going to throw for six touchdowns, but we knew what he was capable of doing. That's the type of game it was. He came out there, it was a shootout, and we were able to throw the ball and make some plays down the field."

Prior to this contest, Flynn had made one career start—an impressive three-touchdown performance during a 2010 loss in New England. Flynn had thrown just 88 career passes, appeared in only 18 games mostly in mop-up duty, and was an enigma to much of the National Football League.

But Flynn changed all that against the Lions.

"We have a great offense," Flynn said. "We have great coaches and [McCarthy] has been here for a number of years now and I've been here for four and I've seen the offense progress each year, little things we do differently here and there that we've learned from the past that didn't work.

"The offense has grown and we're in an offense that's the best play available. So if we have a play called and we don't have a good look and we have a better look somewhere else, we can change it. We have the freedom to do that. I think that's what really helps us, not to mention the weapons we have all around us."

Flynn certainly made the most of his weapons with a variety of first-rate throws.

Flynn threw a nifty jump ball that Jordy Nelson adjusted to and hauled in for a 36-yard TD. Flynn also threw a perfect ball down the seam to Nelson for a 58-yard score.

Flynn hit Donald Driver on a crossing route for a 35-yard TD and fired a gorgeous fade to James Jones on the game-winning drive. Finally, Flynn capped off his big afternoon with a back shoulder bullet to Jermichael Finley for the game-winning score.

"It was unbelievable," Nelson said. "We're extremely excited for Matt in this locker room, especially after the way he played last year in New

England and didn't get to come away with the win, and then come out here and reset the records that he broke today, and get the win."

Flynn finished with TD passes of 7, 80, 36, 58, 35, and 4 yards. And Flynn joined Dan Marino and Kurt Warner as the only players to throw three or more touchdowns in their first two starts.

Flynn also joined Y.A. Tittle (1962), Joe Namath (1972), and Joe Montana (1990) as the only quarterbacks to ever throw for 475 yards and six TDs in the same game. And Flynn's 480 passing yards broke Dickey's team mark of 418 set in 1980.

"It's humbling," Flynn said. "I'm honored to have the opportunity to do it and just think about all the great quarterbacks that have come through here. It's very humbling and I thank everybody around me and everything.

"I couldn't have done it, obviously, by myself, but there's weapons all around me and the line did a great job. It was just one of those games where it got to be a shootout. We just kept matching each other and that's kind of why you saw the numbers that you did."

Flynn's timing was perfect, as well.

Flynn became a free agent after the 2011 season. And that off-season, Flynn signed a three-year contract with Seattle with $10 million guaranteed.

Following his record-setting performance against the Lions, Flynn knew deep down he had just made himself a lot of money.

"That is a mind game that you're going to have to stay away from," Flynn said. "Preparing for the game I looked at it as just one game. I didn't look at it as trying to prove anything to anybody or trying to prove myself to the rest of the NFL. I didn't look at it like that."

In the end, though, Flynn proved plenty. And he gave Packers fans a show that won't be forgotten anytime soon.

"I don't want to say we're extremely amazed because I think that takes away what he's able to do," Nelson said. "But I don't think anyone could have said he'd come in here and break the records he broke.

"It's awesome, we're excited for him; glad he played well. He made plays and helped us win a game. It was great."

DON MAJKOWSKI

D on Majkowski could be 50, 75, even 100 years old. And the former Green Bay Packers quarterback is sure of one thing.

He's unlikely to ever pay for another drink in tiny Green Bay,
Wisconsin.

Majkowski hasn't had to pick up a tab around Titletown since
November 5, 1989. That's when Majkowski had one of the most unforgettable touchdown passes in team history in a contest that immediately became known as "The Instant Replay Game."

"That's probably my defining moment as a Green Bay Packer, my
most famous play," said Majkowski, who was given the nickname
"Majik Man." "And I'm proud to be remembered from that game."

With good reason.

The Packers hosted hated-rival Chicago on a warm Sunday afternoon that was 53 degrees at kickoff. The Bears entered that game with
an eight-game winning streak against Green Bay, their longest streak
in a series that dates back to 1921.

The Packers had been a league laughingstock since the glory years
of Vince Lombardi in the 1960s. And Chicago had become the bully
of the NFC Central, winning the division five straight years.

Late in the contest, it appeared the Bears were about to extend
their streak over Green Bay to nine games. Chicago led 13–7, with
just 41 seconds left, and the Packers faced a fourth-and-goal from the
Bears' 14-yard line.

Majkowski dropped to pass, then was forced out of the pocket and
scrambled to his right. Majkowski got perilously close to the line of

scrimmage, then fired back across his body 7.0 seconds after taking the snap from center Blair Bush.

Ace-wideout Sterling Sharpe worked from left to right, got himself free, and caught an apparent game-winning 14-yard TD pass between three Bears defenders. The Packers celebrated like they'd won the Super Bowl. But that excitement was quickly tempered when Majkowski was penalized for crossing the line of scrimmage.

Chicago's offense came back on the field and television analyst Dan Fouts said, "No magic for Majik today." But the play went to the review booth, and replay official Bill Parkinson spent five minutes breaking down the tape from every possible angle.

Finally, referee Tom Dooley told the 56,656 fans at Lambeau Field, "After further review, we have a reversal. Touchdown!"

And just like that, another loss to the Bears became a 14–13 victory.

"Mike Singletary walked up to me and whispered, 'Sorry, kid. Too bad it won't count,'" Majkowski said of the Bears' standout linebacker. "He was a great player. He stared at me with those intense eyes during games for six years, and I stared right back. When the call was made, I didn't trash talk or anything like that. I just winked at him."

Parkinson said the deciding factor in his reversal was where the ball was released from, not where Majkowski's feet were.

"On stop and start on the instant replay, the initial line feed showed that the ball did not cross the line of scrimmage, the 14-yard line," Parkinson said. "This was a very important play. The ballgame hinges on this play. We took our time and looked at both feeds."

The Bears have never agreed with either feed. Chicago bemoaned the ruling afterward, and to this day, the Bears' media guide has an asterisk next to that game.

"It was a bad call—period," Bears coach Mike Ditka said. "Remember one thing: instant replay was put in to get the call right. I don't care how long it takes, but get the call right. Of course it was controversial, and we were very disappointed at the time. It was agonizing for both teams to wait while they reviewed it.

"But human beings make mistakes, and the call went Green Bay's way. It is what it is. You win some, you lose some. It was just one game in a long series between the Bears and the Packers. A series based on competition, which got out of hand for a couple of years. I was proud to be a part of those competitions and that rivalry."

That was the crowning moment in a magical season for Majkowski.

Majkowski threw for 4,318 yards that year—which at the time was the third most in franchise history. He led the Packers to a 10–6 record, their most victories in 17 years. And Majkowski reached the Pro Bowl and finished second to Joe Montana in the MVP voting.

"That whole year was just awesome," said Majkowski, a 10th-round draft choice in 1987. "We were in the playoff hunt for the first time in years. The whole community was so charged up. It was just a great time to be a Packer."

Majkowski's rise to the top of the football world was short-lived, though.

Majkowski tore the rotator cuff in his right shoulder in 1990 and never regained the arm strength he previously possessed. Then, Majkowski suffered ligament damage to his left ankle against the Bengals on September 20, 1992.

Young gunslinger Brett Favre came on for Majkowski that day and led the Packers to a stirring 24–23 win. From that day forward, Majkowski became Favre's backup.

"I could have been bitter," said Majkowski, who ranks sixth on the Packers' career passing yardage list. "But he was just a guy getting paid to do his job, so I tried to help him along the best I could.

"I knew my stint in Green Bay was done. So all I tried to do was help him the best I could while he was in his learning stages."

But Majkowski's place in Packer lore was safe by then.

Fans will talk about "The Instant Replay Game" for generations to come, and Majkowski is unlikely to ever need his wallet when he travels back to Green Bay.

"That game had such significant meaning to the Packers fans because the Bears of the mid- and late '80s were so dominant," Majkowski said. "And to finally end the streak at home on the last play of the game in such dramatic fashion is pretty memorable. And to this day, that game goes down as one of the five most memorable games in Lambeau Field."

AARON RODGERS

It was roughly an hour before kickoff on September 8, 2008. Aaron Rodgers was about to become the first quarterback not named Brett Favre to start a game for Green Bay in nearly 16 years. He was set to replace a living legend and the finest player in franchise history. And he was trying to win over a fan base that was still largely bitter over Favre's departure.

So as Rodgers plopped down next to teammate Ruvell Martin, he was clearly bouncing off the walls, right?

"Nope," Martin said. "He was calm as can be."

Which is just how he proceeded to play.

Rodgers finished the night 18-of-22 for 178 yards, threw for a touchdown, ran for another and posted a passer rating of 115.5. He also rushed for 35 yards and wasn't sacked a single time.

Most importantly, Rodgers led the Packers to a 24–19 win over archrival Minnesota.

"It feels great," Rodgers said. "You've got to remind yourself it's just one win, but it was a big one. I think the talk this week was a lot about the Vikings and I don't think enough about the kind of team that we had. So we definitely wanted to play well tonight and I think we did."

Rodgers certainly did his part on a night where all eyes were directed at him.

Rodgers became the first quarterback other than Favre to start a game for Green Bay since September 20, 1992. Following Favre's messy divorce with Green Bay, Rodgers immediately found himself under more pressure and scrutiny than any NFL player in years.

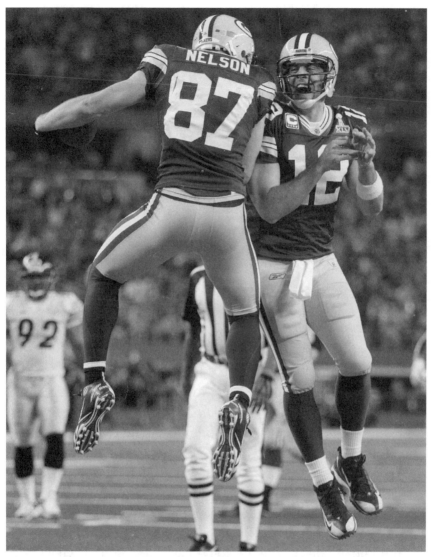

Aaron Rodgers and Jordy Nelson celebrate after the two hooked up for a touchdown in Super Bowl XLV against the Pittsburgh Steelers.

All Rodgers had to do in his first start was fill the shoes of the NFL's all-time leader in passing yards, touchdowns, and wins. Making things even more uncomfortable for Rodgers was the fact Favre had excelled in his New York Jets debut with a passer rating of 125.9.

But Rodgers never blinked during his entrance.

For the most part, Rodgers kept his passes short and simple. The Packers used more max protection than in past years, largely to slow Minnesota's vaunted pass rush. And Rodgers took very few chances in the passing game.

Still, he did enough to lift his team to a huge win.

"He did what he had to do," Vikings cornerback Cedric Griffin said of Rodgers. "Nothing special. Nothing great. But he executed real well and they won the game. Congratulations to him."

Minnesota linebacker Chad Greenway agreed.

"I'd say he did his thing," Greenway said. "He didn't kill us, but he kept the chains moving and kind of picked away at us. He was efficient."

That he was.

Green Bay's offense was brutal early on, some of it the fault of Rodgers, but much the responsibility of his reworked offensive line. The Packers had five first-quarter penalties—all on the offensive line—and managed just 43 yards of total offense.

Rodgers and Green Bay's attack finally got going in the second quarter, though, when they went to work on a Minnesota passing defense that ranked 32nd in football in 2007.

On the Packers' first play of the second quarter, Rodgers unleashed a bomb for Greg Jennings. Green Bay's top wideout adjusted nicely and made a 56-yard reception in front of Minnesota reserve-corner Charles Gordon at the Minnesota 6-yard line. That set up a one-yard TD pass from Rodgers to fullback Korey Hall on third-and-goal that gave the Packers a 7–3 lead.

"You know, I don't think he could have handled this whole situation better," said Hall, who scored his first career touchdown. "You can't imagine the amount of pressure he has on his shoulders right now and he went out and he was collected and calm.

"He played great, made good decisions, and I think he won the respect of a lot of people. I think a lot of people have more faith in him now. I think he's going to have a great season."

Later in the second quarter, Rodgers engineered an eight-play, 63-yard march that set up a 42-yard Mason Crosby field goal and gave Green Bay a 10–3 advantage. At halftime, Rodgers had completed 75.0 percent of his 16 attempts for 139 yards with a passer rating of 121.6.

Rodgers wasn't asked to do much in the second half, thanks to a 76-yard punt return for a TD by Will Blackmon and a 57-yard run by Ryan Grant to the Vikings' 2-yard line. Grant's burst set Rodgers up for a one-yard TD that made it 24–12 and provided what proved to be the game-winning points.

"I thought Aaron Rodgers played well tonight," Packers coach Mike McCarthy said afterward. "Number one, I thought he managed the game…I thought he did a good job managing the game without taking chances. Playing with the play call and taking what the defense gave you and so forth. So I was pleased with his performance."

In the years that followed, McCarthy's pleasure level would only increase.

Rodgers sat and watched behind Favre for three years. Then after Favre retired in 2008—and later changed his mind—it appeared Rodgers may never get his chance.

But the Packers opted to trade Favre and roll the dice with Rodgers. And Rodgers made that decision pay off.

Rodgers threw for 86 touchdowns and 31 interceptions during his first three seasons as a starter. He led Green Bay to the playoffs twice, then got white hot in the 2010 postseason and guided the sixth-seeded Packers to an improbable Super Bowl championship.

But Rodgers took his play to even greater heights in 2011, as the Packers went 15–1 during the regular season before losing to the New York Giants in the postseason.

During the 2011 season, Rodgers set franchise records for touchdown passes (45), passing yards (4,643), completion percentage (68.3), and yards per attempt (9.25).

Rodgers set a new NFL record with a 122.5 passer rating. And during that 16-game window, Rodgers arguably played the quarterback position as well as anyone had ever seen.

So when the season ended, it came as no surprise that Rodgers was named the NFL's Most Valuable Player.

Rodgers received 48 of the 50 votes and became the first Packer to win the award since Brett Favre, who won three straight between 1995 and 1997. Rodgers became the fifth Green Bay player to win the award, joining Paul Hornung (1961), Jim Taylor (1962), Bart Starr (1966), and Favre.

"I'm not sure there's ever been anybody better here," Packers wide receiver James Jones said. "I'm not saying he's better than Brett, but Aaron's my quarterback and I'm always going to have his back. And I'm saying I'd take him over anybody because I got his back like that. He's my quarterback and I'll take him over anybody that's playing today, yesterday, or in the future."

Rodgers had eight games in 2011 with more than 300 passing yards, which was a new team record. He threw just six interceptions, and his touchdown-to-interception ratio of 7.5-to-1 was a new team record.

Rodgers became just the third quarterback in NFL history with 10 games with at least three touchdown passes. And he became the first 4,000-yard passer in NFL history to throw six or fewer interceptions.

Rodgers continued to excel in 2012, throwing for 39 touchdowns and just eight interceptions. And through his first eight years in the league, Rodgers had 171 touchdowns, just 46 interceptions, and a passer rating of 104.9.

"People really count on me to be consistent each week, to play well," Rodgers said. "Knowing that my performance, the fact that I touch the ball every play, I have a direct impact on the game, the way I play. And if I'm playing consistent and doing things I know I'm supposed to do, we've been able to have some success because of it."

Few, except perhaps Rodgers himself, could have ever predicted this level of success.

Rodgers was an undersized high school player from Chico, California, who drew virtually no attention from collegiate recruiters. Rodgers attended Butte Junior College for a year, then earned a scholarship at the University of California.

After two standout seasons with the Bears, Rodgers declared for the NFL Draft a year early and hoped the hometown San Francisco 49ers would use the No. 1 overall selection on him. The 49ers passed, though, and Rodgers plummeted all the way to Green Bay at pick No. 24.

McCarthy was one of the prominent decision makers in San Francisco when the 49ers passed on Rodgers. Ironically, McCarthy later ended up being Rodgers' head coach. And many times, Rodgers talked about proving McCarthy wrong.

"I think there's a lot more in life that drives him than that," McCarthy said. "That's part of his history. It's always going to be there. It's not going to go away. So I'm very happy the way it worked out.

"Things happen for a reason. Life's about opportunities and it's about what you do with them. I never really worried too much about the opportunities I wasn't given. I always focused on the ones I have been given and he's a great example of that.

"I think he has fun with it more than anything. It's definitely an experience he can use, but also it's an experience to be a great role model with. It's a great story. If you want to look at an illustration of a successful person that's had hurdles in his life to overcome, what a great example."

These days, Packer Nation almost takes Rodgers and the quarterback position for granted. But back in 2008, Rodgers was still earning his stripes.

"It was a pretty special night," Rodgers said.

In Rodgers' case, it was the first of many.

Bart Starr

Twenty minutes.

That's how long it took for Bart Starr to know his life was about to dramatically improve.

In the summer of 1959, Starr was 20 minutes into his first meeting with new head coach Vince Lombardi. And that's when Starr knew things were going to be different in tiny Green Bay, where losing had become the norm.

At his first opportunity, Starr ran to the phone to call his wife, Cherry.

"I said, 'Honey, we're going to begin to win,'" Starr recalled.

There's no way Starr knew just how much.

Between 1961 and 1967, Green Bay not only won, it dominated. The Packers captured five championships, including three in a row from 1965 to 1967, and became the only team in NFL history to win three consecutive titles.

And Starr proved to be the ultimate triggerman.

Starr was named to the Pro Bowl four times and was the Most Valuable Player of Super Bowls I and II. Starr was the NFL MVP in 1966, when he had a quarterback rating of 105.0, threw 14 touchdown passes and just three interceptions.

Starr led the NFL in passing in 1962, '64 and '66, and set almost every quarterbacking record in Packer history before Brett Favre came along.

Most importantly, though, was the fact Starr helped guide Green Bay to a 74–20–4 regular season record between 1961 and 1967. For his remarkable accomplishments, Starr was inducted into the Pro Football Hall of Fame in 1977.

"You couldn't find a quarterback better suited for our offense than Bart," running back Jim Taylor said of Starr. "For my money, he's the best quarterback of all time."

More than five decades after his career exploded, it still seems remarkable that Starr is in the discussion of greatest quarterbacks of all time.

Starr was sidelined for much of his junior and senior seasons at the University of Alabama due to back injuries, and with NFL brass leery of him physically, he wasn't even chosen until the 17th round of the 1956 draft.

Starr endured three rather nondescript seasons in which he played under coaches Lisle Blackbourn and Scooter McLean and threw 13 touchdown passes and 25 interceptions. In that time, Starr never could win the starting job outright.

Before Lombardi's arrival, Green Bay's offensive playbook was a hodgepodge of plays gathered from various coaches through the years.

"Gobbledygook," Starr called it.

Immediately, that changed. Lombardi brought a system that was clean, simplistic and disciplined.

That four-inch playbook McLean used was now an inch and a half. While there were fewer plays, there were more options within each one as Lombardi spoke of the relentless chase for perfection on every down.

By the end of Lombardi's first year, Starr had won over his new coach with sensational performances in victories over the Los Angeles Rams and San Francisco 49ers to help Green Bay close the year 7–5.

"In Bart Starr, we're going to have one of the great quarterbacks in football," Lombardi told Frank Gifford on his radio show following the season.

Boy, was Lombardi right.

The son of a career Air Force master sergeant, Starr had the mental fortitude necessary to succeed under the demanding Lombardi.

While Starr's arm was far from cannon-like and he didn't scare anybody physically, few have ever been smarter. He understood every intricacy of Lombardi's offense, recognized all the complexities a defense could throw at him, and almost always made the right decision.

Starr led the Packers to the 1960 NFL Championship Game, where they lost to Philadelphia 17–13. It would be the only postseason game Starr ever lost.

Starr finished his brilliant career with a 9–1 playoff record and ranks as the greatest postseason quarterback in history.

Although Green Bay was always a run-first operation under Lombardi, Starr was always there to make a play when the Packers needed one.

"Bart almost never made a mistake," said Jerry Kramer, the Packers right guard at the time. "He was a caretaker for the offense, but he could be more than that if we needed him to be. Bart was exactly what we needed at that position."

Unfortunately for Starr—and the Packers—things weren't as rosy when his playing days ended. Starr coached the Packers from 1975 to 1983, when his teams struggled and went just 52–76–3.

"Going back to coach in Green Bay was the biggest mistake I ever made in my life," Starr said. "I was approached by the organization and it turned out to be an enormous mistake. I was extremely disappointed. I disappointed the Packers and their fans."

Starr retired following the 1971 season. Four years later, he was back as coach and general manager of a franchise heading south in a hurry.

Starr was inexperienced and overmatched early in his tenure. He was also left with an aging roster that lacked top draft picks after former coach Dan Devine traded five picks for over-the-hill quarterback John Hadl.

And in Starr's nine-year tenure, the Packers played in the postseason just once—the strike-shortened 1982 season.

"I accept all responsibility. I just didn't get it done," Starr said. "I haven't ever really sat and analyzed what went wrong.

"Early on, my inexperience hurt us, but in the later years, we had some good draft choices and we were beginning to make progress.

But I don't want it to sound like I'm making excuses. I just didn't get it done."

Starr almost always got it done on the field, though. But trying to get Starr to talk about himself is tougher than feeding vegetables to a toddler.

"The reason we had success is because that was a great football team," said Starr, who is among 12 players from Green Bay's Glory Years in the Pro Football Hall of Fame. "I was just one part of a great team.

"You look at the quality players and look at the leadership we had, and it's easy to understand why we won. I was just so blessed to be in Green Bay when I was and to be led by a gentleman [Lombardi] that's difficult to describe."

Describing just one moment as the best is impossible for Starr. Heck, when you're choosing between the Ice Bowl, Super Bowl championships and playing for the legendary Lombardi, you can see why it wouldn't be easy.

"I really think just the honor of playing on five championship teams in seven years is the best thing," said Starr, 79. "Being part of a team that was so unselfish was amazing. What we were able to accomplish was very meaningful, [especially] the fact that we were able to get it done as a team."

Starr still talks to as many former teammates as possible. And needless to say, his heroics on the field will make him a Packer legend for generations to come.

"I'd like to pay tribute to what are unquestionably the world's greatest fans," Starr said. "They are very loyal and very rabid. And I had the time of my life when I played in front of them."

DAVID WHITEHURST

Quarterback controversies carry a sexy, soap opera–type story line to them. But aside from making good copy and providing entertaining drama, they typically tear at the fabric of a football team, causing an organization to battle both internally and externally.

Back in the late 1970s, Packer fans were split on whether Lynn Dickey or David Whitehurst should be the team's leader. And while the Dickey-Whitehurst debate might not have drawn the attention of classic QB controversies such as Steve Young-Joe Montana, Phil Simms-Jeff Hostetler, or Brett Favre-Aaron Rodgers, it certainly struck a nerve with Packer fans.

"Lynn challenged me every day to be as good as I could be and I hope I did the same with him," said Whitehurst, who works as a home builder in Duluth, Georgia, today. "But through it all, I think we were really close."

Whitehurst means personally, although their play on the field was tight, too.

When Dickey suffered a broken leg in Week 9 of the 1977 season, the door swung open for Whitehurst, a rookie eighth-round draft pick out of Furman. Whitehurst's first start came the next week during a 10–9 loss to Washington on *Monday Night Football*.

Over the next four games, Whitehurst had a pair of memorable performances.

Whitehurst went 17-of-22 and led the Packers to a 16–14 victory over San Francisco. Whitehurst also guided Green Bay to a 10–9 win over Detroit.

For a Packers team that was 2–7 when Dickey went down, the finish—which raised Green Bay's record to 4–10— excited the coaching staff and fans.

"I thought I played decently for a rookie," Whitehurst said. "I was just happy to be there and all of a sudden I was the starter."

That didn't change the following year.

With Dickey still out for the entire 1978 season, Whitehurst started all 16 games and engineered Green Bay's 7–2 start. But the Packers fell flat on their collective faces over the final nine games, finished 8–7–1, and missed the playoffs.

Still, the fans didn't seem to blame Whitehurst, voting him the team's Most Popular Player in a 1978 fan poll.

Whitehurst's popularity began to slip, though, during a 5–11 campaign in 1979. There, he started the first 13 games before Dickey returned for the final three.

Whitehurst admits the fishbowl-type atmosphere that exists in Green Bay began to take a toll on him.

"All I wanted to do was play football, but I always felt I had people looking over my shoulder," he said of the fans. "I had 'em cheer me and I had 'em boo me and all I wanted to do was play.

"Back then, I didn't want the distractions. Now, I don't feel that way. But back then I did. I was too immature at 22 or 23 to recognize that. The fans in Green Bay are the greatest in the country."

All in all, Whitehurst started 34 consecutive games between 1977 and 1979, passing for nearly 5,000 yards and 21 touchdowns. So when 1980 rolled around, he fully expected to beat Dickey out for the starting position.

"At that point, I didn't think he was better than me," Whitehurst said of Dickey. "But once we started practicing and playing, he proved he was pretty quickly. And then he just kept it going."

Dickey did just that, starting all but three games over the next four seasons and shattering several Packer passing records in the process. Whitehurst, meanwhile, played the role of good soldier and quietly served as a backup through the 1983 season.

"I wish I had been more mature and appreciated the starting job more than I did when I had it," he said. "I look back and that was just a great time in my life.

"I played hard and worked hard and had a blast. Those are times you wish you could recapture for just a moment."

Despite Dickey's stellar play, Whitehurst did have a few shining moments after losing the starting quarterback job.

In 1981, he helped the Packers go 6–2 down the stretch and finish the year 8–8. In a Week 9 victory over Seattle, Whitehurst rallied the Packers from behind on three occasions, before they finally prevailed 34–24.

The following week, Whitehurst came off the bench and hit John Jefferson with a 41-yard pass late in the game that set up a Jan Stenerud game-winning field goal in a 26–24 victory over the New York Giants. And the next week, he returned to the starting lineup and threw for three touchdowns in a 21–17 win over Chicago.

Whitehurst's play was primarily in mop-up duty the next two seasons, but he did have one shining moment in 1983. In the season opener, he relieved an ailing Dickey and guided an overtime drive that led to Stenerud's game-winning 42-yard field goal in a 41–38 victory over the Houston Oilers.

When Whitehurst's career as a Packer ended, he had joined Bart Starr, Tobin Rote, Arnie Herber, and Dickey as the only quarterbacks in Green Bay history to exceed 6,000 yards passing.

"To be honest, I was a below-average talent, but I had the intangibles to make me an average football player," said Whitehurst, who played all seven of his seasons in Green Bay for Bart Starr. "To get what I did out of my career with my talent, I am happy.

"I played for one of my childhood heroes in Bart. And I was able to be around him at a time in my life where I was influenced very easily. And it's tough to find a better influence than Bart was."

Whitehurst has watched with great pride as his son, Charlie, has reached the NFL, as well.

Charlie was a standout at Clemson and a third-round draft pick of San Diego in 2006. Like his father, Charlie has been mostly a backup in the NFL.

While watching Charlie has been a thrill, Whitehurst admits nothing can compare to his time in Green Bay.

"Anytime I look back, I wish I would have appreciated it more," Whitehurst said. "Because that was a great time in my life."

2

PLAYMAKERS

DON BEEBE

Super Bowl XXXI was about to end.

Green Bay had dominated New England and was set to close out a 35–21 victory for the franchise's 12th world championship.

Quarterback Brett Favre took the final snap, dropped to one knee, then turned to wide receiver Don Beebe, who was in the game as a personal protector.

"After the last play, Brett turned to me," Beebe recalled, "and I asked if I could have the ball. Brett said, 'If anyone deserves it, it's you.'

"So I took the ball and ran through all the craziness to the corner of the stadium and found my wife and my family. I gave my wife the ball, then had my oldest daughter in one arm and my son in the other. It was a pretty special moment. And I still have that ball in my den today."

Favre was right.

While the 1996 Packers were filled with stars like Favre, Reggie White, LeRoy Butler, and Antonio Freeman, Beebe played an enormous role in Green Bay's rise to greatness.

And if it wasn't for his performance against the San Francisco 49ers in Week 7 that season, there's a chance those Packers would have never reached the Super Bowl.

Beebe was Green Bay's No. 3 wideout that year, and when he came to Lambeau Field for that Monday Night showdown against the 49ers, Beebe figured to be a role player, at best. Instead, he had one of the most unforgettable nights in Packers history.

"It was just one of those nights where I was touched by an angel," Beebe said.

And how.

On the game's first play, starting wide receiver Robert Books suffered a season-ending knee injury, and Beebe stepped into the spotlight.

The diminutive speedster caught 11 passes for 220 yards and guided the Packers to a dramatic 23–20 overtime win over the 49ers. Beebe's 220 receiving yards still rank third in Packer history, while his 11 catches in a game are tied for fifth.

Considering what was at stake that night, Beebe's performance was even more impressive.

Had Green Bay lost, the 49ers would have finished with the NFC's best record and earned home-field advantage throughout the play-offs. Instead, the Packers finished one game ahead of San Francisco, had the NFC's top record, and rode their home-field advantage all the way to a Super Bowl XXXI championship.

"When a guy goes down, you have somebody else who has to come in and play," said Beebe, who had been on the losing side of four Super Bowls with the Buffalo Bills earlier in his career. "And I had a lot of experience in the playoffs and big games with Buffalo, and it certainly helped me."

Nobody could ever have predicted how much Beebe would help on that critical night against the 49ers.

Midway through the third quarter, Beebe dove and hauled in a 28-yard pass from quarterback Brett Favre. San Francisco corner-back Marquez Pope also went to the ground and presumably touched Beebe's knee when both players were down.

The referees, though, didn't see the contact and Beebe wasn't sure if he was touched or not. So when Beebe didn't hear a whistle, he sprang up and went the final 31 yards for a 59-yard touchdown. The play stood because there still wasn't instant replay in the NFL.

"I was always taught to go until I heard the whistle and I didn't hear a whistle," Beebe said. "It was a big play, but there were a lot of big plays in that game."

Beebe had his share of them that night, catching two passes as the Packers drove for a tying field goal late in regulation. Then in overtime, Beebe had a huge 13-yard reception to set up the eventual game-winning field goal.

"This is a game that, honestly, I thought we had lost, and then I thought we had won it, and then I thought we had lost it again," Favre said afterward. "The Bills gave up on [Beebe], I guess, but right away we could see that he still had great speed and an uncanny ability to get open and get the ball."

Beebe, who played collegiately at tiny Chadron State, always had blinding speed. In the six times he ran the 40-yard dash coming out of college, he was clocked between 4.21 and 4.31 seconds.

Beebe played six seasons in Buffalo and had one of the most noteworthy plays in Super Bowl history.

During the fourth quarter of Super Bowl XXVII, Cowboys defensive tackle Leon Lett picked up a Bills fumble and began rumbling for a Cowboys score. As Lett neared the end zone, though, he began to celebrate prematurely and held the ball out to his right side.

The Bills trailed 52–17 at the time, but that didn't stop Beebe from playing his heart out.

Beebe streaked down the field and knocked the ball out of Lett's hands just before the goal line. The loose ball went through the end zone and out of bounds, which caused a touchback and prevented a Dallas score.

"I was always taught that it didn't matter what the score was," Beebe said. "You play until the final whistle."

Beebe certainly did that throughout the 1996 season, finishing the year with 39 catches for 699 yards and four TDs. Along the way, Beebe became one of the Packers' leaders.

"The day after we beat Carolina in the NFC Championship, Mike [Holmgren] asked if Jim McMahon and myself would both speak to the team," Beebe recalled. "We were the only two guys on the team that had played in a Super Bowl.

"Jim of course had won one and I had been to four, but lost them all. Mike said, 'Don, you tell the guys what *to* do down there and Jim you tell them what *not* to do.' So that was pretty funny."

That entire season wound up being a blast for Beebe and the Packers. For Beebe personally, though, nothing will ever compare to his magical night against the 49ers.

"That was a great, great night," he said. "But really, the whole year was just so special.

"Having been part of four Super Bowl losses, then getting a chance to win one, I think I'll always cherish that victory more than anybody else. I think what I'll remember most is the camaraderie and the leadership we had that year. It was just a fantastic time."

ROBERT BROOKS

Donnell Woolford could fly. Or so we believed.

Woolford, the Chicago Bears standout cornerback, ran the 40-yard dash in 4.40 seconds when he left Clemson University.

When Robert Brooks left the University of South Carolina, his 40-yard dash time was 4.58 seconds.

But when Brooks and Woolford squared off on September 11, 1995, you'd have sworn their times had been reversed.

We met the Bears on *Monday Night Football* in a critical early season battle. Early in the second quarter, we had a 14–0 lead, but we faced a third-and-10 from our own 1-yard line.

Mike Holmgren called a play named "Sluggo"—in which Brooks ran a slant and go. Brooks lined up wide right and was one-on-one with Woolford. Quarterback Brett Favre took a three-step drop and pump faked.

Brooks faked an inside slant and both Woolford and safety Mark Carrier bit on Favre's fake. Brooks then wheeled back to the outside and caught Favre's perfectly placed rainbow at the 32-yard line.

When Brooks caught Favre's pass, Woolford was at the 31-yard line and had an angle on Brooks. But the next 69 yards would show 40-yard dashes don't always measure true football speed.

By the time the pair hit the 50-yard line, Brooks' cushion was two yards. At the Bears' 30-yard line, Brooks led by three yards.

Woolford used his angle to try cutting Brooks off, but that failed too. By the 15-yard line, Woolford had given up and Brooks was on his way to a franchise-record 99-yard touchdown.

We didn't have a speed guy back then. Coming from South Carolina, I knew Robert. He was a fast guy; he might not have timed that fast, but he ran routes with sharp and piercing stops.

And there were about five teams that Robert used to destroy. Chicago was one of those and he used to have those guys literally scared of him.

They used to double him with Donnell Woolford, who was an All-Pro cornerback, and Mark Carrier, who was a great safety, and it wouldn't even matter. He smoked them both.

He certainly did on that night.

Brooks' heroics that night helped us eventually claw out a 27–24 win. And we went on to win the division that year for the first time since 1972.

At the heart of our resurgence was Brooks, who was just 6′ and 180 pounds. Brooks wasn't big and he certainly wasn't a blazer. But his routes were precise and his speed with pads on was comparable to his track speed.

I remember saying to him, "Man, they told me you were 4.5, 4.6, 4.7." And he said to me, "Don't always believe what you read."

That was the case with Brooks for much of his career.

During the summer before the 1995 season, all Brooks was reading and hearing was that Green Bay's passing game was about to fall apart. That's because Pro Bowler Sterling Sharpe had been released following a career-ending neck injury.

"I had a chip on my shoulder," Brooks said. "I came from South Carolina, where Sterling played too, and I had heard the same thing back then. 'What are we going to do without Sterling Sharpe?' I took that personally."

It showed.

Brooks had one of the greatest years in team history during that 1995 season, catching 102 passes for 1,497 yards and 13 touchdowns. Brooks' receiving yards that year remain a franchise record and his reception total ranks third in team history.

Brooks proved that season he belonged in the discussion of the NFL's elite receivers. And of course, the highlight was that 99-yard TD reception from Favre.

"I was training harder than ever before leading into that year," Brooks said. "That was the most memorable time. I was just out there having fun and smiling and felt strong the entire season. And everything worked out just right."

Brooks also fondly remembers his two touchdown catches— including a 73-yarder—in the NFC Championship Game against Dallas that year. More painful, though, is the memory of Green Bay's 38–27 loss that day.

"I'll never forget after that game, we were devastated," Brooks said. "But in the locker room, guys like Reggie [White] and Keith [Jackson] said, 'We're good enough to go the Super Bowl.' Our minds were set. The next year it was going to be Super Bowl or bust."

The 1996 campaign turned out to be a glorious one for us, as we won Super Bowl XXXI. Unfortunately for Brooks, he wasn't on the field for it.

Brooks began that season just where he left off in 1995, and we were averaging 34 points per game in our first six contests. But in a Week 7 overtime win over San Francisco, Brooks suffered a horrific knee injury.

Brooks was blocking downfield against 49ers cornerback Tyronne Drakeford. Drakeford pulled Brooks to the turf on the play and Brooks suffered a torn anterior cruciate ligament and a torn patellar tendon that ended his season.

"In '96 [against New England], I was there too," Brooks said. "And even though I didn't play, I'd say it was better to not play and win than playing and losing. When we won that Super Bowl, that was a whole team that won. And even though I was on the sidelines, that was a great team to be a part of."

Brooks made a tremendous recovery and won the NFL Comeback Player of the Year the following season after catching 60 passes for 1,010 yards and seven touchdowns. But the injury was still having an effect.

While Brooks' knee was sound, his running stride was affected, which put a great deal of undue stress on his back. Brooks suffered through a painful 1998 season, in which he suffered a herniated disc in his back. He retired the next year, then made a brief comeback with Denver in 2000 before retiring again.

"My career was shortened and I think about it all the time," Brooks said. "I wonder had I played a 14- or 15-year career, what could have my stats been like. I think I need to come back and pad my stats."

That won't happen now. But Brooks did enough during his seven seasons in Green Bay to earn a trip to the Packer Hall of Fame.

"I was a little surprised," Brooks said. "You never know with stuff like that. A lot of different things go into the criteria. It's an honor. I'm just very grateful people in the organization and the Hall of Fame realize the impact I had."

One the Bears experienced firsthand on a memorable Monday night.

FRED CONE

When Fred Cone found out he was going to the NFL, he thought he'd hit the big time.

The Clemson star fullback and kicker was drafted by the Green Bay Packers in the third round in 1951. He signed a contract for $6,500 his rookie year.

And he couldn't wait to get started. Only when Cone arrived in Green Bay, he couldn't believe what he saw.

"You could tell the franchise didn't have much money and was in a lot of trouble," said Cone, who was born in 1926. "Our equipment at Clemson was better, a lot better.

"We got to training camp and they gave us old tattered sweatshirts. The helmets, shoulder pads, hip pads, all that stuff was better at Clemson. We even had to buy our own shoes for games. They were on the verge of going broke."

They sure were. In 1950, the Packers had held a stock sale across the state and raised $125,000 to stay solvent.

But the effects of that cash influx hadn't trickled down to the players when Cone arrived. Still, they didn't seem to mind.

"I've told a lot of people, we would have played for room and board," said the 5′11″ Cone, who played at 195 pounds. "Guys from my era just loved to play the game."

Cone was certainly one of those.

A hard-nosed fullback and solid kicker in his day, Cone played seven years with the Packers. He never made more than $7,500, had to work in the off-season, and played on mostly losing teams during his time in Green Bay.

The Packers rarely flew back then, meaning train trips to the West Coast would often take $3\frac{1}{2}$ days each way. And home games were played at tiny Green Bay East High School.

Still, Cone was living a dream.

He was playing a game he adored. He met his wife, Judy, during his time in Green Bay. And he competed with players who shared his passion for the game.

"I'm glad I played when I did," said Cone, who's retired and living in Blairsville, Georgia, today. "Even though we didn't make a lot of money and we weren't winning, it was a great time to be playing.

"I remember the few times we did fly were usually to Detroit on Thanksgiving. We'd get back to the airport and usually we'd have just got slaughtered. But the fans would be lined up cheering us as we got off the plane.

"I know today the money's better and the food's better and everything's probably better. But I wouldn't trade when I played."

Cone wasn't Green Bay's starter at fullback. But because the rosters contained just 33 players back then, he often played as much as starter Howie Ferguson.

Cone also handled the kicking duties, and led Green Bay in scoring six of his seven seasons with the team. The only downer was the Packers won so infrequently.

Cone's first three seasons came under Gene Ronzani, a time in which the Packers went 11–24–1.

"He was a nice fellow," Cone said of Ronzani, "but there was a lot of player movement back then, and he was highly suspicious that guys would take our offense back to [Chicago Bears coach George] Halas.

"So during meetings, he'd hold up the plays on a big cardboard sheet. And he'd only hold it up long enough for you to write down what your job was. His way of presenting things wasn't real good."

Things didn't get much better under Lisle Blackbourn, who went 17–31 over the next four years. Green Bay's best season under Blackbourn was 6–6.

"Blackbourn wasn't as likeable as Ronzani," Cone said, "but he was a real sound, fundamental coach. I don't want to say anything bad about Ronzani, but Blackbourn knew football much, much better.

"It's just that when you don't have a lot of talent, there's not much you can do. That was our biggest problem."

There were countless good times, though.

Cone was part of a traveling caravan that went around Wisconsin in 1957, trying to get people throughout the state to buy season tickets and keep the franchise alive. He met Richard Nixon in 1957, when the vice president came to town for the Packers' first game at City Stadium.

Cone once ran for more than 100 yards against the Chicago Cardinals, kicked a game-winning field goal against the Los Angeles Rams and had a career-long 47-yard field goal against the Baltimore Colts.

He was also part of one of the all-time great pranks. He and some teammates rigged a bucket of water to fall on end Bill Howton, who was coming in late for curfew.

"He was just soaked and screaming," Cone said of Howton. "Plus, he had a wet bed to sleep in. But he shouldn't have been breaking curfew."

Cone thought his football career was over after the 1957 season, and he coached at a high school in Mobile, Alabama, the next two years. But Dallas summoned him out of retirement to handle its kicking in the 1960 season.

Clemson, Cone's alma mater, came calling in 1961. And Cone returned there as the Tigers' kicking coach and head recruiter—a position he stayed at until 1978.

But in 1979, Clemson head coach Danny Ford restructured his staff, and Cone was asked to head up the intramural program at the university, something he did until his retirement in 1988.

"Once Danny Ford got there, they moved me over to intramurals," Cone said. "Rather than fire old coaches, it's a lot easier to put them out to pasture.

"But I enjoyed that a lot. When I was recruiting, I was on the road most of the week, then would wind up wherever Clemson was playing on Fridays. This way I got a lot more time at home. It was like a vacation."

Playing back in the 1950s was nothing like a vacation. But Cone wouldn't change a thing.

"Those were some great, great times," he said. "You always wish you could have won a little more. That would have been nice. But playing in Green Bay was one of the best things that ever happened to me."

DONALD DRIVER

Donald Driver's remarkable Green Bay Packers career spanned 14 years and included 743 receptions and 61 touchdowns.

But if anyone is ever looking for a play that best sums up Driver—and his remarkable rags-to-riches story—all they need to do is pop in a tape from December 5, 2010.

Few will remember that the Packers defeated the San Francisco 49ers 34–16 that day. What no one will forget was Driver's 61-yard touchdown that ranks among the Packers' top individual efforts in recent memory.

"That was one of the best plays I've ever been a part of," Packers quarterback Aaron Rodgers said afterward.

No one was arguing.

Green Bay led the visiting 49ers 14–13 early in the third quarter and clearly needed a spark.

Enter Driver.

On Green Bay's opening drive of the second half, the Packers faced a second-and-16 at their own 39. Driver lined up in the right slot and found a hole in San Francisco's zone defense.

Driver hauled in a strike from Rodgers at the 49ers' 38-yard line and immediately spun away from safety Reggie Smith at the 30. Driver then ducked under a tackle attempt by safety Dashon Goldon at the 22.

Cornerback Nate Clements had an angle on Driver, but Driver simply shoved him out of the way at the 10. Three 49ers finally corralled Driver at the 4, but he dragged them into the right corner of the end zone for an improbable 61-yard TD and a 21–13 Green Bay lead.

Donald Driver breaks away for a 31-yard touchdown against the Panthers in 2002.

The Packers went on to an easy win that day, and two months later, they won the 45th Super Bowl.

"I thought Donald Driver's touchdown was the biggest play in the game," Packers coach Mike McCarthy said that day. "I thought it ignited our football team. We needed that.

"We had some plays where the ball probably didn't bounce our way or a call that didn't go our way and that's football. But I thought Donald Driver's play was clearly the biggest play in the game and then we were able to take off from there."

Rodgers agreed.

"It was incredible," Green Bay's quarterback said. "Donald made one of the most amazing catches and runs I've ever seen. When he was at about the 20 I was thinking, *Go down, go down, don't get drilled.* And then when he broke another tackle I was hoping he'd get it in the end zone. Like I said, one of the most amazing plays I've ever seen here."

Driver had been left for dead by many prior to that play.

The Packers' veteran wideout was in the middle of a quiet, two-month stretch. After catching 18 balls the first three games of the season, Driver had just 16 receptions between Weeks 4 and 12. Driver had also been hampered with a quadriceps injury and was the target of fewer balls from Rodgers.

Many had started to wonder if age had finally caught up to this Packer great. During that remarkable catch-and-run, the 35-year-old Driver offered his rebuttal.

"My whole thing is that sometimes you don't want to be denied," Driver said. "This week…last month you could say everybody was just writing me off, saying I was done. My thing is I felt like I had to prove something.

"Every year I've been playing in this league it seems like I have to prove something…and I'm okay with that because it just makes me who I am. Today was one of those things. I saw the ball, made the catch, and I wasn't going to be denied going to the end zone. Whatever I had to do. When I saw it, I wasn't going to go down."

That had always been Driver's modus operandi.

Driver was an undersized, overlooked, seventh-round draft choice back in 1999. And his first three years in the league he had just 37 catches and three touchdowns.

Many questioned whether Driver belonged in the NFL, but Driver always used the critics as his No. 1 source of motivation.

"I love it. I love the doubters," he said. "That's always been my thing. If you're not going to believe in me, I don't need you to. I believe in myself and my family believes in me.

"I don't get any newspapers. I don't see any of that other stuff. I just get to a point where I don't pay attention. I have friends that will send me emails that say, 'Hey, this person said something about you.' But at the end of the day, it's no big deal. People are going to say what they're going to say. There's nothing I can do about it. Just try and continue to prove 'em wrong."

Driver did just that.

When Driver moved into the starting lineup in 2002, he became Brett Favre's top target and earned a spot in the Pro Bowl. Driver would eventually play in three Pro Bowls and went on to set a bevy of franchise records.

Driver ranks No. 1 in franchise history in receptions (743) and receiving yards (10,137). Driver holds the team record with seven seasons of 1,000 yards receiving and is second in team history in games played (205).

Driver, who became a national celebrity after winning the coveted mirror ball trophy on *Dancing with the Stars,* stayed in remarkable physical shape. The 193-pound Driver kept his body fat around 4 percent, worked out twice a day, and ate only baked and organic foods.

"Donald's an unusual athlete," Packers general manager Ted Thompson said. "Remarkable in some ways."

Father Time eventually catches everyone, though, and Driver was no different. Following the 2012 season, Driver called it quits after a brilliant 14-year career.

"Even though I feel that I can still play the game, God has made the answer clear to me, the time is now," Driver said the day of his retirement. "I have to retire a Green Bay Packer. I've always said I never wanted to wear another uniform, but always the green and gold."

Never was Packer Nation more happy to call Driver their own than during his remarkable run-and-catch against the 49ers in 2010.

When Driver enters the Packers Hall of Fame someday—which is a foregone conclusion—that clip will undoubtedly be played over and over.

"He's Hercules," Packers offensive coordinator Joe Philbin said that day. "It was a great run. You've got to give him a lot of credit. They couldn't drag him down and I'm real pleased about it."

Just like the Packers were always pleased to have Driver on their side.

ANTONIO FREEMAN

When Free first got here, he was one of the best return guys I'd ever seen. I used to read this scouting report and it said, "Not real fast, about 4.65 40-yard dash." So why did he keep getting deep on our corners in practice?

We had a book on our own guys, and I told our coaches, "You're all full of crap. This guy is running past our guys all day long." And when they put him on the inside, on the slot—whew!

To me, Donald Driver was the toughest guy in the world and that's the entire NFL because he caught 70 percent of his passes between the white lines. A lot of guys don't do that.

But I don't think I've seen a smarter receiver when it comes to knowing coverages than Antonio Freeman. Once he released, he knew what coverages you were in.

I said to him once, "Come here, man. You were a return guy at Virginia Tech. How did you know that was Cover 2?"

He said he looked at footwork, looked at vision, because he always had a two-way go. He'd run this if we were in Cover 2 and run that if we were in Cover 4. A lot of receivers don't do that.

We called him Quack Man because he ran like a duck. But he was smart as hell. Damn, he was smart. He knew it. There were two people besides Brett who *always* knew what they were going to do—Mark Chmura and Free.

Freeman used to catch balls over the middle. I remember San Francisco safety Tim McDonald coming up to me and saying, "Where'd you'd all get that boy from? They told us he was just a return guy."

I said, "You better quit believing those reports. He's a full-fledged receiver on the outside and on the inside."

People kept telling us he was slow. In the Super Bowl he went 81 yards for a touchdown. He outran their whole secondary, but everyone kept saying he was slow. He had deceptive speed.

We have this thing—and it's a compliment to receivers if they can get it because not all of them can get it—called a number tree. A 2 is a slant, a 9 is a go. It's a number tree.

The reason why Jerry Rice was the best was that he would run the number tree at the same speed. Slant? Same speed. Go? Same speed. Antonio was one of the few guys who could do that. Not everybody could do that, so I could never guess what he was running.

His pad speed and his football speed were the same. Absolute same. And that's hard to cover. We knew what Randy Moss was doing and when he was loafing. We knew what Cris Carter was doing. With some guys, you just know.

But with Free, when he came off the ball, you didn't know what he was running and that's a tribute to him. And even today, I tell all little league receivers to go watch No. 86 because he's doing it all at the same speed.

Freeman was damn good. He used to rip Tampa Bay apart and they'd be doubling him the whole time. He'd say, "Roy Lee (that was my nickname), it don't matter."

Freeman? Damn, he was good.

JIM GRABOWSKI

Jim Grabowski was born and raised in Illinois. He played collegiately at the University of Illinois, spent a year with the hometown
Chicago Bears, and broadcast Fighting Illini games on the radio for
more than three decades.

But Grabowski's loyalties wound up resting with the team to the
north.

"There's no question, I always rooted for Green Bay," Grabowski
said.

With good reason.

Grabowski, a first-round draft choice in 1966, played fullback for
the Packers for five seasons and helped Green Bay win the first two
Super Bowls. And while Grabowski never developed into the Pro
Bowl player many thought he would, his career was extremely solid.

"I don't have any regrets," Grabowski said. "It was a good ride."

Packers coach Vince Lombardi took aim at his backfield of the
future when he selected Grabowski with the ninth overall selection
in the 1966 draft. Lombardi had drafted Donny Anderson in the first
round the previous year, and hoped the pair would be the next Jim
Taylor and Paul Hornung.

"That was a tough act to follow," said Lee Remmel, Green Bay's former executive director of public relations and the team's unofficial his-
torian. "I don't know of a lot of guys that could have lived up to that."

Grabowski and Anderson were known as the "Gold Dust Twins."
That's because Grabowski was given a $400,000 signing bonus, while
Anderson—the seventh pick overall the previous year—received a
$600,000 signing bonus.

At the time, NFL teams were bidding against clubs from the American Football League for talent, which drove the price to heights previously unseen. And that didn't always sit well with veterans.

"I know Taylor wasn't real happy about that," Remmel said. "But that's how it worked then if you wanted to get a player."

Grabowski certainly walked into an ideal situation. During his rookie year, he got to sit and learn behind Taylor and even scored a touchdown on an 18-yard fumble recovery in Green Bay's 34–27 victory over Dallas in the NFL Championship Game.

Two weeks later, the Packers routed Kansas City 35–10 in the first Super Bowl.

"I was just in absolute awe," Grabowski said of his rookie season and playing under Lombardi. "Here I come from the city of Chicago and I get to play with the world champion Green Bay Packers. I was half scared and half excited. It was an unbelievable experience."

By Grabowski's second year, Lombardi had cut ties with Hornung and Taylor. And the rushing load fell in the lap of Grabowski and Anderson.

Early in the season, Grabowski set what was then a franchise record with 32 carries against Chicago. Later, he ran for 123 yards to help Green Bay defeat the New York Giants 48–21 in Lombardi's return home.

By the end of the year, Grabowski led the team in carries (120) and yards (466). And once again, the Packers were Super Bowl champions.

"I just thought this is going to go on forever," Grabowski said. "And in some ways, the second Super Bowl team was probably more gritty than the first one.

"We probably weren't as talented. But we had guys step up and play well at the end of the year and do what they had to do to help us win.

"And in retrospect, as I look back on it, the best part was the guys that made up those teams. There were just so many class guys, guys that still epitomize class. It was an incredible time."

But Lombardi saw he had an aging team on his hands that was probably fortunate to defeat Dallas in the 1967 NFL Championship

Game on its way to a Super Bowl victory. So he bolted and handed the reins to Phil Bengtson.

The following season, Green Bay failed to qualify for the playoffs.

"Even with Vince, I don't think we would have made the playoffs," Grabowski said. "There were a lot of guys that had been around quite a while. We had a lot of injuries occur.

"And in Phil's defense, he was considered by almost everybody to be one of the brightest defensive minds around. We just had a lot of guys that had been around a while that weren't at the same level."

After rushing for a career-high 518 yards in 1968, Grabowski ran for a combined total of just 471 during his final two seasons in Green Bay. Grabowski, who played at 220 pounds, was known more as a fullback who was quick off the ball rather than the punishing type. But a knee injury caused him to lose some of his burst and explosiveness.

Grabowski finished his career in a Chicago uniform, but to this day he's a Packer through and through.

He still returns to Green Bay every September for Alumni Day. He doesn't miss the Lombardi Legends events. And he still talks to former teammates with great regularity.

"There's no place like Wisconsin and football in Green Bay," Grabowski said. "There's not many guys out there like Willie Davis and Bob Skoronski and some of the others I played with. That's why Green Bay will always be special to me."

RYAN GRANT

The order for goat horns was on its way.

But Ryan Grant wanted no part of that delivery. Grant thought he'd look better with an "S" on his chest rather than horns on his head.

So Grant—a Green Bay Packers running back—changed history with one of the most stunning turnarounds the game of football has ever seen.

In a 2007 divisional playoff game against Seattle, Grant lost two fumbles in the first 69 seconds of the contest. And less than four minutes into this enormous game, the Packers trailed 14–0 and their faithful were ready to dig Grant his own tomb.

What followed was a comeback that rivaled John Travolta.

Grant ran for 201 yards and three touchdowns to lead the Packers back to a stirring 42–20 win on a snowy evening at Lambeau Field. Grant's rushing total set a new franchise postseason record, and his rushing mark was also the seventh highest in NFL postseason history.

Not bad for a guy who was going to have to wear fake glasses and a wig around town during the off-season.

"It's unfortunate what happened," Grant said of the two early fumbles. "But I really appreciate everybody backing me. They backed me the whole time.

"From the training staff to the coaches to the players, everybody just said, 'Stay with it. You know what you've got to do. Let it go.'"

Grant clearly did just that. And by the end of the day, the largest crowd in Lambeau Field history (72,168) was ready to throw a parade in Grant's honor.

"I'm an even-keeled person," Grant said. "I don't really get too high, too low, so the whole time I was saying it's a long game and I understand you've got to be able to stay middle ground when things are high, things are low, and I was able to do that."

The Packers lost to the New York Giants in the NFC Championship Game the following week. But fans will never forget Grant's performance in lifting Green Bay into the conference title game.

"Ryan's a talented young man," Packers coach Mike McCarthy said that day. "Ryan's very consistent. That's what I like about Ryan. You have the same player every day. He works extremely hard. There isn't a whole lot of variance in his performance. That's very useful for a coach, particularly in the game plan.

"I think his consistency is the thing I like best. He plays with a lot of confidence. He's very confident. I never questioned him and we did not blink."

What may have been most surprising was Grant's early woes. During Grant's 218 touches during the regular season, he fumbled just once.

On the first play of the game, though, Grant caught a swing pass in the right flat, fell and tried getting up. When he did, Seattle's Leroy Hill forced a fumble. Lofa Tatupu recovered and returned it to the Packers 1-yard line to set up a TD.

On Green Bay's next possession, Grant ran for eight yards off left tackle on first down. But on his next carry, Grant fumbled again and Seattle cornerback Jordan Babineaux recovered.

Just 69 seconds into the biggest game of his life, Grant had lost two fumbles and the Packers were quickly down two touchdowns.

"The good thing about spotting them 14 was that we did it so quick, we still had plenty of time left and I knew Ryan could have a big game," Packers quarterback Brett Favre said. "Any time he touches the ball he can have a big game.

"And I came over, he was on the bench and I said—hey, you know what, believe me if there's one person that knows what it feels like to be in his shoes, it's me. I said, 'Forget about it. You're going to have plenty of opportunities.' He gave me the old, generic answer: 'Yeah, I know.' Same thing I would have said. But I said, 'Go down swinging, man. Don't worry about it.'"

Grant certainly didn't seem to.

Two series later, Grant ripped off a 26-yard run that seemed to fully restore his confidence. Grant finished that drive with a one-yard TD run, then had a three-yard touchdown shortly before halftime that gave the Packers a 28–17 lead.

Then in the second half, Grant ran wild.

Grant busted a 24-yard run that set up Green Bay's first touchdown of the second half, giving the Packers a 35–17 lead. Then Grant ripped off a 43-yard run late in the third quarter that set up his third TD, one that put Green Bay ahead 42–20.

"We feel confident with this team and we know when we don't turn the ball over and we don't make mistakes on our end, we're pretty dangerous as an offense," said Grant, who was traded to Green Bay in 2007 for a sixth-round draft choice. "I've been playing football for a long time and I understand there are ups and downs and I've got to keep fighting no matter what."

Grant did just that. And by the time the day was over, his list of accomplishments also included: most rushing TDs (three) in a playoff game in franchise history, second most points in a playoff game (18) in team history, and an amazing transformation from goat to hero.

The Packers had studied Grant that preseason, when he was a member of the New York Giants. The Giants had a surplus of backs, and the Packers eventually shipped a sixth-round draft pick to New York eight days before the season-opener.

"What a day," said Packers director of pro personnel Reggie McKenzie, the man largely responsible for finding Grant. "He's fun to watch. He's fun to watch. He runs hard, he runs tough, and he's fast. He's fast.

"We just saw something in preseason and he made us say, 'We need to add this guy to our stable.' And he's been outstanding. We put his foot in the door and the rest was up to him. And he showed himself and proved himself."

Grant went on to rush for 4,143 career yards in Green Bay, which ranks fifth all-time. He led the Packers in rushing three times and had two 1,000-yard seasons.

But when Packer Nation thinks of Grant, they'll always flash back to that magical day in the 2007 playoffs.

"What he did was remarkable," Packers right guard Jason Spitz said. "Remarkable."

AHMAN GREEN

Wesley Walls played with Hall of Famer Roger Craig and a young and gifted Ricky Watters when he was a member of the San Francisco 49ers.

Bubba Franks played alongside the great Edgerrin James, as well as Clinton Portis and Willis McGahee while he was at the University of Miami.

William Henderson blocked for Dorsey Levens when he was in his prime, and Nick Luchey helped clear holes for Cincinnati standout Corey Dillon.

All of those former Packers also played with Ahman Green. And each and every ex-Packer said what Green did in 2003 trumped anything they'd ever experienced.

"I think Ahman is probably the best back I've played with," said Walls, a Packers tight end in 2003. "Those other guys I played with were really good. I mean really good. But I think Ahman had a little more burst."

Franks, a Packers tight end from 2000 to 2007, agreed.

"It's close. I mean real close," Franks said when comparing Green to James. "But I'd give [Green] the nod."

It's easy to see why.

During the 2003 season, Green didn't just have the best season ever by a Green Bay Packers running back. He had one of the top years in NFL history.

Green rushed for 1,883 yards, shattering Jim Taylor's former franchise record of 1,474 yards that had stood for 41 years. As of this writing, Green's 2003 rushing total was tied for the ninth-highest single-season mark in NFL history.

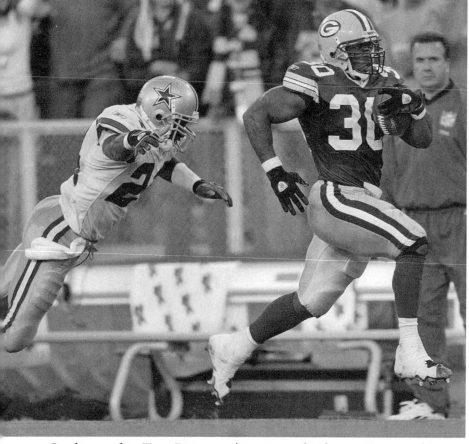

Cowboys safety Tony Dixon can't quite catch Ahman Green on his way to a 90-yard touchdown run at Lambeau in 2004.

Green also set a new Packers record with 20 touchdowns and averaged 5.30 yards per carry that season.

"Everything just kind of went right that year," Green said. "The line was great that year and I was healthy and we were just in sync. That year was a lot of fun."

Green went on to set the Packers' career rushing record with 8,322 yards. He eclipsed 1,000 yards in six different seasons and had 33 100-yard rushing games, which are both franchise records.

But nothing could hold a candle to what he did in 2003.

Green had 10 100-yard rushing games that season, highlighted by a 218-yard effort against Philadelphia and a 192-yard effort against Detroit. Those remain the two top regular season rushing games in team history.

Green eclipsed 100 yards four consecutive games, which set a franchise record. He found the end zone in seven straight games, which tied Paul Hornung's mark set in 1960.

Green had a 98-yard touchdown run against the Broncos that season, and also busted off TD runs of 65 yards against Detroit, 60 versus Chicago, and 45 against Philadelphia. But Green was much more than just a home run hitter.

He delivered punishing blows to linebackers and safeties throughout that memorable season. And by the end of games, those players wanted nothing to do with Green.

"A year like that is something else," said Tom Rossley, who was Green Bay's offensive coordinator from 2000 to 2005. "You just won't see many like it."

Rossley was dead on.

As of this writing, only Eric Dickerson of the Los Angeles Rams (2,105 yards in 1984), Minnesota's Adrian Peterson (2,097 in 2012), Baltimore's Jamal Lewis (2,066 in 2003), Detroit's Barry Sanders (2,053 in 1997), Denver's Terrell Davis (2,008 in 1998), Tennessee's Chris Johnson (2,006 in 2009), Buffalo's O.J. Simpson (2,003 in 1973), and Houston's Earl Campbell (1,934 in 1980) had run for more yards in a single season. Green tied Sanders' 1994 total (1,883).

"When you're going through a season like that, you really don't think about all the numbers," Green said. "You're just playing football, trying to win games.

"But when it's over, you can kind of look back and take pride in what you did. I'd say that's what happened for me."

Perhaps the most remarkable part of Green's 2003 season was that he became the No. 1 option in the Packers' offense. That's something no one felt would ever happen with the great Brett Favre still around.

But that season, the Packers ran the ball 51.7 percent of the time. The last time Green Bay had more rushes than passing attempts in a season was 1987.

A big reason for Green's success was the dynamic offensive line of Chad Clifton, Mike Wahle, Mike Flanagan, Marco Rivera, and Mark Tauscher. But Green—who possessed a rare combination of speed and power—did plenty of damage himself.

"I think Ahman has a style almost of his own in regard to his explosiveness and his power," Packers coach Mike Sherman said. "His ability to burst, his ability to run over people, around people. I don't look at him and see anybody else. I think he's unique in his own way."

No one could have ever imagined Green having that type of impact in Green Bay.

During the 2000 off-season, then–Packers general manager Ron Wolf sent cornerback Fred Vinson to Seattle for Green in a swap of disappointing players.

Green was a third-round draft pick of the Seahawks in 1998. But fumbling problems landed him in Mike Holmgren's doghouse.

Vinson was a second-round draft pick of Green Bay in 1999. But after just one season, the Packers soured on Vinson and swapped him for Green.

"People talk about my trade for Brett [Favre] as my best ever," Wolf said. "And they're right. That was a great trade. But our trade for Ahman isn't far behind."

That's for sure. And when it comes to Green's 2003 season, it doesn't take a backseat to any in Packers' history.

"That year was really, really special," Green said. "It kind of brought me back to my days at Nebraska.

"I felt really good the whole season. The line was amazing and everything just kind of clicked. That was a lot of fun."

PAUL HORNUNG

Today, the concept seems almost preposterous. Back in 1961, it was par for the course.

Packers do-it-all Paul Hornung was the NFL's MVP in 1961 after scoring a league-high 146 points. But as Green Bay readied to face the New York Giants in the NFL Championship Game that year, Hornung was called to duty by the Army.

Packers head coach Vince Lombardi called President John F. Kennedy and asked that Hornung be granted leave for the title game. Amazingly, Kennedy obliged.

"Paul Hornung isn't going to win the war on Sunday," Kennedy said. "But the football fans of this country deserve the two best teams on the field that day."

And at that time, Hornung was the best of the best.

Hornung scored a then–playoff record 19 points that day. And Green Bay routed the Giants 37–0, before a team-record 39,029 at Green Bay's City Stadium.

"That was a great day and a great game," Hornung said. "It would have been hell to miss that game."

It would have been hard on the Packers, too.

The Giants entered that game with the No. 1 defense in football. But that didn't seem to bother Hornung and his teammates.

Hornung had a six-yard touchdown run in the second quarter to start the scoring. By the time it was over, Hornung had added three field goals, four extra points, and totaled 19 points.

"That was a great time for us," Hornung said. "That's right when we were starting to take off."

Hornung was a huge reason why the Packers began rising from obscurity.

Hornung, dubbed "the Golden Boy," was an All-American and Heisman Trophy winner at Notre Dame. Green Bay used the No. 1 pick in the 1957 draft on Hornung.

Hornung was one of the most versatile players in the game, but then–Packers coach Lisle Blackbourn mistook Hornung's flexibility for shortcomings. Blackbourn—and later coach Ray "Scooter" McLean—couldn't decide on a position for Hornung. And after two short seasons, Hornung had seen enough and wanted a trade.

But when McLean was fired after the 1958 season, the Packers hired the legendary Lombardi. And that move may have saved Hornung's career.

Lombardi viewed Hornung as a halfback with great power. He also saw Hornung as a player who could throw on the run—two traits that would open up the playbook.

"I suggest that you report to training camp at a maximum of 207 pounds," Lombardi told Hornung in a letter dated May 14, 1959. "You will be heavy enough at that weight, and the left halfback in my system must have speed in order to capitalize on the running pass option play."

Under Lombardi, Hornung developed into a standout running back, but also posed danger as a passer, kicker, receiver, and lead blocker.

Hornung won three straight NFL scoring titles between 1959 and 1961 and set a league record with 176 points in 1960. That mark stood for 46 years before San Diego's LaDainian Tomlinson broke it in 2006.

During that 1960 campaign, Hornung scored 15 touchdowns, kicked 15 field goals, and made 41 extra points. He also threw for two touchdowns that season, meaning he had a hand in 188 points—or 15.7 per game.

To this day, Hornung holds three of the top four scoring days in Packer history. And it seems unlikely that his 33 points against Baltimore on October 8, 1961, will ever be topped.

Lombardi later called Hornung "the most versatile player in football" and "the best clutch player I have ever seen."

Perhaps. But Hornung's off-the-field antics often outweighed his on-field achievements.

Hornung had a reputation as one of the country's most successful ladies' men. Hornung and teammate Max McGee were both hard drinkers who liked to party together.

Lombardi could live with that. The gambling was another story.

NFL commissioner Pete Rozelle suspended Hornung and Detroit's Alex Karras for the entire 1963 season for gambling. With Hornung out of the lineup that year, the Packers' run of two straight NFL championships ended as well.

"Oh, we missed him," Packers quarterback Bart Starr said. "There's no doubt about that."

You bet they did, especially Hornung's incredible versatility.

After missing the 1963 season, Hornung scored 107 total points in 1964. But he also missed 26 of 38 field goal attempts that year.

Don Chandler replaced him as the team's kicker in 1965, and Hornung's last two seasons were injury plagued and rather nondescript.

By the time his terrific nine-year career ended, Hornung had scored 760 points, including 62 touchdowns, 66 field goals, and 190 extra points.

"You have to know what Hornung means to this team," Lombardi said in George Sullivan's book, *The Great Running Backs.* "I have heard and read that he is not a great runner or a great passer or a great field goal kicker, but he led the league in scoring for three seasons.

"In the middle of the field he may be only slightly better than an average ballplayer. But inside the 20-yard line, he is one of the greatest I have ever seen. He smells that goal line."

Hornung was beginning to wonder if he'd ever smell the Hall of Fame, though.

Hornung was kept out of the Hall the first 14 years his name was on the ballot. While his statistics were sublime, voters couldn't get past the fact Hornung was suspended an entire season for gambling.

Finally, on his 15th try, Hornung got the necessary support. Today, he's one of 22 Packers in the Hall—11 that played under Vince Lombardi.

"Let's put it this way, I didn't give up hope," Hornung said. "But it was a long time in coming.

"I thought I might have been used somewhat like a political football because the story was, 'Why wasn't Paul Horning getting into the Hall of Fame' rather than most of the people who were getting in? But naturally, I'm happy to be in it now."

EDDIE LEE IVERY

Not every Green Bay Packer has happy stories to tell from their playing days. In a sport packed with violence, injury, and temptation, there's a greater chance of things going bad than good.

Eddie Lee Ivery is the perfect example of that.

Ivery, a running back who the Packers selected in the first round in 1979, tore his ACL twice. He developed addictions to drugs and alcohol.

But Ivery turned his life around after football. And today, Ivery is back as an assistant football coach in his hometown of Thomson, Georgia.

While Ivery's playing days weren't what he hoped for, his story appears to have a happy ending.

"I'm blessed. Absolutely," Ivery said. "I'm clean. I'm happy. I have no complaints."

The balance, stability and steadiness Ivery possesses today are things he didn't have during his days in Green Bay.

When the Packers took Ivery with the 15th overall pick in 1979, they thought they had their franchise back for the next decade. Instead, a combination of injuries and his own addictions stymied what had all the makings of a tremendous career.

In his first game ever with the Packers, Ivery tore his left ACL against Chicago at Soldier Field. The most infuriating thing about the play was Ivery wasn't even touched. Instead he was cutting back against the grain on what appeared would be a 67-yard touchdown run.

"I'd played my entire college days on turf," Ivery said. "And nothing bad happened. And then to do that to my knee on grass. Man!"

Ivery battled back and led the Packers in rushing with 831 yards in 1980. But the following season, Ivery experienced déjà vu of the worst kind when he again tore up his left knee.

For the second time in three seasons, the play happened in Green Bay's season opener. It happened against the Chicago Bears. And it happened at Soldier Field.

"I look back at my career and think it could have been different if it wasn't for those injuries," Ivery said. "But I also know I should have worked harder in the off-season. I took way too much time off, and in that elite league, you can't do that."

Ivery did go on to lead the Packers in rushing in both the strike-shortened 1982 season (453 yards) and in 1985 (636 yards) and is currently 12th on the Packers' all-time rushing list. But he was struggling with his addictions, too, something that caused him to miss the final eight games of the 1983 season and nearly ended his Green Bay career.

But Ivery credits then–coach Bart Starr for helping him through his problems, even though it wound up being temporary.

"I was in big-time denial," Ivery said. "But Bart was like a father figure to me. He called me into his office one day, and I couldn't lie to him.

"I cried in his arms like he was my dad and he hugged me. And he allowed me to take the time I needed to get my life in order."

The Packers sent Ivery to the Hazelden Foundation in Minnesota for a 28-day drug treatment program.

Back in Green Bay, Starr was fired following an 8–8 season and replaced with Forrest Gregg. And when Ivery returned, he was sure his days as a Packer were about to end.

"When Bart left, I was sure my career with the Packers was over," Ivery said. "Two knee surgeries, drug problems, I figured my days were numbered. But with Forrest, it wasn't about what you had done. It was what could you do for me. And he gave me a chance."

Ivery played well for Gregg. He led the Packers with six rushing touchdowns in 1984. He led Green Bay with 636 rushing yards in 1985 and caught 31 passes for 385 yards in 1986.

Ivery was released after that season, though, and retired in 1987. And without football, Ivery's battle with drugs and alcohol only intensified.

Ivery tried getting himself clean and sober on three occasions by entering recovery centers, but each time the effects were short term.

His addictions destroyed his marriage, harmed other relationships, and left him downright miserable. So in the fall of 1998, Ivery knew he really only had two options.

"It was either beat this thing or go six-feet under," Ivery said. "And I wasn't ready to go six-feet under."

So for the first time in Ivery's life, he seriously committed to getting better. Instead of the 30-day programs he previously took part in, he spent 14 months at Oakhurst Recovery Center in Decatur, Georgia.

When it was finished, Ivery felt like a new man. One with a new lease on life. One ready to make the most of his second chance.

Today, he's doing exactly that.

Ivery worked for eight years as the assistant strength and conditioning coach at his alma mater, Georgia Tech. He remarried and had a daughter; he turned his life around.

"I always felt without drugs and alcohol you couldn't have a good time," Ivery said. "But just being around young kids and young people has kept me young. And doing what I'm doing doesn't feel like work anymore. One of the things I always had a passion for was sports and now it's my job, too."

Ivery has also gotten out in the community and shared his story.

It's certainly not the story Packer Nation hoped for when Green Bay drafted Ivery, but at the end of the day, Ivery's tale has had a happy ending.

"The one thing I try and share with them is there's going to be a lot of peer pressure," Ivery said. "But you don't have to do what others are doing.

"Three things can happen when you get involved with drugs and alcohol: jail, institutions, and death. And not necessarily in that order. If I can help one person, then going out and speaking is worth it."

GREG JENNINGS

Greg Jennings was a highlight reel waiting to happen during his seven years in Green Bay.

Jennings caught Brett Favre's 421st career touchdown, which helped Favre break Dan Marino's record of 420. Jennings had an 82-yard TD reception from Favre during a memorable overtime win in Denver in 2007.

Jennings played in two Pro Bowls. And he's just one of five receivers in team history with three consecutive 1,000-yard seasons (2008–2010).

But when Packer Nation remembers Jennings, it will likely be for his heroics in the 45th Super Bowl.

Jennings caught a pair of touchdowns, becoming just the 15th player in league history to record multiple TD catches in a Super Bowl. And Jennings' biggest play was arguably a 31-yard reception from quarterback Aaron Rodgers with the Packers clinging to a 28–25 lead late in the fourth quarter.

Rodgers won the MVP that day, as the Packers defeated Pittsburgh 31–25. But Green Bay would have never claimed its 13th NFL title without the performance of Jennings,

"When you're humble, God gives you favor with men and he'll raise you up," Jennings said the night the Packers became Super Bowl champs. "He definitely raised this team up. We took full advantage of this game and this opportunity.

"We overcame some adversity, even within this game. It kind of defines our season. We are a team with a certain dynamic that a lot of teams don't have. What separated us from the other 31 teams was that dynamic and that will to overcome adversity."

Jennings was a huge reason the Packers overcame countless obstacles and became NFL champions during that surprising season.

Green Bay was devastated by injury throughout the 2010 campaign, but rallied late in the regular season to reach the postseason. The Packers followed with upset road wins over Philadelphia and Atlanta, then toppled host Chicago in the NFC Championship Game.

Now, in the 45th Super Bowl, quarterback Aaron Rodgers was red hot. And Jennings was a big reason why.

Late in the first half, the Packers held a 14–3 lead when Rodgers and Jennings hooked up and made music.

On a first-and-10 from Pittsburgh's 21, the Packers lined up four wide receivers; the Steelers rushed four and dropped seven. Jennings lined up in the left slot and ran a deep seam route.

Jennings got behind linebacker James Farrior and in front of safety Ryan Clark, but Rodgers' window was small and his pass had to be perfect. It was.

Rodgers delivered a dart that Clark missed by inches. Jennings took a wicked shot from safety Troy Polamalu, but he was already in the end zone.

With just more than two minutes remaining in the first half, the Packers had surged to a 21–3 lead.

"It was like they were a hair faster than we were all night," Clark said.

Jennings certainly seemed to have another gear that night.

Early in the fourth quarter, Green Bay's lead had been trimmed to 21–17. The Packers drove to Pittsburgh's 8-yard line, and on second-and-goal, they employed an empty backfield.

After the ball was snapped, Rodgers quickly looked left. Rodgers had no intention of ever going left, mind you. He was simply trying to get Polamalu—the NFL's Defensive Player of the Year—to drift that way.

It was a continuation of a 60-minute battle that Rodgers waged—and won—with Polamalu.

"He's a guy that you have to be aware of him, where he's at all times," Rodgers said of Polamalu. "He's a great player, had a great season, but guys have to respect where my eyes are looking so it was important to me to use good eye control on the field and not stare anybody down because he can cover a lot of ground quickly."

Rodgers was sublime on this play. Polamalu watched Rodgers' eyes and cheated back to the left, which allowed Jennings to come free in the right corner. Rodgers lofted another perfect ball and Jennings' TD grab gave Green Bay a 28–17 lead.

"It was a corner route," Jennings said. "I had a corner route the entire time and they dropped me and let me run free the play before. They dropped me on another corner route and we came back to it and scored on that play."

The Packers weren't out of the woods, yet.

Pittsburgh closed within 28–25, and after Green Bay started on its own 25, quickly faced a third-and-10. The Steelers rushed just three, which meant Rodgers would have to be razor sharp to beat the eight-man coverage in back.

Jennings, working from the left slot, ran another seam route against Steelers' No. 1 cornerback Ike Taylor. The ball was out of Rodgers' hands in 2.8 seconds, and he had perhaps a 12-inch window to squeeze the ball into.

He did. It was arguably the throw of Rodgers' life, one that went for 31 yards and kept the Steelers' offense grounded.

"It seemed like it brushed off the tip of Ike Taylor's glove," Jennings said. "But it just got over the top enough where I could make a play on it."

That play helped the Packers run additional clock and eventually add a field goal that gave them a 31–25 lead. And when Green Bay's defense held, the Packers were Super Bowl champions again.

"It feels awesome," Jennings said that night. "Awesome game."

Jennings played just two more injury-plagued seasons in Green Bay. Then he signed a free agent contract with bitter rival Minnesota after the 2012 season.

But the Packers got seven highly productive seasons from Jennings—and one memorable night in the 45th Super Bowl.

"I'll definitely be in touch with these guys throughout my career," Jennings said before leaving Green Bay. "That's the one thing that you take away from it.

"Everything else just kind of falls to the wayside a bit, which is unfortunate. But you build relationships, long-standing relationships, and you establish them for after football."

GARY KNAFELC

When Gary Knafelc arrived in Green Bay in 1954, he had a terrible stuttering problem.

Completing a full sentence took what felt like a fortnight to Knafelc. And writers were brutal, often referring to him as "K-K-Knafelc" in their stories.

It's surprising that a man who had such a hard time speaking eventually took the path he did.

From 1954 to 1962, Knafelc was a standout wide receiver and later a tight end for the Packers.

Then in 1964, Knafelc was Vince Lombardi's personal choice to be the stadium's public address announcer. Knafelc held that position from 1964 to 2004, giving him 50 years of service with the organization.

"It was a lot of fun," Knafelc said. "The seasons just started getting too long. I have a winter home [near Orlando] that I wasn't getting to use as much as I wanted. But it was great to be a part of it for so long."

If it weren't for a bad hamstring injury, Knafelc probably would never have become a member of the Packers. The rival Chicago Cardinals made Knafelc the second wide receiver taken in the 1954 draft, but when he suffered a nasty hamstring injury that year in a postseason all-star game, the Cardinals released him.

The Packers were more than happy to claim Knafelc, and by 1955, he was one of Green Bay's starting wide receivers. At 6'4", 220 pounds, with 10.3-second speed in the 100-yard dash, Knafelc had a fantastic combination of size and speed and enjoyed some terrific moments in Green Bay.

In 1955, Knafelc led the Packers with eight touchdown receptions, including a thriller in a season-opening 20–17 victory over Detroit. On the game's final play, Knafelc ran a post down the middle and quarterback Tobin Rote delivered a strike for a 28-yard touchdown pass that remains among the most dramatic plays in franchise history.

Afterward, Knafelc was carried off the field.

"I'm not about tooting my own horn," Knafelc said. "But I was carried off the field that day, and as far as I've been told, that's never happened to another player. Coaches have been carried off, but apparently I'm the only Packer player that's ever happened to."

Knafelc is also an important part of Packer history due to this little bit of trivia:

When the Packers closed old City Stadium on November 18, 1956, Knafelc caught the final TD pass in a 17–16 loss to the San Francisco 49ers. When the Packers moved across town to the new City Stadium—which was later renamed Lambeau Field—the following year, Knafelc caught the first touchdown pass there.

But Knafelc was much more than a trivia answer.

He developed into one of the Packers' most dynamic receiving threats. And he was also making a lot of noise off the field.

Knafelc worked hard to overcome his stuttering, and became the first Packer player to host a television show. Along with Lew Carpenter and later Bart Starr, Knafelc hosted a weekly show called *Packerama*.

Later, he was in a movie called *Palm Springs Weekend* that, according to Knafelc, "still plays on the late, late, late show. Usually after *King Kong* or something like that."

Knafelc was also an extremely successful businessman, building a company called Coleman School Supply before merging it with Valley School Supply—a company owned by former Packers Willie Davis, Bob Skoronski, and Ron Kostelnik—in 1974.

Knafelc later became the president of a commercial furniture company called Interplan. As successful as Knafelc's off-the-field career was, the on-field losing took a toll early in his career.

Knafelc played four years under Lisle Blackbourn, who Knafelc called "a very good coach who didn't get along with the executive committee. I think he would have won if they would have allowed him to go along."

But when the Packers compiled just a 17–31 record in Blackbourn's time, he was dismissed.

The Packers made the enormous mistake of promoting Ray "Scooter" McLean, who went 1–10–1 in his one year as head coach.

"Oh man," Knafelc sighs when McLean's name is brought up. "Scooter would play poker with the players the night before the game. And what was worse is he wasn't even good at it. [Max] McGee would just take him to the cleaners."

When Lombardi finally arrived in 1959, he cleaned things up in a big way. And by 1961, the Packers were NFL champions.

"I had been on such terrible teams," Knafelc said. "We definitely needed someone like him. We hadn't even been in the playoff hunt, much less playing for championships."

Lombardi moved Knafelc to tight end in 1959, and Knafelc started there two years before Ron Kramer beat him out in 1961. Through it all, Knafelc's relationship with Lombardi was always uneasy.

"I was definitely one of his whipping boys," Knafelc said. "He screamed at me constantly. I didn't like the guy and physically he frightened me.

"But I'll take everything he gave me. I wish I had another five years with him because he made me a much better player."

The relationship between Lombardi and Knafelc ended—at least temporarily—following the Packers' 1962 championship. Lombardi asked Knafelc to return as a player/coach and tutor Green Bay's new tight end, Marv Fleming.

Knafelc asked Lombardi to guarantee him he'd play in three games, which would qualify as a full season, giving Knafelc 10 years in the league and the right to collect a pension. When Lombardi balked, Knafelc walked and played his final season with San Francisco.

Coincidentally, the Packers closed out the 1963 season at San Francisco and Lombardi allowed Knafelc to fly home with the team, because he still maintained a residence in Green Bay.

On the flight, Lombardi asked Knafelc if he'd be a Packers public address announcer the following year. Knafelc wound up doing it for four decades.

"Of all the players I've seen pass through, Brett [Favre] is by far the best," Knafelc said. "I think he's one of the top five players to ever play the game. I still blame [Mike] Holmgren for the one Super Bowl they lost [XXXII]. That still bothers me."

But not much else in Knafelc's five-decade run with the organization has been a bother. In fact, it's been just the opposite.

"What a blast," he said. "What an absolute blast."

DORSEY LEVENS

It might be a Wednesday morning practice, it might be a Friday walkthrough—didn't matter. When Dorsey Levens took the field, the only gear he knew was fifth. And at times, some of us tried getting him to downshift.

He ran hard in our scrimmages, our practices, all the time. Sometimes I'd say, "Choke it down, Horse. Take it down. We need to have you for Sunday."

Oh, Sundays weren't a problem either. Just ask Carolina.

After a 29-year wait, we were back in the NFC Championship Game in 1996. It was the first title game Green Bay had hosted since the legendary Ice Bowl in 1967.

And Levens made this his personal coming-out party.

The second-year running back from Georgia Tech had 10 carries that frigid afternoon for 88 yards. He also caught five passes for 117 yards.

Levens' huge afternoon helped us topple Carolina 30–13. Two weeks later we drubbed New England 35–21 in Super Bowl XXXI.

Prior to Levens' breakout game against Carolina, his rushing high was 86 yards and his previous receiving highs were five catches for 83 yards. Talk about your poster child for the "timing is everything" campaign.

"I thought I would contribute a little bit," Levens said. "I never dreamed of having a game like this. This is definitely a career game. I'm in the game plan every week, but usually not this much."

But Levens punished the upstart Panthers—a franchise in just its second year of existence—throughout. And as Levens kept hurting Carolina, Mike Holmgren called his number more and more.

Dorsey Levens leaps over fullback William Henderson and a Buccaneers defender during a 1997 playoff game.

"He was special in a special game," Holmgren said that day.

And we needed Levens to be special.

Carolina struck for a 7–0 lead early on. Then Levens made one of the biggest plays of the game.

On the first play of the second quarter, we had a first-and-10 from Carolina's 29-yard line. We split two wideouts left, lined tight end Keith Jackson next to right tackle Earl Dotson, and split Levens out wide right.

Levens got a clean release and was left one-on-one with All-Pro cornerback Eric Davis. Favre released the ball 3.05 seconds after the snap, and when he let it go, it appeared Levens was covered up by Davis.

But Levens adjusted perfectly to Favre's pass, won the jump ball over Davis, and hauled in an enormous 29-yard touchdown that knotted the game 7–7.

I'll never forget the pass he caught against Carolina in the championship game, up over Eric Davis. He was covered when Brett threw that ball, but Brett knew his pass-catching skills. That was a big catch.

Levens had plenty of those throughout.

Late in the third quarter, we were clinging to a 20–13 lead and we had a second-and-6 from our own 30-yard line.

Favre flipped a screen pass to Levens in the right flat. The guard, Adam Timmerman, was the first one to throw a key block. Frank Winters and Antonio Freeman followed with terrific blocks of their own.

Levens erupted down the right sideline for a 66-yard reception and wasn't caught until he reached the Panthers' 4-yard line. One play later, running back Edgar Bennett scored to give us a commanding 27–13 lead.

"It was perfect," Favre said that day. "Dorsey did a great job of cutting back and getting in the open field and then using his speed. That was a great call for the blitz.

"Kevin Greene came from the outside and I just dumped it over his head and there is no one out there really, and it's up to our line to block people and Dorsey did a great job of running the football. When he ran that down there I felt pretty good about the outcome of the game. I felt pretty good about where we were."

Rightfully so. The offense piled up a then–team playoff record of 479 total yards.

Favre had a big day, completing 19 of 29 passes for two touchdowns and 292 yards, and our tandem of Levens and Bennett combined for 187 rushing yards. Altogether we racked up 201 total rushing yards.

"All year everyone said the weakest part of the team was the running game," Levens said. "We wanted to prove a point. Nobody gave us any respect all year. We wish quarterbacks had no arms so we could run every time."

Over the next few years, Packer Nation loved the sight of Levens running the football.

Levens had a career year in 1997 with 1,435 rushing yards—the third highest total in team history—and 12 total touchdowns.

Levens' career was slowed when he suffered a broken leg in 1998. Levens ran for 1,034 yards in 1999, but never was quite the same player again. Dorsey and I both left after the 2001 season.

But the Horse, for two or three years, he was just awesome. The combination of his speed and size and catching ability—wow.

Dorsey was something we'd never seen before with that size and power and speed. But he was toughest coming out of the backfield catching the ball. When you're talking about a guy who could come out of the backfield and catch a lot of passes and read zone blocking and loved to play the game, it was Dorsey. He was something else.

And he was never better than in that NFC Championship Game against Carolina.

"That was the game that showed we had arrived," former Packers general manager Ron Wolf said. "I'll never forget it. Playing in our stadium in front of our fans and going up to the podium to accept that [NFC championship] trophy. That was some kind of experience."

One Levens helped make possible.

MAX McGEE

On the field, he produced one highlight after another. Off the field, Max McGee might have assembled even more.

Whether McGee was playing for the Green Bay Packers or broadcasting their games, he was as colorful as anyone who ever passed through the organization.

A standout wide receiver during the Packers' "Glory Years," McGee built a reputation for having as much—or more—fun away from the field as he did on it.

"Yeah, I think that's safe to say," McGee said shortly before his death in 2007. "I was fortunate to spend my whole time in Green Bay because we had a hell of a time. Now, it's just a money game, but back then we had loyalties."

McGee was loyal to Green Bay for more than three decades.

McGee was a top-notch wide receiver during his 12-year career. He was part of the remarkable transformation under Vince Lombardi, won five NFL championships, and was inducted into the Packers Hall of Fame in 1975.

When McGee's playing days ended, he was a smashing success as Green Bay's radio color commentator from 1979 to 1998.

"It was a great ride," McGee said. "Every step of the way was a blast."

For McGee, nothing was more fun than his adventures at Super Bowl I.

McGee had been a Packer standout for years after coming to Green Bay in the fifth round from Tulane in 1954. He was called into the Air Force in 1955–56, then returned to Green Bay in 1957.

McGee led the team in receptions in 1958 and from 1960 to 1962. He was a Pro Bowl player in 1961 and remained a starting wide receiver through 1964, as the Packers dominated the rest of the NFL.

By the time Super Bowl I rolled around, though, on January 15, 1967, McGee was a little-used reserve who had caught just four passes all season. But when Boyd Dowler went down with a separated shoulder on Green Bay's second series, it was McGee to the rescue.

McGee had to borrow a teammate's helmet because he left his in the locker room. But just a few plays later, he made a brilliant one-handed catch, sprinted past Chiefs defender Fred Williamson and raced for a 37-yard touchdown, the first in Super Bowl history.

Over the remainder of the afternoon, McGee produced one of the greatest games in Super Bowl history, catching seven passes for 138 yards and two touchdowns as Green Bay bested Kansas City 35–10.

"After I had scored those two touchdowns, [Paul] Hornung came over to me and said 'You're going to be the MVP,'" said McGee, who lost out on MVP honors to quarterback Bart Starr. "Well I wasn't, but it was a heck of a game."

And a heck of an evening beforehand.

Because McGee believed he had virtually no shot of playing in the game, he says he risked the $15,000 fine and snuck out the night before to meet up with two stewardesses. McGee claimed he was out all night and went into Super Bowl I with a hangover and almost no sleep.

Dave "Hawg" Hanner, who was in charge of bed checks, claimed that McGee's story of dodging curfew was sheer fiction. McGee, though, said that Hanner was covering his own tail.

"Hawg's one of my favorite buddies, but he's trying to cover his ass on this one," McGee said. "I was rooming with Hornung and Hornung didn't want to risk going out because the fine was the same as our game check was going to be.

"But when Hawg stuck his head in, I said, 'Are you going to be checking late?' He screamed, 'You damned right I am,' then he stuck his head back in and shook it no. Well I almost ran him over trying to get out."

McGee was notorious for such antics. He and Hornung both loved the nightlife, and often seemed to divvy up as much in fines as they brought home.

While McGee would often drive coach Vince Lombardi nuts, there was a mutual respect between the two.

"Not to pat myself on the back, but he was very confident when I was playing that I could give him some big plays," McGee said.

One such play that proved how McGee could push Lombardi's buttons came in the 1960 NFL Championship Game in Philadelphia.

McGee, who also punted, loved to fake a punt and take off running under former coaches Lisle Blackbourn and Scooter McLean. But when Lombardi arrived, he told McGee that wouldn't be tolerated unless the order came from him.

With Green Bay needing a spark in the fourth quarter, McGee took off running on a fake punt from his own goal line and picked up 40 yards. The play was remarkably bold, considering Lombardi didn't authorize it.

McGee later capped the drive with a seven-yard TD reception from Bart Starr for a 13–10 Green Bay lead. Although the Eagles rallied back for a 17–13 victory, McGee's run remains legendary.

"If I hadn't made it, I would have never played another down in Green Bay," McGee said. "I know that much."

Luckily for the Packers—and McGee—he made it that day.

McGee would go on to post 345 career receptions for 6,346 yards and 50 touchdowns. McGee also punted 256 times for 10,647 yards, an average of 41.6 yards per punt.

"When I first got there, the Packers were a disaster," McGee said. "We weren't winning. We didn't have enough talent. Who would ever thought things would end up the way they did?"

McGee certainly didn't think he'd remain part of the Packers family when his playing days ended, either.

McGee retired after the 1967 season and became a successful restaurateur. McGee also dabbled in some television and radio broadcasting, before getting a call from the Packers in 1979.

Jim Irwin and Lionel Aldridge were doing the Packers radio broadcasts at the time. But when Aldridge became ill, McGee got the call.

"They told me the game was in L.A.," McGee said. "And I said, 'I'll be there. Maybe I can find those stewardesses again.' Had it been in St. Louis or something, I would have probably said no."

Many Packer fans feel fortunate he didn't. Over the next 20 years, McGee and Irwin developed a cult following that lasted until their retirements following the 1998 season.

"I never claimed to be an announcer," McGee said. "What it did was give me a platform to tell people the truth and what was really going on.

"We saw a lot of bad football early on and I'd tell people when a guy made a dumb-ass play. And I'd tell jokes and be funny and Jim was kind of a homer who people liked. I think it worked perfectly."

Just like McGee's career.

"I'm glad I got to play when I did," McGee said. "I don't even like football anymore because every time a guy gets a hand in on a tackle, he's doing a backflip or pounding his chest.

"I played at a great time with some great guys. And even though the money wasn't close to what it is like today, we had a great time."

Few more so than McGee.

Don McIlhenny

Don McIlhenny would have loved to win an NFL championship. And the former Green Bay Packers halfback might have done just that had he stayed in one place a little longer.

McIlhenny played his rookie year of 1956 in Detroit. The following year he was one of four players traded to Green Bay for quarterback Tobin Rote. That 1957 season, the Lions won the NFL championship, the last time that franchise has captured a title.

McIlhenny played in Green Bay from 1957 to 1959, then was taken by Dallas in the expansion draft in 1960. Sure enough, by 1961 the Packers began their run of five world championships in seven years.

Even the Cowboys would go on to great things, but that was long after McIlhenny had retired.

"Every time I left someplace, they got awfully good," said the 78-year-old McIlhenny, who's retired and living in Dallas today. "My timing wasn't the best."

Still, McIlhenny considers his timing impeccable for winding up in Green Bay. He had been the Lions' third-round draft choice out of Southern Methodist University in 1956 when the Packers dealt for him.

He led Green Bay in rushing in 1957 with 384 yards, had 239 the following season, and caught 38 passes in those two seasons. But the Packers went just 3–9 under Lisle Blackbourn in 1957 and 1–10–1 under Ray "Scooter" McLean in 1958.

"Blackbourn was a real impersonal guy," McIlhenny said. "There was no zip or anything.

"Scooter should not have been moved up. I remember in the last week of 1958, we were out on the West Coast and we had just got out butts kicked.

"We had a team meeting and one guy said, 'I got a problem.' Scooter started scratching his bald head and said, 'Take your problems to Jesus, son. Scooter's got problems of his own.'"

That truly was the case as McLean was fired a few days later and replaced by the legendary Vince Lombardi. As McIlhenny soon found out, things had changed for the better.

"It was fun playing for Vince, but for different reasons," McIlhenny said. "It was a wonderful, wonderful turnaround. I was very fond of him.

"All he asked is you stay out of trouble and work hard. I thought that was very simple. If you were a jerk, he'd treat you like a jerk. But we had a couple of private moments that were very special."

One of those came after Green Bay suffered its fourth consecutive loss in 1959, a 28–17 setback at the hands of the hated Chicago Bears.

"Vince was just furious in the locker room," said McIlhenny, who ran for 231 yards in 1959. "He was slamming lockers and really furious and people were just trying to stay out of his way.

"I had gone into the shower, and the shower facilities at Wrigley Field were really tiny. All of a sudden I looked up and Vince was standing next to me in the showers and he said, 'You played a hell of a football game today.' I didn't know what to say."

The next time McIlhenny had such a moment with Lombardi came prior to the 1962 season when he was two years removed from his Packer days.

Texas was home to McIlhenny, so when the Cowboys were given an expansion team in 1960, he told Dallas coach Tom Landry he'd like to play there. It turned out to be a mixed bag, though, as McIlhenny was cut after just one season.

He played the 1961 campaign in San Francisco and wasn't sure if he wanted to retire or not. After watching the Packers practice in Dallas prior to the 1962 season, McIlhenny thought he had the itch and called Lombardi.

"I went to his hotel room and I sat on one bed and he sat on another," McIlhenny recalled. "I told him I wanted to come back and play, and he said, 'I think we can work it out. Why don't you join us back in Green Bay?'

"Well, I think it's like when you want someone to say they love you, but you don't want to get married. I just realized it wasn't for me. So I called him back and he was very gracious and he wished me well."

McIlhenny certainly did well for himself. After a few years in the real estate world, he was an independent producer in the oil business.

Today, McIlhenny keeps close tabs on the Packers, and sometimes wishes his timing had been a little better.

"Green Bay was a bunch of nice people," said McIlhenny, who once played for Curly Lambeau in the College All-Star Game. "It was a very hospitable town and you knew all the store owners and they knew you. We had a great time there. I wish I would stayed around a few years more when they got so good."

CHUCK MERCEIN

Chuck Mercein is wrapped up in another crazy day on Wall Street. His phone never stops ringing. Clients' demands never cease. And Mercein, a sales trader for many years, is going at a frenzied pace.

But in the midst of the hustle and bustle, three simple words can still put Mercein in an almost trance-like state and bring the bedlam around him to a stop: the Ice Bowl.

"Every minute, every second of that final drive, I can still remember it," Mercein said of Green Bay's 21–17 win over Dallas in the 1967 NFL Championship Game. "I remember it like it was yesterday."

And why not? In arguably the most unforgettable game in NFL history, Mercein was arguably the most valuable Packer.

That day, when the kickoff temperature was 13 degrees below zero and the wind chill was minus-46 degrees, Green Bay took the field with 4 minutes, 50 seconds left, trailing the Cowboys 17–14.

"I still remember [Ray] Nitschke walking off the field yelling at the offense, 'Don't let me down,'" said Mercein, a fullback playing in just his seventh game with Green Bay. "Well, I sure wasn't going to be the one to let Nitschke down."

He didn't. The Packers proceeded to put together one of the greatest drives in league history, a 12-play, 68-yard march that quarterback Bart Starr capped with a one-yard touchdown dive with 13 seconds remaining.

Without Mercein, though, Green Bay would have never been in that position. On the drive of all drives, Mercein accounted for 34 of the Packers' 68 yards and put them in position for one of the greatest victories in franchise history.

"It was just great to be placed in a position to make a contribution," said Mercein, who was born in Milwaukee, moved to Chicago when he was in junior high, and later attended Yale. "You always hope to be up to bat with the bases loaded and two outs. That's all I could have asked for."

The Packers certainly couldn't have asked for any more from Mercein.

He got Green Bay's initial first down on the drive with a seven-yard run around right end. After the Packers drove to the Dallas 30-yard line with 1:35 remaining, Mercein made the biggest catch of his life.

Mercein noticed during the drive that he was being left open in the left flat. He then did something extremely rare: he suggested to Starr in the huddle that the quarterback look his way.

Sure enough, Mercein was open. And on a day when the conditions were nightmarish, Mercein made a fantastic adjustment, hauled in the pass, and got out of bounds after a 19-yard gain to the Dallas 11.

"Nobody talked in that huddle except Bart," Mercein said of Starr, who called all the plays. "But I told him, 'I'm open in the left flat. Look for me if you need me.' It was a tough adjustment, but I had decent hands and made a big catch."

Mercein followed that with a big run. The Packers ran a play called "give 54" that looked like a variation of the Green Bay sweep and was designed to take advantage of the aggressiveness of Cowboys Hall of Fame tackle Bob Lilly.

Starr faked the sweep and Lilly followed the guard, leaving a huge hole for Mercein who rumbled eight yards to the 3-yard line.

"Starr made a brilliant call," Mercein said of the give play. "It was a very, very gutty call and I almost got in."

Mercein thought he'd get his chance to score after the Packers moved to the 1-yard line and took their final timeout with 16 seconds left. In the huddle, Starr called "35 wedge," a play designed for Mercein to get the ball.

But Starr worried that the icy conditions could lead to Mercein slipping. And without telling anyone, Starr decided to run a quarterback sneak.

Mercein got a good start and didn't slip. And when Starr kept it and scored, Mercein was initially stunned. But to this day, Mercein doesn't have a single regret with how the final play unfolded.

"Honest to goodness, I wouldn't change a thing," Mercein said. "It would have been great to get the last yard. It would have been the cherry on top of the icing. But Bart was so intelligent and so smart, it was the right percentage move."

Turns out, coming to Green Bay was the right move for Mercein, too.

Mercein began his career with the New York Giants in 1965 and was the team's leading rusher in 1966. But he didn't see eye-to-eye with Giants coach Allie Sherman, who placed Mercein on waivers in 1967.

Mercein wasn't quite ready for a 9-to-5 job, so he stayed sharp working with the Westchester Bulls, a farm team of the Giants. Midway through that 1967 season, Mercein was all set to sign with the Washington Redskins, when he got an unexpected phone call.

"It was a Sunday night and coach Lombardi called and he said, 'I understand you're talking to the Redskins,'" Mercein recalled. "He said, 'We lost both our backs today [Elijah Pitts and Jim Grabowski] and we could really use your help. How would you like to play for the world champion Green Bay Packers?'

"I told my wife to unpack that car. I was going to the Packers. That was a wonderful moment for me."

And for the Packers.

Mercein was starting at fullback the next week, and of course, he helped the Packers go on to win Super Bowl II and their third straight world championship.

"I really had a bruised ego when I got there," said Mercein, who played with Green Bay through the 1969 season before finishing up his career in Washington and with the New York Jets. "But going there and playing well was such a validation of my ability.

"I did what I was capable of doing and helped them win a world championship. It was one of the greatest experiences of my life."

Mercein's life after football was awfully successful, too. But he's the first to admit the thrill of Wall Street never could match the highs of football.

And nothing could ever match the 15 minutes of fame the Ice Bowl brought.

"Those are moments that will never be forgotten," Mercein said. "I still get stuff to sign every week. It was just a privilege to be part of it all."

It's safe to say Packer fans feel the privilege was theirs.

BARTY SMITH

Barty Smith was going to be the next great running back in Green Bay.

He was set to grab the torch from John Brockington, who had taken it from Jim Taylor and Paul Hornung. As Green Bay's No. 1 draft pick in 1974—and the 12th overall selection that year—many predicted greatness for Smith.

But before Smith ever put on a Packers uniform, his career seemed cursed. Playing in the Coaches All-America Game in 1974, Smith suffered a major left knee injury that sidelined him most of his rookie year and caused him to play through great pain over the next seven years.

"I had come to rookie camp that year fat and happy and was not in good condition," said Smith, who played in Green Bay from 1974 to 1980. "So I made a commitment to get ready to play before camp and I had myself in super shape.

"But that was all blown out of the water. After that game, my knee was a mess."

It got even worse.

Smith was plagued by that same knee throughout his seven-year Green Bay career. After Smith's playing days ended, he had eight knee surgeries before eventually getting his left knee replaced.

But you won't hear Smith complain.

Smith became a senior vice president of sales for Loveland Distributing, a beer wholesaler in his hometown of Richmond, Virginia. Smith remarried and has three sons from that marriage.

"Things are going great. I feel really blessed," he said "I enjoy going to work and I think there are few people who can truthfully say that. I have an absolutely great family. Really, I'm blessed and couldn't be happier."

Smith would have been happier if his football days had followed a different path.

At 6′3″, 228 pounds, Smith was a true power runner in his day and was compared to Miami's Larry Csonka when he was coming out of Richmond. But after injuring his knee during the Coaches All-America Game, Smith wasn't the same.

The injury took away much of Smith's rookie season, and when he returned that year, he was moved permanently to fullback and used primarily as a blocker. Smith began seeing a bigger role in the offense over the next few seasons, and by 1977 the coaches felt confident enough in him that they released Brockington.

In 1977, Smith led Green Bay in rushing yards (554) and receptions (37) and he followed that up with 567 rushing yards and 37 catches in 1978.

Following the 1977 season, Smith was named Green Bay's Offensive Player of the Year by the Wisconsin sportswriters. While his stats that year were far from Pro Bowl–caliber, they were the best on a 4–10 Packers team.

"Just to show you how bad it was [in Green Bay], those stats were not very good," Smith admitted. "But it was a sad testimony to our team, I guess."

Smith's knee though, was in a constant state of deterioration and the pain was becoming too much to play with. By 1980, Smith's role was extremely limited and he knew he couldn't pass a physical, causing him to retire.

Smith finished his Green Bay career with 1,942 rushing yards, 979 receiving yards, and several thoughts of what could have been.

"I think I had an acceptable career. I'm not at all ashamed of it." Smith said. "But it could have been a lot better if it wasn't for the knee.

"The pain there never went away, particularly in the latter stages of my career. I just didn't have any confidence or strength in it, plus in my left thigh I was developing atrophy. And that all just does something to your psyche."

The constant losing certainly didn't help.

During Smith's seven years in Green Bay, the Packers' lone winning season came in 1978 when they went 8–7–1. Overall, Green Bay was 37–65–2 in Smith's time.

"I don't think anyone likes losing and that was not a good situation," Smith said. "Everyone there is coming from high school success and college success and all of a sudden, the bottom falls out."

That doesn't mean Smith doesn't have many fond memories.

As a boy in Virginia, Smith grew up idolizing Bart Starr and was thrilled to get the chance to play for him in 1975.

But Smith admits Starr was in over his head when he began. Former head coach Dan Devine left an empty cupboard for Starr after he gave away five high draft picks for over-the-hill quarterback John Hadl.

"I was awestruck to play for a legend like Bart," Smith said. "I had an awful lot of respect for him. He was very dedicated and hours meant nothing to him.

"But he was at such a huge disadvantage after that trade. That was a huge hole to climb out from. We gave it our best, but the talent level wasn't what it needed to be."

Smith includes himself in that category, mainly due to the injury.

And even though his teams were never successful and he still battles chronic pain, Smith doesn't have a single regret.

"No way," said Smith, who played for $150,000 his rookie year and $90,000 his final season. "I never looked at it as a job. I enjoyed the sport and the competition and the contact and wouldn't trade it.

"The fans were unbelievable to us. Even though we struggled on the field, they were great to us. Green Bay's a special place. It's nice to see them doing so well now."

JAMES STARKS

Three games.

Twenty-nine rushing attempts.

One hundred and one yards and an average of 3.48 yards per carry.

These were James Starks' mediocre statistics during the 2010 regular season.

So when the Packers traveled to Philadelphia for a wild-card playoff game, Starks probably wasn't anybody's choice to play hero, right?

"Probably not," Starks said. "But I was ready. Came into the game ready to play, ready for an opportunity."

And it showed.

In one of the most unlikely performances in Packers postseason history, Starks erupted for 123 rushing yards—22 more than his total for the entire season. Starks' heroics lifted the Packers past the Eagles by a score of 21–16, and put him in the record books, as well.

Starks' total established a Packers' rookie postseason record, breaking the old mark of 88 yards by Travis "the Roadrunner" Williams set in 1967. Four weeks later, the Packers were Super Bowl champions—and Starks' performance that first playoff game was a big reason why.

"James was a difference-maker," Packers coach Mike McCarthy said of Starks. "He was a difference-maker for us just the way he was running the ball. He's a gifted athlete, he's a longer-levered individual and he falls forward, and I just love running backs that fall forward, especially when they're 6'2"."

Starks missed the first 11 games of the 2010 season with a hamstring injury. He saw action in three games, but was a healthy inactive in Week 16.

But in one afternoon, Starks—a sixth-round draft pick out of Buffalo—etched his name in the Packer history books.

"The way that James Starks was running the ball tonight was maybe one of the most important factors in this win," Packers quarterback Aaron Rodgers said that night. "He ran great and I am so happy for him. He is a great kid and he has really grown a lot in the past couple weeks. He was big tonight."

Starks certainly wouldn't have been a trendy pick to play hero.

He had a coming-out party, of sorts, with a 73-yard effort against San Francisco in Week 13. But over the final month of the season, Starks had just 11 carries and was inactive in two of Green Bay's final three games.

"All you can do is be ready," Starks said. "That is what I did. Just wait for my opportunity and when it arrives, I try to make the best of it."

McCarthy liked several elements of Starks' game. But Green Bay's head coach didn't fully trust Starks late in the year because his practice habits were sloppy.

"I just haven't been practicing well," Starks said late that season. "It's something I've just got to get used to.

"Coming from college to the NFL has been a lot different. Practice tempo is a lot different. Now, coaches harp on that, and that's something I have to get better at. The best players pick themselves up. I'm just going to keep practicing and keep getting better."

Starks did exactly that against the Eagles.

Starks ripped off a 27-yard run on his first carry of the day, setting the tone for things to come. Starks ran for 36 yards on that drive, one that ended with a Rodgers touchdown pass to tight end Tom Crabtree.

By halftime, Starks had 51 yards on eight carries—then he really cranked it up in the second half.

After the Eagles trimmed Green Bay's lead to 14–10 early in the third quarter, the Packers answered back with an 11-play, 80-yard TD march. Starks had five carries for 32 yards on that drive, including a 19-yard burst off left tackle.

Starks had 15 carries in the second half alone and accounted for 79.3 percent of the rushes by Green Bay running backs.

"Yeah, he surprised me a little bit," Eagles defensive tackle Antonio Dixon said of Starks. "But it's the NFL. Anything can happen any week."

Green Bay, which entered the game running the ball just 43.6 percent of the time, ran it 54.2 percent against the Eagles. The Packers often operated with a full-house backfield, in which fullbacks Quinn Johnson and John Kuhn led the way for Starks.

"Obviously, that was probably the biggest difference," Eagles safety Kurt Coleman said of Starks. "They just kept running the ball and they ran the ball well. He found a lot of holes, and kept on running and got the tough yards."

That didn't stop for Starks either during the 2010 postseason.

Starks averaged 70 rushing yards per game in Green Bay's next two playoff contests—a pair of wins that helped the Packers win the NFC. Starks then had just 11 carries in the 45th Super Bowl, but averaged 4.7 yards per carry.

Starks' performance in those 2010 playoffs helped the Packers offense gain some balance. And Starks was a huge reason the Packers eventually became Super Bowl champions.

"Hard work really does pay off, I'm a very firm believer in that," Starks said. "I'm a hard worker. I'm going to go in and give my all. I'm very confident in my ability.

"I'm going to prove for a lot of people that if I'm healthy...I can do a lot of things that [some people thought I couldn't do]. So I'm going to continue to work hard, continue to try and get better and be the best athlete I can for the team. When my number's called I'll be ready."

Starks was certainly ready against the Eagles. And for that, his place in Packer history will forever be secure.

JIM TAYLOR

The game-time temperature was 13 degrees and falling. Winds gusted up to 40 miles per hour, and many players said the conditions were worse than the legendary Ice Bowl.

The field was hard and frozen. And when players fell, there were pieces of dirt that cut like glass.

Jim Taylor didn't have gloves that day for the 1962 NFL Championship Game. Players didn't wear them back then.

But if ever there was a 60-minute performance that defined Taylor, that was it.

Taylor ran for 85 yards that day on 31 carries and scored the game's lone offensive touchdown. And his remarkable toughness helped Green Bay defeat the host New York Giants 16–7 for their second straight NFL championship.

"That was just a brutal, brutal football game," Taylor said. "We didn't wear gloves back then and my hands were almost frozen, so that made it even worse. But we accepted it and just went out and did our job."

Taylor did his job as well as any running back the Packers have ever had, and was Green Bay's all-time leading rusher until Ahman Green passed him in 2009. Taylor finished his Packers career with 8,207 yards, had five consecutive 1,000-yard seasons between 1960 and 1964, and ran for a career-best 1,474 yards in 1962.

Taylor was named the NFL's Most Valuable Player that 1962 season. He went on to win four championships with the Packers, earned a trip to five Pro Bowls and was inducted into the Pro Football Hall of Fame in 1976.

Vince Lombardi congratulating Jim Taylor after Taylor was named Player of the Year in the NFL by the Associated Press.

Taylor had a myriad of terrific games. But few contests displayed his grit and toughness better than the 1962 Championship Game.

In the first quarter, Taylor was drilled by legendary Giants linebacker Sam Huff, tore up his elbow, bit his tongue, and was swallowing blood the rest of the half.

"That had never happened to me before," Taylor said. "It was rough."

But so was Taylor. After getting stitched up at halftime, Taylor played on—and played at a remarkably high level on a miserable day for football.

"Did everything I could to that [expletive]," Huff recalled later.

Taylor just stared at him, though, and said, "That your best shot?"

That's how Taylor always played the game.

Taylor came to Green Bay out of Louisiana State University as the 15th overall pick in the 1958 draft. At 6' and 214 pounds, Taylor wasn't a big back by any means. He also didn't have blazing speed.

But few players could match Taylor's toughness.

"That was probably my greatest attribute," Taylor said. "It was going to be tough for another player to get the best of me."

That's for sure.

Taylor led the Packers in rushing for seven seasons (1960–66), a mark topped only by Clarke Hinkle, who did so between 1932 and 1941.

Taylor had 26 games with more than 100 yards rushing, which ranks second in team history. Taylor also averaged 4.53 yards per carry, which ranks second all-time to Gerry Ellis (4.58).

Taylor set a team record with 19 touchdowns in 1962, a mark that stood for 41 years. Taylor had four touchdowns in a game three times, and his 91 career touchdowns ranks second to Don Hutson (105).

But perhaps the statistic Taylor remains most proud of is his fumbles—or lack thereof. In 2,166 career touches, both rushing and receiving, Taylor had just 34 fumbles. That equates to just one fumble every 63.7 touches, a mark that stood until Detroit's Barry Sanders shattered it with one fumble every 83.8 touches.

"I was very conscious to maintain my hold on the ball," Taylor said. "I was always very conscientious of maintaining the football.

"And that's a record I always cherished. I feel I was above average in maintaining the football."

Taylor was above average in every aspect of the game.

He was a bruising runner who sought out defenders as much as they searched for him. He wasn't elusive, but bringing him down often took multiple defenders.

Throw in the fact he operated behind one of the greatest offensive lines ever assembled and the passion Vince Lombardi had for the running game, and you can see why Taylor excelled.

"I was clearly running behind the best offensive line in football," said Taylor, who was also inducted into the Packer Hall of Fame in 1975. "And Coach Lombardi stressed that part of the game more than anything.

"We were going to run the ball 65 percent of the time, or so, and Bart [Starr] was only going to have to throw it about 15 times a game. But as I look back, I can say I feel good about the contribution I made to the Packers era and the Lombardi era. I feel good about it."

He should.

But after years of excelling, Taylor and Lombardi reached an impasse. Prior to the 1966 season, the Packers had given youngsters Jim Grabowski and Donny Anderson big contracts to be their back-field of the future.

Taylor, who was always one of the staunchest negotiators among Packer players, became determined to play out his contract, then search for big money. So after the 1966 campaign, he returned home and played one frustrating year with the New Orleans Saints.

"I took a position and just felt I was making the kind of contribution I wanted to be rewarded for," Taylor said.

The move proved beneficial. After his career ended, Taylor spent 18 years working as a color commentator and later as a scout for the Saints.

He and Lombardi also patched up their differences, and when Taylor went into the Hall of Fame, he asked Marie Lombardi to give the introductory speech.

"After Vince went to the Redskins [1968], we had dinner one night," Taylor recalled. "And after that, everything was great again."

Almost as great as Taylor's days with the Packers.

"When I got drafted by Green Bay, I didn't know anything about it or where Green Bay even was," Taylor said "But for me, it turned out to be a stroke of luck because they needed running backs and Coach Lombardi came along the next year.

"At the time, I just said I'll go there and do my job and I think things worked out fine."

Anyone who saw Taylor play would certainly agree.

3

ON THE LINE

PAUL COFFMAN

Paul Coffman can still hear the cheers.

All he has to do is close his eyes and flash back three decades to when he was catching touchdowns for the Green Bay Packers.

Or, he can still simply walk through the Lambeau Field parking lot.

"My daughter and I were walking through the parking lot after a game," Coffman said. "And people started recognizing me and yelling, 'Paul Coffman, you were the greatest!'

"Now, I was losing my hair and it was graying and these people still don't forget you. They embrace their Packers with unconditional love. It's just incredible."

Most would describe Coffman's time in Green Bay as rather incredible. And even though Coffman hasn't donned a Packer uniform since 1985, it's easy to see why he's never been forgotten.

An undrafted free agent out of Kansas State, Coffman played in Green Bay from 1978 to 1985 and made three trips to the Pro Bowl. Coffman caught 322 passes and 39 touchdowns in a Packer uniform. He also teamed with quarterback Lynn Dickey and wideouts James Lofton and John Jefferson to form one of the NFL's deadliest passing attacks in the early '80s.

In the strike-shortened 1982 season, the Packers averaged 25.1 points per game and all three pass-catchers were named to the Pro Bowl.

The following year, Green Bay averaged 26.8 points per game, which was its fourth-highest total since it joined the NFL in 1921.

"Man, that offense was fun to be part of," said Coffman, who was inducted into the Packer Hall of Fame in 1994. "We had four guys catch over 50 passes one year [1983]. All three of us wound up in the Pro Bowl and Lynn did a great job of getting us the ball. That was something else."

Coffman was something else himself. But few would have ever predicted it.

Coffman was so lightly regarded coming out of Kansas State in 1978 that he had to persuade former Packer assistant coach John Meyer to give him a tryout when Meyer visited the campus to work out a different Wildcats player.

After Coffman wasn't selected in a 12-round draft, the Packers signed him as a free agent. Coffman played little his rookie year, but burst onto the scene with a 56-catch season in 1979. That was a team record for tight ends until 2012, when Jermichael Finley caught 61 balls.

Year in and year out, Coffman was one of the NFL's most productive tight ends. Aside from the strike-shortened 1982 campaign, Coffman had at least 42 catches and 496 yards in every season following his rookie year and he played in all but two games during his Green Bay career.

Coffman lacked great speed, and at 6'3" and 225 pounds, he was never going to be an overly physical presence. But he had a phenomenal football I.Q., competed harder than most and had sensational hands.

When his accomplishments are brought up, though, Coffman is a picture of modesty.

"Bob Schnelker paid so much attention to detail," Coffman said of his former offensive coordinator. "He didn't assume anything. He was one of the first people to utilize the tight end and he was a big reason our offense produced as well as it did."

Coffman's production was never better than in 1983, when he caught 54 passes for 814 yards and 11 touchdowns. Those 11 touchdowns were the most by a Packer receiver since Bill Howton had 12 in 1956. And the only receivers in the NFL with more touchdowns that year were St. Louis' Roy Green [14], Philadelphia's Mike Quick [13], and the Raiders' Todd Christensen [12].

Included in that memorable season was Coffman's huge night in the Packers' 48–47 victory over Washington on *Monday Night Football*. In that game, Coffman caught six passes for 124 yards and two touchdowns.

Coffman added to his solid career, catching 43 balls with nine touchdowns in 1984 and 49 passes with six touchdowns in '85.

Then the inexplicable happened. During training camp in 1986, head coach Forrest Gregg determined the Packers needed a youth movement. So he cut the 30-year-old Coffman, along with Dickey.

To this day, Coffman remains upset about how his Green Bay days ended.

"Forrest, he's someone I have nothing to say about," said Coffman, who split his final seasons between Kansas City and Minnesota. "When James [Lofton] went into the Hall of Fame, he mentioned him. But I guess he's just got more class than I do."

Coffman has spent the last several years watching his two sons follow their football dreams. Chase Coffman has bounced around the NFL, while Carson Coffman is playing in the Arena Football League.

Both players have a long ways to go, though, to catch their old man. And if they don't believe it, all it might take is a return trip to Lambeau Field.

"Going back there and still getting recognized is really neat," said Coffman, who grew up in tiny Chase, Kansas. "Just playing there was unbelievable.

"From my perspective, I was living my dream. From the time I was a little kid, all I wanted to do was play in the NFL. And I was a small-town guy and I would have been lost in New York or L.A, so Green Bay was the perfect place for me."

Packer fans still feel the same way.

RON HALLSTROM

Ron Hallstrom's views certainly weren't the norm. But that was just fine with the Green Bay Packers 1982 first-round draft choice.

Hallstrom, a guard, didn't hit it off with then–coach Bart Starr. Hallstrom and Forrest Gregg peacefully co-existed. And later, Hallstrom butted heads with general manager Ron Wolf.

Interestingly, Hallstrom's views were 180 degrees from many Packers from that era.

"That's just how it worked out for me," Hallstrom said.

Starr, the Packers head coach and general manager, took Hallstrom in the first round of the 1982 draft with the 22nd overall pick. At the time, Hallstrom was part of a changing of the guard at the guard position.

He was a big man who could move. He had great feet and was extremely fast within a 15-yard box.

Hallstrom entered the league at 300 pounds and later played at 320. And because Starr liked his linemen smaller, Hallstrom sat his first two years.

"That was tough," Hallstrom said. "I never totally understood why Bart drafted me in the first place."

When Gregg took over in 1984, though, he made the switch to bigger linemen. And Hallstrom was a fixture at right guard the next nine years. While Hallstrom never made a Pro Bowl, he was tough, physical, reliable, and one of Green Bay's better linemen of that era.

"I have great respect for Forrest because he gave me my start," Hallstrom said. "I can't say anything bad about him. I did have some different experiences with him, things we should probably keep out of the paper. But he did a lot of things that helped mold me into an NFL player."

The problem was Gregg never did mold Green Bay into a winning NFL team, going 25–37–1 in his four years on the job. In fact, the Packers were above .500 in only three of Hallstrom's 11 years in Green Bay and made the playoffs just once, in 1982.

"The losing was hard," said Hallstrom, who had just one surgery during his playing days. "That can really take a toll. That's the one thing I wish I could change."

That's not totally true. In 1990, Hallstrom and teammates Ken Ruettgers and Rich Moran were all looking to change their contracts.

Green Bay had broke the bank on Tony Mandarich the previous April, and Mandarich never saw the field during the Packers' 10–6 season in 1989. So the trio of offensive linemen held out that year.

"Tony was a product of his environment," Hallstrom said. "He was the prototypical guy who knew how to sell a contract. It was the Brian Bosworth effect."

Eventually, they all were signed before the season began and Hallstrom tripled his previous salary. But head coach Lindy Infante punished them all with benchings. Ruettgers was the first to start, but Moran sat much of the year behind Billy Ard, and Hallstrom sat the longest, playing behind Keith Uecker.

Those decisions by Infante played a large role in Green Bay's 6–10 campaign. And it may have been the beginning of the end for Infante, who won just 10 games over the next two seasons and was fired.

"With Lindy, too many people thought the success we were having was because of them," Hallstrom said. "It was too individual. And that led to the demise of the team."

The demise of Hallstrom's Green Bay career came after the 1992 season.

The NFL was in its first year of full-fledged free agency and Hallstrom was hoping for one big final contract. The Los Angeles Rams had offered him $1 million a year, but he truly wanted to stay in Green Bay, so he turned it down.

Hallstrom went to then–Packers general manager Ron Wolf asking for $1 million—figuring that was where the bar had been set. But Wolf wouldn't budge off $800,000 and refused to add a series of incentives to hit the $1 million mark.

So Hallstrom played one year in Philadelphia—a move he regrets to this day.

"Our egos didn't hit it off well," Hallstrom said of he and Wolf. "And I learned don't let a personal relationship make a business decision for you. I should've just sucked it up.

"I really wanted to finish my career in Green Bay and should have done that. Instead, I left the league the way you should leave it. Pissed off."

At the time, Hallstrom was going through plenty of personal crisis. His younger brother had passed away. He found out his mom had cancer. And he was in the process of a divorce with his wife, Mary Pat.

"That year, everything kind of came into perspective," Hallstrom said. "And football kind of took a backseat."

Hallstrom's career, though, doesn't need to take a backseat to anyone's. In a time where Green Bay's franchise lacked stability and steadiness, he was a rock.

"I'd never take back or change what happened," Hallstrom said. "It was a great experience. It was really a kick start to what I'm doing today. I have no qualms."

It's easy to see why.

When Hallstrom arrived in Green Bay years ago, he didn't hunt or fish. He didn't know anything about snowmobiles or four-wheelers. Personal watercrafts were a mystery to him.

Today, Hallstrom's a resident expert on it all as the owner of Ron Hallstrom Sports and Marine in tiny Woodruff, Wisconsin, located just outside Minoqua. It's not the post-football career he ever envisioned coming out of Iowa.

"After I retired, I looked into a bunch of things," Hallstrom said. "I didn't know anything about this. But it's been good."

To some extent, the business parallels football. Six months a year—three during both summer and winter—are crazy and intense. The other six are more laid back.

In many respects, the Woodruff area is similar to Green Bay—quiet, peaceful, and steeped in family values. And it's just what Hallstrom wanted after his 12-year career ended.

"I love Minoqua and my family loves it," Hallstrom said. "I think you have to be ready for it in your life, and I was. And by that point, I had lived the life of 20 men."

A life he's still grateful for today.

"I had a great time in Green Bay," Hallstrom said. "Not everything was perfect. It never is. But looking back, I have no complaints. It was a great experience."

BOB HYLAND

Bob Hyland wishes Packer fans would remember him as a rookie part-time starter during Green Bay's Super Bowl championship season of 1967. Or perhaps as a versatile offensive lineman that enjoyed a solid, 11-year NFL career.

But Hyland knows that's unlikely.

Hyland's claim to fame is—and likely always will be—breaking Green Bay coach Dan Devine's leg in the 1971 season opener.

"It was just one of those fluky things," Hyland said.

That it was.

Green Bay had made Hyland, an All-American offensive lineman at Boston College, the ninth overall pick in the 1967 draft. He was supposed to be the Packers' center of the future, but after three somewhat tumultuous years in Green Bay, Hyland was traded to Chicago and was with the Giants in 1971.

The season opener that year marked Devine's first as Green Bay's head coach and Hyland's first in a Giants uniform. It was a wet and rainy day, and at one point, Packers defensive back Doug Hart intercepted New York quarterback Fran Tarkenton.

Hyland took off in pursuit, and helped knock Hart out of bounds on the Green Bay sideline.

"It was sloppy and muddy and I couldn't stop," Hyland said. "I kind of went careening into a bunch of people."

It wasn't until after the game that reporters informed Hyland that one of those people was Devine. And Hyland's hit had shattered Devine's leg in several places.

To this day, Packer fans bitter about Devine's failed tenure joke it was the best thing Hyland ever did for the Green Bay organization. But it's the last thing Hyland wanted.

"When reporters came to me after the game and told me what happened, I was like, 'Jesus.' I felt awful," Hyland said. "But Devine was a class act.

"He had read my comments and saw how bad I felt and sent me a telegram. He told me not to feel bad and that he always stood too close to the field, anyhow. It was a crazy play."

Hyland's time in Green Bay was somewhat crazy, too.

Hyland came to Green Bay in 1967, and was expected to step in at center or guard. By the midway point of his rookie season, Hyland had become the preferred starter at center over Ken Bowman. But throughout the year, he bumped heads with Ray Wietecha, the Packers offensive line coach.

"Ray Wietecha and I never did get along from Day 1," Hyland said. "He had it in for me. He didn't like my style of play for some reason."

Packers coach Vince Lombardi seemed to like Hyland's play just fine. The 6'5", 260-pound Hyland was big for his era, and weighed about 20 pounds more than Bowman. Lombardi liked Hyland's size and physicality, and started him much of the second half of that season.

Hyland played most of the Western Conference Championship Game against Los Angeles that year, a 28–7 Green Bay win. And although Bowman became famous for his block in the Ice Bowl the next week, Hyland seemed in line to start Super Bowl II.

"I had been practicing with the No. 1s that week right up until the end," Hyland said. "And with about five minutes left in practice, Bart [Starr] bobbled a snap. I don't know if it was my fault or his fault, but Lombardi decided to make the change.

"I think Wietecha had been in his ear, but I was steamed. And I just walked right off the field. I figured [Lombardi] would fine me, but he didn't. So unfortunately, the Super Bowl wasn't the greatest of memories for me. It was great to win, but I was just so darned disappointed."

The rest of Hyland's career in Green Bay was somewhat disappointing for him, as well.

Lombardi stepped down as head coach after the 1967 season. Hyland never could crack the starting lineup under new coach Phil Bengtson. Bowman refused to give up his job at center, and the Packers used a first-round draft choice on guard Billy Lueck in 1968, blocking Hyland's path there.

"Without Vince, it just wasn't the same," Hyland said. "I played some guard the next year, but then they drafted Billy Lueck. And with Wietecha around, I was out of there."

Indeed he was. Hyland was traded to Chicago following the 1969 season, and after a year with the Bears, he was traded to his hometown team—the New York Giants.

Hyland moved to left guard with the Giants and played the most minutes on the team in 1971. But in '72, an old foe reappeared.

"I had one really good year with the Giants and then they hired a new offensive line coach," Hyland recalled. "And guess who it was? Good 'ol Ray Wietecha.

"And that was after I had let a lot of people and a lot of sportswriters know how I felt about him. I learned the hard way not to burn your bridges. Because he got his revenge."

That he did. Hyland spent most of the 1972 and '73 seasons on the bench.

But by '74, it was crystal clear to management that Hyland was one of the team's best five linemen. And despite Wietecha's presence, Hyland started the next two years.

To this day, though, Hyland holds a grudge against Wietecha. And he wishes it was Wietecha—and not Devine—on the sideline that day in Green Bay.

"That would have been beautiful," Hyland said.

Hyland actually came back to Green Bay and played the 1976 season behind starting center Larry McCarren. He asked for his release following that year, then played half of the '77 campaign in New England before retiring.

"It actually felt good to go back," said Hyland said. "I had enjoyed Green Bay a lot and felt it was a quality organization, so it was good to go back to a familiar place."

One that will always remember him as the man who broke Devine's leg.

"I'd rather be remembered with Bowman and [Jerry] Kramer for the block in the Ice Bowl," Hyland said. "But it is what it is."

GREG KOCH

For nine years in Green Bay, Greg Koch made a ton of noise on the football field. He was one of the better right tackles in the game, and was an enormous part of the Packers' record-setting offenses of the early 1980s.

Fortunately or unfortunately for Koch—depending on your perspective—he made just as much noise off the field. As one of the more outspoken Packers of his era, Koch always told the truth, which ruffled a fair share of feathers along the way.

"I gave whatever answers I felt and sometimes that hurt me," Koch said. "People thought I was outspoken. But I won't apologize for the things I said. They were things I believed."

It should surprise few that Koch is just as outspoken today. Only now his debating comes in a courtroom and on the radio.

When his playing days ended, Koch returned to the University of Arkansas to get his law degree. He's been a practicing lawyer since. In addition, Koch does a daily radio show in Houston with former NFL defensive end N.D. Kalu.

"I never could stand the dumb-jock connotation," said Koch, who was a chemistry major during his undergraduate days at Arkansas. "Larry McCarren and I would go on trips and bring a *Newsweek*. And just for argument's sake, we would argue every story that was in there.

"Even if we didn't necessarily believe in something, one of us would argue the opposite point just to play devil's advocate. We were going to solve all the world's problems."

Koch was always trying to solve the Packers' problems—both on and off the field—during his time in Green Bay.

Koch criticized management for failing to sign No. 1 draft pick Bruce Clark in 1980 and later losing defensive end Mike Butler.

"It was all about money back then," Koch said. "They were not trying to win with those executives. They got Ron Wolf in there, starting spending some money, signed Reggie White, and they won a Super Bowl."

Koch wasn't shy when it came to ripping some coaching decisions Forrest Gregg made.

"He ran down the football team in the media," Koch said of Gregg. "Then, if you do well, it's the coach that looks good. But the truth is he was not a good football coach."

Koch continued to pile on Gregg, even when his Packer days had ended. Gregg cut several veterans before the 1986 season, including Koch, quarterback Lynn Dickey, and tight end Paul Coffman.

Two seasons later, after Koch had landed in Minnesota, Gregg left Green Bay to take over an SMU program that had just been handed the "death penalty." A reporter asked for Koch's opinion of the hire.

"I said, 'He's the perfect guy for the program,'" Koch recalled. "The reporter said, 'There isn't a program.' And I said, 'Exactly.'"

Looking back, Koch regrets just one thing he said. After Gregg cut him in 1986, Koch was signed by Miami and was asked the biggest difference between the two cities.

"I said in Green Bay, you've got a great wardrobe if you've got 10 bowling shirts," Koch said.

That zinger made *Sports Illustrated's* top 100 all-time quotes, but Koch said it was taken out of context.

"I was trying to poke fun of myself, but it was a stupid remark and I wish I had never said it," he said. "I've been apologizing for it ever since."

Koch had nothing to apologize for when it came to Green Bay's offense in the 1980s.

Koch and the Packers qualified for the playoffs during the strike-shortened season of 1982. That was Green Bay's first trip to the postseason in 10 years and the only time in Bart Starr's nine-year coaching tenure the Packers reached the playoffs.

In 1983, Koch and Green Bay's high-flying offense scored 429 points and ranked second in the NFL in total offense.

"We had some great players on that team," Koch said. "A lot of weapons."

Koch was certainly at the heart of Green Bay's success, starting for eight years, and at one point making 78 consecutive starts.

Koch, a second-round draft choice out of Arkansas in 1977, possessed tremendous strength and could bench press 520 pounds in his heyday. And he was arguably the top pass blocker on a Green Bay offensive line that give Dickey and his talented core of wideouts time to shine.

"That offense was a lot of fun to play on," Koch said. "We didn't really think anyone could stop us, and a lot of times, we were right."

Koch talks fondly of Green Bay's 48–47 win over Washington on *Monday Night Football* in 1983. He still smiles when talking about the Packers' 41–16 playoff win over St. Louis in 1982.

And thinking about Green Bay's aerial circus—one that featured Dickey, wideouts James Lofton and John Jefferson, and tight end Paul Coffman—remains a great source of pride.

It wasn't always paradise. But the good certainly outweighed the bad.

"I had nine great years in Green Bay and absolutely loved my time there," Koch said. "I made a lot of great friends there. Some people say the best friends you make are in high school. But those are guys I sweated my guts out with and took a lot of flak with."

And in Koch's case, gave his share of flak, too.

JERRY KRAMER

Today, Jerry Kramer is fondly remembered as one of the greatest offensive guards to ever play for the Green Bay Packers.

Kramer made arguably the most memorable block in NFL history during the Ice Bowl. And Kramer's 11-year stint in Green Bay included three Pro Bowl selections, a berth on the 1960s All-Decade team and five NFL championships.

But when he looks back, Kramer laughs when he thinks how close he came to having his career in Green Bay cut short.

Kramer, Green Bay's fourth-round draft choice in 1958, played his first season under the loosey-goosey Scooter McLean. And when Vince Lombardi came in the following year, his in-your-face approach initially didn't sit well with Kramer.

In the early 1960s, the *Chicago Tribune* had just published a story calling Kramer and Fuzzy Thurston the best pair of guards in football. Later that same week in practice, a Packer sweep went nowhere and Lombardi went ballistic.

"He came running up screaming 'The best pair of guards in football, my [expletive],'" Kramer said. "And I was already playing hurt. I had broken two ribs the week before in San Francisco, and I just snapped.

"I was dead-set on punching him in the mouth. I got off the pile and I thought, 'Okay, I'll be suspended. I'll get docked my salary. And I'm sure I'll get traded.' And I just said, '[Expletive] it!' I'm going to hit him. I was so angry and so out of control. So I walked over by him and he wouldn't look at me. He just stayed turned away.

"Finally I got over my anger and decided to walk the sidelines. Well after five or six minutes, just the right amount of time for me to cool off, Lombardi came down, pats me on the shoulder, and rubs my hair. It was good for both of us that I didn't hit him."

That it was.

With Kramer playing right guard, Green Bay won NFL championships in 1961, '62, and '65. The Packers also won Super Bowl titles in 1966 and '67.

Kramer received some form of All-Pro honors on six occasions and was named to the All-NFL First 50 Years Team. And Kramer's block on Dallas' Jethro Pugh sprung quarterback Bart Starr for a game-winning touchdown in the Ice Bowl, one of the most famous football games ever played.

To this day his omission from the Hall of Fame is one of the greatest mysteries of the sport.

"Out of every guy that was on the first 50 years all-football team, I'm the only one not in the Hall of Fame," he said. "Does it bother me? A little bit, but not a lot."

Don't let Kramer completely fool you. There's a part of him that's extremely agitated, and many have taken measures to help Kramer reach the Hall of Fame someday.

Kramer's very own website (jerrykramer.com) makes a case for him. Kramer's daughter, Alicia, also started a nationwide campaign to get support for her father's enshrinement.

So far, though, Kramer's been left out in the cold.

"The way I look at it is football has been so good to me," Kramer said. "It's given me so many presents. After so many years, it would seem a little childish to be [expletive] off over an honor you didn't get."

That's about the only honor Kramer didn't get. But when history remembers Kramer, he will always be linked to the Ice Bowl.

Trailing 17–14 to Dallas in the 1967 NFL Championship Game, the Packers were out of timeouts and faced a third-and-goal from the Cowboys' 1-yard line with 16 seconds left. Lombardi bypassed a potential tying field goal, electing to go for the victory instead.

No. 64 Jerry Kramer clears the way for Paul Hornung during an intrasquad game in 1959.

The play was supposed to be a handoff to Chuck Mercein, but Starr was leery of Mercein slipping and decided to run a quarterback sneak instead. Kramer found a rare piece of field that wasn't iced over, came off the ball fast and hard and immediately leveled Pugh with a perfect cut block.

Center Ken Bowman finished Pugh off, giving Starr the wedge opening he needed. Starr snuck in, the Packers had one of the most dramatic victories in league history and Kramer was part of the NFL's most legendary block.

"People want to always talk about that play. But what personifies the character and makeup of that football team was the drive," Kramer said, referring to the 12-play, 68-yard march to win the game. "That was a perfect example of what those teams were all about.

"On that drive, we were absolutely brilliant. Chuck Mercein, Donny Anderson, Boyd Dowler, Bart, the entire offensive line. They were all outstanding."

The legendary play also provided the ideal ending for a book Kramer and sportswriter Dick Schaap were working on.

Throughout the 1967 season, Kramer kept a diary of the Packers' season, one that ended with a victory in Super Bowl II.

The publicity generated by the Ice Bowl—a game that was later voted the greatest game in NFL history—helped *Instant Replay* become one of the best-selling sports books of all time.

"It was an interesting experience and it was fun to see that world," Kramer said. "Pro football is a very closed world. You're either part of the team or you're not. But the whole experience was pretty great."

Kramer's post-football experiences have been awfully great, too. And despite multiple efforts, Kramer hasn't been able to bring himself to retire.

Kramer went into the commercial diving business, then built apartments with former Packer Don Chandler. He started a film company in Los Angeles and dabbled in the restaurant business. He also worked with oil and gas exploration, coal mining, telecommunications, and nutrition, and did consulting work for a security company and a hospital group.

"I've tried it like three or four times and it just didn't sit very well with me," Kramer said. "There's so many things I still want to do and I'm not slowing down at all. In fact, I'm as busy as I've ever been. But I'm enjoying the hell out of it."

But Kramer's the first to admit nothing compares to playing on Sundays.

"Those were incredible times and some incredible men," Kramer said. "You won't get groups of guys like that very often."

Nor will you get many people like Kramer.

RON KRAMER

R on Kramer doesn't regret his decision for a single second. He's never wavered, never looked back.

But oh, how Kramer wishes circumstances could have been different.

The former Green Bay Packers standout tight end had the decision of a lifetime to make before the 1965 season. His son, Kurt, had lost an eye while playing with a pair of scissors. His daughter, Cassie, was terribly sick with allergies.

And Kramer's family wouldn't come to Green Bay. So the former Packers great did what he believes any family man should do—he returned to his.

"I would love to have stayed my whole career in Green Bay," Kramer said before his death in 2010. "I loved all of my teammates… but I look at my children, and I'm so proud of the decision I made.

"If I could have played in Green Bay all those years, I would have. But I made the decision that had to be made.

"It's not noble when it comes to your family. I had to make sure the kids would be okay. And even though the marriage didn't make it, the kids and I did."

Kramer, who played out his option after the 1964 campaign, returned to Detroit to be with his family. Shortly thereafter, Kramer succeeded in getting traded to the Lions to be closer to home.

Under the old Pete Rozelle Rule, the Packers were awarded a No. 1 draft choice, which they used to select fullback Jim Grabowski in 1966.

"Every time I see Grabowski, he kisses me and thanks me for letting him become part of two more championship teams," said Kramer, who played in Detroit from 1965 to 1967. "It was tough because my years in Detroit were awful.

"The head coach [Harry Gilmer] was the dumbest guy I ever met. People didn't come on time, and people didn't care. It was polar opposite of where I came from.

"But I did what I had to, and Coach Lombardi was great. He said, 'I understand that you have to do what you feel is right. I can't replace you, but I'll understand whatever decision you make.'"

Kramer, who was inducted into the Packer Hall of Fame in 1975, was in the midst of a brilliant career with Green Bay at the time. The fourth overall pick of the 1957 draft out of Michigan, Kramer possessed a frightening combination of size, strength, and agility.

Kramer tore up his knee as a rookie, then spent the 1958 season as an officer in the Air Force. When Kramer returned in 1959, though, his play skyrocketed at the same time Green Bay's did.

Between 1961 and 1964, Kramer caught 138 passes for 2,202 yards and 15 touchdowns. He was named All-Pro in both 1961 and 1962 and was named to the Pro Bowl in '62.

In the 1961 NFL Championship Game, Kramer caught four passes for 80 yards and two touchdowns.

That marked the first of five titles Green Bay would win under Lombardi between 1961 and 1967.

"He was the best coach ever, and I think few would question or argue that," Kramer said. "He always had you ready to go, mentally and physically.

"All you had to do was watch him and emulate him, and you'd be ready to play. Plus, he was just a tremendous teacher, very thorough. It was an honor to play for him."

Green Bay won titles in 1961 and '62 and later 1965–67 under Lombardi. Most agree, though, that the 1962 team Kramer was part of was the best of them all.

That group went 14–1—including the postseason—and again defeated the New York Giants for the NFL championship, 16–7.

"That team was incredible," said Kramer, who finished his career with 299 receptions for 3,272 yards and 16 touchdowns. "Everybody was in their prime, everybody had a great year."

In spite of a few rough seasons in Detroit, Kramer's great years continued after he left Green Bay.

Kramer retired following the 1967 campaign. He then worked for Paragon Steel Corp. in Detroit for 22 years, working his way up to vice president. In addition, he was an analyst for University of Michigan football until 1997, called some preseason Detroit Lions football games, and was an analyst for Big Ten Football for WTBS-TV.

"I loved it," Kramer said. "I would watch the game, and I think I could recognize a lot more than most people because of the great training I got under Lombardi."

Kramer also began a business called Ron Kramer Industries, where he dealt in specialty advertising.

Kramer was inducted into the College Football Hall of Fame in 1978. And in 1999, *Sports Illustrated* published a list of "The 50 Greatest Sports Figures from Michigan" (in all sports), and ranked Kramer seventh on the list.

Through it all, Kramer tried like heck not to look back on his decision to leave Green Bay.

"I'd go back and do it all over again," said Kramer, who had been living with Paul Hornung and Max McGee prior to leaving Green Bay.

"I loved Green Bay, and nothing compares to the Green Bay experience anywhere. I would have loved to spend a little more time there, but I never regret what I did for a minute."

NORM MASTERS

It was more than 50 years ago that Norm Masters received a letter that always stayed near and dear to him.

It was January 4, 1963, and Green Bay Packers coach Vince Lombardi was thrilled his team had just won its second NFL championship, defeating the New York Giants 16–7 in a game played at Yankee Stadium. So Lombardi sent everyone on the Packers a letter thanking them for a glorious season that saw them go 14–1 and repeat as world champions.

Masters, an offensive tackle, found the letter inspirational. And up until his death in 2011, Masters kept a copy in his study at his Bloomfield Hills, Michigan, home.

"I'm one of the few guys who saved that letter," said Masters, who played with the Packers from 1957 to 1964. "Even Vince Lombardi Jr. asked me once where I got it and I said, 'Your dad sent it out to the team.' It's really special to me."

In the letter, Lombardi opened by saying that words will never express his gratitude. He talked of how success is more difficult to live with than failure.

He said the Giants tried intimidating the Packers, but Green Bay prevailed thanks to its mental toughness. He said the Packers are made up of men of great character and reminded the players there is no substitute for victory. Then, he told each player that he was sending them a color television.

"A color TV was big time back in those days," Masters joked shortly before his death. "But really, that letter has meant a lot to me. I've used it many times in my life and I used so much of what coach Lombardi taught us."

Like many players from his era, Masters went on to great success after football. He began his career in the insurance industry, but moved into the fast-food business. For more than 40 years, he was a franchise owner of Kentucky Fried Chicken, Long John Silver's, and Taco Bell.

Up until his death at age 77, Masters was a managing partner with Van Masters Management Inc./KFC Franchise.

"I've always thought if you have a passion for what you're doing and you still have the flame, why not?" he said.

Masters certainly had a passion for football. But little did he know he'd ever be playing the game in tiny Green Bay.

Masters, who played collegiately at Michigan State, was drafted by the Chicago Cardinals. But he played the 1956 season with the British Columbia Lions because the pay in the Canadian Football League was much better than the NFL.

NFL teams didn't retain draft rights back then, so when Masters decided he wanted to play closer to home, he signed with the Detroit Lions. But Detroit quickly traded Masters and three others for Green Bay quarterback Tobin Rote.

Masters came to a franchise in disarray. There was talent, but virtually no direction or leadership, which is why Green Bay went 4–19–1 in 1957–58 under Lisle Blackbourn and Ray "Scooter" McLean.

"What was happening was we had some talent," Masters said. "But we needed someone to get us organized."

That someone, obviously, was Lombardi. The Packers were 7–5 during his first season in 1959, winning their final four games that year. And by 1961, they were NFL champions.

"He had prepared for that job for a long time," Masters said of Lombardi. "He came in and he had a plan and we used his criteria as a leader. He demanded that people respond to his program and he convinced us that we'd be successful if we listened to him. And we were.

"He set standards to create a winner and he knew what the end result would be. From Day 1, you knew from how he presented himself that he had a strong grasp. And as we started to win, we all became believers."

Regardless of what their individual situations were. For example, Masters was a starter at left tackle his first two years in the league while Bob Skoronski was in the service. The two split time at the position in 1959, then Masters eventually became Green Bay's top backup lineman as Skoronski reclaimed the job.

"The big thing is we played as a team," Masters said of the Packers' success. "You never really saw any friction of any type. And if you think about it, what people remember are the great teams.

"It's because of that team, not any individuals, that we still get such great notoriety. And Lombardi always preached that whole team concept. He was the kind of guy that pushed you hard and you didn't realize until afterward, but he made you better than you thought you could be."

Masters' time in Green Bay was better than he could have ever hoped.

Not only did he win two titles, he made countless friends that he always remained close to. Masters also returned to Green Bay at least once a year for an alumni-related function and was extremely grateful he wound up a Packer.

"I can't tell you how much I liked Green Bay," Masters said. "It's one of the Meccas of sports and just a great place to play football.

"I think about how lucky I was to play there and take what I learned and have some success in the business world. It's been a wonderful life. It really has."

BOB SKORONSKI

The Beatles had Ringo. The Fab Five had Ray Jackson. Led Zeppelin had John Paul Jones.

Every great group always seems to have an anonymous member. And the fantastic Green Bay Packer offensive lines of the 1960s were no different.

While players such as Jerry Kramer, Forrest Gregg, Jim Ringo, Fuzzy Thurston, and Ken Bowman received much of the attention, durable left tackle Bob Skoronski was about as dependable as they came. And even though he didn't get the glory, Skoronski was as vital as any other member of the line.

"The coaches used to grade out every performance we had, and I'll tell you what, I sleep pretty well at night," Skoronski said. "The line didn't operate with four guys, and we used to run important plays everywhere, not just to one side or the other.

"I don't think any player ever thought anyone was better than anyone else. And in my own way, I'm very satisfied with my career."

With good reason.

The Packers drafted Skoronski in the fifth round out of Indiana in 1956. After starting most of that year, he had to fill a two-year ROTC commitment.

When Skoronski returned for the 1959 season, Lisle Blackbourn—his previous coach—had been fired. So had Scooter McLean—the man who had replaced Blackbourn.

In stepped Vince Lombardi, and Skoronski soon realized that things would never be the same again. And that was a great thing for everyone involved.

"If I could put one word on it, it would be discipline," he said. "Discipline in our study. Discipline in the execution. Discipline in how we prepared. There was a chain around us all the time.

"Plus, [Lombardi] got us in the kind of physical shape that when the game was decided in the fourth quarter, we were in shape to do it. He brought an attitude about winning and a professionalism that we lacked. And if you weren't prepared for every play, it was a calamity."

Lombardi didn't just reverse the Packers' sorry fortunes on the football field. He did it away from the gridiron, too, buying every player a jacket, slacks, and a tie.

"He told us we're not some stumblebums," Skoronski said of Lombardi. "He wanted us to look as good as the doctors or the lawyers in town.

"His philosophies weren't just like a father and a teacher. We were all part of something special, and didn't even know it was happening."

What began to happen was a complete reversal of fortune that saw Green Bay win five NFL championships between 1961 and 1967. And Skoronski was in the middle of it throughout.

It took Skoronski just a few games to replace Norm Masters at left tackle after he returned in 1959, and he remained there throughout the 1963 season. When the Packers sent Ringo to Philadelphia in 1964, Skoronski was shifted to center for a time before Bowman was ready.

"They called me down and asked me to snap the ball," Skoronski recalled. "I did it maybe eight or 10 times, and they said, 'Okay. We've seen enough.'

"Well, then next thing I know they trade Ringo and I'm the center. I had no idea what they had been up to."

Skoronski certainly knew what was happening on the field, though. After Bowman was ready to take the reigns at center, he moved back to left tackle where he started though the 1968 season—his final one in the league.

Skoronski was a punishing run blocker and received some recognition when he was voted to the Pro Bowl by the coaches in 1966. He was also named to the Packer Hall of Fame in 1976.

Like many of his linemates, Skoronski will always be most closely identified with Lombardi's signature play—the Packer sweep.

"I think when he first got there, we broke it down for a week," Skoronski said of the play. "I never saw anyone, anywhere go though something more thoroughly than he did that one play.

"And the one thing about Lombardi was you didn't sleep much after the Sunday games if you had any mistakes. Now, no one ever plays a perfect game, but we tried to be as close to perfect as you can be."

And to a large extent, they succeeded. While few will rattle off the name Skoronski when reciting the stars of Green Bay's glory days, he deserves a lot of credit for helping the Packers accomplish all they did.

"Once we started to win, we were all satisfied," he said. "It didn't matter who got the credit. No one on that team was any more important than the next guy, and I think that's a big reason we did as well as we did."

ED WEST

They called him "the Toolbox."

And Ed West definitely had a little bit of everything in his arsenal.

A gritty blocker, a reliable pass catcher, West was the ultimate jack-of-all-trades during a surprising 14-year NFL career that included 11 seasons in Green Bay.

"Brett Favre gave me that nickname," West said. "And it was a pretty good one, too. He said I brought my toolbox to work every day and that's how I got the job done."

Favre was dead-on with that assessment.

West went undrafted coming out of Auburn in 1984, but had roughly 10 teams interested in him as a "street" free agent. He picked Green Bay, though, due to its small-town values.

"I came from a small town," said West, who was raised in Leighton, Alabama. "There was one red light in the whole place. Green Bay was perfect."

It also was the perfect place for West to make a roster.

Green Bay had one of the NFL's top starting tight ends in Paul Coffman, but the Packers lacked depth, and when West had a solid training camp, Packers coach Forrest Gregg took notice. West was actually released on the final cutdown. But when he cleared waivers and a roster spot opened up, the Packers brought him back.

West had a major impact his first season, too. Green Bay featured him near the goal line, and four of West's six catches that season went for touchdowns.

"I was like, 'Are you kidding me?'" he said. "First year in the NFL and I scored four touchdowns. That's amazing."

Gregg was enamored with West's toughness and blocking ability. And after two years as a reserve, West became a starter in 1986 when Gregg released Coffman, the longtime starter.

"I remember that was a lot of pressure," West recalled. "Coffman had been there forever and was a fan favorite.

"But that just made me work harder. A lot of people didn't think I could do the job, and if someone tells you that you can't do something, it just makes you work harder."

West proved all doubters wrong, holding the starting position the next nine years. West was never particularly gifted in one area, just solid in most.

West was a better blocker than receiver and averaged just 18 receptions per season during his 11-year Packers career. But during the 1988–89 seasons, West found the end zone on 10 of his 49 receptions (20.4 percent).

"I think it's pretty safe to say that I got everything out of my talent," West said. "I'm proud of that."

Late in his Packers career, West became more of a situational player, as Green Bay used Jackie Harris as its primary receiving tight end and West in more of a blocking role.

But when Harris left for Tampa Bay following the 1993 season, West proved he could still get it done. When West became the team's primary tight end again in 1994, he had 31 catches for 377 yards—both career highs.

"I was one of those guys who a whole lot of people didn't want to give a chance to," West said. "I don't think anyone would have ever thought I would play 14 years.

"Every year, it seemed I was one of those guys that was on the bubble. Every year in training camp, they'd bring in guys to try and take your job and you'd be fighting off a lot of guys. But I did it."

By the end of the 1994 campaign, though, West had knee and ankle problems and the Packers decided to go with a younger, cheaper alternative in Mark Chmura. West finished his 11-year career in Green Bay with 202 receptions for 2,321 yards and 25 touchdowns.

"I was an older guy who was pretty beat up," West said. "So I didn't hold any grudges.

"Green Bay will always be my first love. But I also wasn't ready to retire when they let me go."

So West went to training camp with Indianapolis, and after being released on the final cutdown there, he was signed by Philadelphia and given the starting job. West played with the Eagles two seasons, and was planning to retire and work in Philadelphia's personnel department.

But West went to the NFL Combine in 1997 and met some Atlanta coaches that persuaded him to play for one more season. West did exactly that, then took a job with the Falcons upon his retirement after the 1997 season.

These days, though, West is retired and living in Lawrenceville, Georgia.

"I know I still want to coach," he said. "But I've learned in life, you go one day at a time.

"Anything can happen. The good Lord has been very good to me, and he might be moving me in another direction."

No matter what direction West heads, his Packers days will always be among his top memories.

"I have so many great memories, man," he said. "So many great memories. Playing with Brett [Favre] and LeRoy [Butler] and Reggie [White]. And all the coaches were great.

"And I came from a background where good things happen to you if you're not afraid to work. And I'm certainly not. So that was just a great time in my life."

4

IN THE BOX

TOM BETTIS

Fact or fiction.

Truth or myth.

Tom Bettis insists it's the latter in both cases.

Bettis, Green Bay's No. 1 draft choice in the 1955 draft, didn't always see eye to eye with head coach Vince Lombardi. And one story had Bettis taking a swing at Lombardi.

Bettis insists that never happened. But Bettis wasn't afraid to tell Lombardi if he felt the stern coach was going too far, and it led to a mini rift between the two.

"In general we got along," said Bettis, who's 83 and living in Katy, Texas. "For the most part, I was one of his guys, but he said some things in a meeting that I didn't think were appropriate and I told him so."

If anyone had justification to be outspoken, it was Bettis.

Bettis was the fifth overall draft pick in 1955, but suffered through some miserable early days with the Packers. So Bettis, a linebacker, deserved what came later.

After the Packers went 14–33–1 in Bettis' first four years with the organization, Green Bay hired Lombardi from the New York Giants. Three years and 27 victories later, Bettis and the Packers won the 1961 NFL championship.

"The early days were miserable in many respects," Bettis said. "And 1958 was a real downer [when the Packers went 1–10–1]. All hell broke loose that year.

"We had some talent, we just needed someone strong and disciplined and [who] treated the players fairly. Lombardi was obviously that guy. He did a magnificent job."

And that began a magnificent stretch of success for Bettis.

He won the 1961 NFL championship in Green Bay. He won his second title with the Chicago Bears in 1963, his final year as a player. Bettis then spent 30 years in coaching, beginning in 1966.

He was on Kansas City's staff when the Chiefs went to Super Bowl I and lost to Green Bay. He was Kansas City's defensive coordinator when it defeated Minnesota in Super Bowl IV. And he had a brief run as the Chiefs' head coach in 1977.

When Bettis finally decided to call it a career after the 1994 season, he knew he'd accomplished as much as he ever could have hoped.

"I got in nine years as a player and 30 as a coach," he said. "I'll take that."

The way Bettis' Green Bay career started out, though, he wasn't sure just how much he could take.

Bettis started at middle linebacker from the get-go and Green Bay went 6–6 his rookie year under Lisle Blackbourn. But the Packers slipped to 4–8 and 3–9 the next two seasons and Blackbourn was fired.

Things got even worse during Ray "Scooter" McLean's one season, when Green Bay went 1–10–1 and Bettis wondered if the Packers would ever get things figured out.

"There was always talent there," Bettis said of Green Bay's roster. "Just not a lot of discipline."

That obviously changed under Lombardi. And while Bettis was on board for most of the changes, he and Lombardi didn't always see eye to eye.

Whether or not that prompted Lombardi to trade Bettis is debatable. By 1961, Ray Nitschke had taken over Bettis' middle linebacker spot, and when the year was over, Bettis was dealt to Pittsburgh.

"I kind of helped coach Ray right out of my job," he joked. "And the trade was kind of both [his and Lombardi's] idea."

After a year with the Steelers, Bettis was traded to Chicago in 1963, and his timing couldn't have been better. The Bears won the Western Conference with an 11–1–2 record and went on to win the NFL championship.

Bettis knew he was near the end, so he went into the advertising business and remained a part-time scout for the Bears. But in 1966, Kansas City coach Hank Stram—who was on the Purdue staff when Bettis was in college—persuaded him to join the coaching ranks.

Stram had tried to get Bettis to retire in 1961 and join his coaching staff, but Bettis wasn't ready to quit playing. This time, though, was different.

"He sold me on it," Bettis said. "[Stram] said I belonged in coaching."

Boy, was Stram right.

Bettis was on the Chiefs' staff from 1966 to 1977 as the team's defensive coordinator, defensive backs coach, and linebackers coach. And when things blew up on head coach Paul Wiggin in 1977, Bettis took over on an interim basis.

The problem was, Bettis was dealt a lousy hand and the Chiefs went 1–6 during his time in charge. Bettis never got another chance to be a head coach.

"I was content with what I was doing," he said. "But I always thought I could be a good head coach. I think I was just hurt by that disastrous year in '77."

Perhaps when it came to being considered for a head coaching job, but Bettis was never hurting for work.

He spent the next seven years with the St. Louis Cardinals, had two stints in Houston, another gig with Kansas City, and tenures in Cleveland, Philadelphia, and with the Los Angeles Rams. That's a lot of stops, but Bettis always had a certain fondness for Green Bay, where everything began for him and later culminated in his first championship.

"My wife and I loved Green Bay," Bettis said. "We bought out first house there in 1959 and stayed there until 1966, even when I wasn't playing in Green Bay anymore. We loved it there."

GEORGE CUMBY

There's a saying that George Cumby holds near and dear to his heart.

He puts it on his office voice mail. It's always near the tip of his tongue. But most importantly, it's advice he lives by.

"My whole philosophy is you must teach today's generation now," said Cumby, the former Green Bay Packer middle linebacker, "because tomorrow isn't promised. You never know when the end might come, so you have to be prepared."

Cumby, who played in Green Bay from 1980 to 1985, was as prepared as any Packer of his era. But there's nothing Cumby could do to ready himself for the Packers' *Monday Night Football* game with Chicago in 1985.

Cumby was just a fraction over 6′ and played at roughly 220 pounds. Even in his era, he was extremely small.

Chicago had started to experiment with 300-pound defensive lineman William Perry—better known as "the Refrigerator"—at the goal line. And Bears coach Mike Ditka—who was always looking for a way to stick it to the Packers—used this prime-time game to roll out "the Fridge."

"My timing wasn't great," Cumby said. "Back then, *Monday Night Football* was a huge, huge deal. It wasn't like now when there's a million games on. Everyone watched on Monday night."

And everyone saw Cumby play the nail while Perry was the hammer.

On three different occasions, Perry bowled Cumby over. Twice Perry flattened Cumby on blocks that cleared the way for Walter

Payton touchdowns. And once Perry carried the ball himself and barreled into Cumby on his way to a one-yard touchdown run.

Cumby will forever be linked with that game. But he says he has tried to make the best of the bad memory.

"I still use that game a lot of times when I go and speak," Cumby said. "When I get a chance to speak to a lot of kids, that kind of breaks the ice. I tell the story and people recognize my name because of that night. So I have found some good in it."

As if that game wasn't bad enough, Perry caught a touchdown pass against Cumby when the Packers played the Bears at Lambeau Field later that season. Perry's offensive exploits were seen as an attempt by Bears coach Mike Ditka to embarrass Packers head coach Forrest Gregg.

Cumby just happened to get stuck in the middle.

"People were trying to isolate me for years," Cumby said. "And for the most part, I lived by my quickness. But my size did hurt me."

While those games stick out to most people, the majority of Cumby's time in Green Bay provided far happier memories.

Green Bay selected Cumby with its second first-round draft choice, the 26th overall pick, in the 1980 draft. He emerged as a steady performer in the middle and played in Green Bay for six seasons.

Cumby led the Packers in tackles once and was their second leading tackler on two other occasions. But the biggest drawback with Cumby was always his size.

So before the 1986 season, coach Forrest Gregg decided Green Bay needed to get bigger at that spot and sent Cumby packing.

"Things just never clicked with Forrest and me," Cumby said. "He always thought I was too small to play the position and he was probably right. I was small.

"But I was okay as long as things didn't come right at me. And at the end, he didn't even give me a chance. He just decided to move on."

During his time in Green Bay, Cumby helped make religion far more acceptable in the locker room. In fact, players such as Cumby, Rich Wingo, John Anderson, Randy Scott, Mark Murphy, and Randy Wright all had a network to support one another.

"Bart was a Christian," Cumby said of former Green Bay coach Bart Starr. "And he lived that way and it was very acceptable.

"I was still very close to all my teammates and developed some great friendships. It's just that when I came in and guys would be talking about what they did the night before, you'd hear a hush and they'd go talk about it in another spot.

"We would all hang out as a team. But when it came time for some of them to go to their gigs, it just [excluded] me."

After Cumby's playing days ended, he worked as a Youth and Young Adult Minister at a Methodist church in Houston. Today, he's the head football coach at Texas College in Tyler, Texas.

Cumby still thinks fondly of his time in Green Bay. He also hopes people remember him for more than those two games against Perry and the Bears in 1985.

"For the most part, I really liked Green Bay," he said. "We didn't win enough games, which was tough. But overall, it was a great time in my life. There were a lot more good games compared to those games against the Bears that people still remember."

WILLIE DAVIS

W illie Davis was driving home in the summer of 1960.
 A third-year defensive lineman with the Cleveland Browns, Davis was playing for legendary head coach Paul Brown. And he loved every minute of it.

That quickly, though, Davis' life changed.

The voice on the radio let the audience—and Davis himself—know he'd been traded to Green Bay.

"The way I heard about the trade was on the radio when I was driving," Davis recalled. "So I wasn't really happy about that to begin with.

"Then, my only knowledge of Green Bay came from Paul Brown telling players he would ship them there if he wasn't happy with them. Green Bay was like a Siberia back then."

For a brief stretch, Davis considered going to play in Canada instead of coming to Green Bay. But within 24 hours, Davis knew he was fooling himself with any thoughts of Canada.

"I got on the phone with Coach Lombardi and he said, 'I hope you're ready to come and be part of our team,'" Davis recalled. "And by the time I hung up that phone, I knew I was going to be a Green Bay Packer. He was that convincing."

Which was extremely lucky for the Packers.

Davis had played both defensive tackle and end for the Browns. But when Lombardi was coaching with the New York Giants, he was enamored of Davis' skills at end.

So he moved him there permanently, and over the next 10 seasons, Davis became as feared as any pass rusher in football.

"I remember Lombardi once said to me, 'I know why you play the way that I coach. It's because you want to prove to the world, and I want to prove to the world, and we both want to prove what we're capable of doing,'" Davis recalled. "And he was right."

It's easy to see why.

Davis was a 15th-round draft pick back in 1956. Today, the draft ends after seven rounds.

But Davis' hunger, drive, and passion helped him become a Pro Football Hall of Famer and help the Packers become the NFL's dominant team of the 1960s.

One of the keys to Davis' success was he kept himself in tip-top shape year-round. And at the end of football games, when many players were exhausted, his tank still had something left.

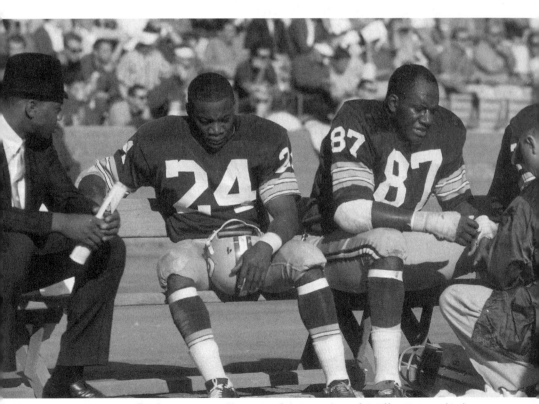

Future Hall of Famers Willie Wood (No. 24) and Willie Davis (87) take a breather during a game against the Rams in 1964.

"To me, I always accepted my personal situation that it was going to be up to me to make plays at the end of the game," said Davis, whose greatest payday came during his final season when he made $46,000. "I could always hear Lombardi above the crowd yelling, 'Get in there, Willie!'"

And more often than not, Davis did just that.

Davis played in 138 consecutive games at one point, and 162 total games during his NFL career.

And while sacks weren't an official stat in Davis' era, John Turney—a member of the Professional Football Researchers Association—has studied Davis' career at length. Turney's extensive research determined Davis had in excess of 100 sacks during his 10-year Green Bay career (1960–69), and "possibly more than 120." Turney also determined that Davis had a minimum of 40 sacks from 1963 to 1965 alone.

Green Bay's all-time sack leader is Kabeer Gbaja-Biamila with 74.5. It's a safe bet that had records been kept during his day, Davis would be the runaway leader.

"I wish they would have kept sacks back then," Davis said. "I'd love to know what the real number is. But they didn't do it and you can't change that. I certainly don't have too many complaints."

That's understandable.

Davis was named to five Pro Bowls and won All-Pro honors five times. He also holds the Packers' all-time record for fumble recoveries with 21.

Davis was named to the Pro Football Hall of Fame in 1981 and was inducted into the Packer Hall of Fame in 1975. Along the way, he helped guide Green Bay to five NFL titles, including three consecutive championships from 1965 to 1967.

Today when Packer fans look at the 21 names that make up the team's Ring of Honor inside Lambeau Field, Davis' name rests between Ray Nitschke and Lombardi.

"For me, playing in Green Bay was a love affair," Davis said. "I couldn't imagine playing any place else.

"That certainly wasn't the case when I first heard the news that Cleveland had traded me away. But things worked out."

Things certainly worked out for Davis in his post-football days, too.

Davis became president and CEO of All Pro Broadcasting, Inc., in 1976, and owns five radio stations, including three in Milwaukee and two in California.

"It's just something that really appealed to me," Davis said. "It gives me the satisfaction of giving something back to the community. Because I truly believe no one serves the community better than we do."

Few have ever served the Packers better, either.

And to this day, Davis is thrilled he wound up in Green Bay instead of heading north of the border.

"I didn't think about going to Canada for very long," Davis said. "It was an option…but then I had that talk with Coach Lombardi. He was a very persuasive man, and after we talked there was no way I was going to Canada. And I guess you'd say things worked out just fine."

MIKE DOUGLASS

Mike Douglass was always ahead of the times.

Before weight training was popular, he lifted regularly. Before eating right was stressed, he counted calories and fat grams.

So it should come as no surprise that the former Green Bay Packers standout linebacker still dedicates his life to fitness.

Douglass owns a health club called Alpine Fitness located just outside San Diego in Alpine, California. Douglas is also a professional low-fat chef and owns Mike's Place, a low-fat restaurant on the second floor of Alpine Fitness.

Douglass is also a personal trainer who's worked with several professional athletes. Recently, he trained Miss California for the Miss America pageant.

In addition, Douglass has won the California Natural Bodybuilding Championship six times.

While others struggle transitioning after their football careers end, Douglass knew right where he was headed.

"I love it," Douglass said. "I've always been into this, even when a lot of guys in the locker room weren't. So it was just a natural thing for me to stay in."

Douglass, a fifth-round draft choice from San Diego State in 1978, was a tackling machine during his eight-year Green Bay career.

Douglass holds three of the top five single-season tackling marks in team history. His 180 tackles in 1981 ranks second all-time, and Douglass also ranks fourth on the Packers' all-time tackling list with 967 stops.

Known as "Mad Dog," Douglass was a presence on and off the field. When he wasn't making big plays on Sundays, he was showing teammates the right way to eat. In fact, by the end of his career, Douglass had started cooking for several of them.

Douglass' devotion to fitness allowed him to play nine years when many didn't think he would last half of that.

Despite weighing just 205 pounds—the size of most safeties today—Douglass was a terror largely due to a sculpted body that had just 7 percent body fat. Being in top physical shape was also a key in his never missing a game in Green Bay.

"There weren't a lot of guys dedicated to fitness back then," Douglass said. "But I always did it and I think it really helped me never get injured."

"I think I got even more out of my career than I could have hoped. You look what I accomplished and I never thought I'd do that when I came into the league."

Largely because of his size, little was expected of Douglass. But then–head coach Bart Starr liked fast linebackers that could flow to the football, especially after the team switched to a 3-4 defense in 1980.

Douglass certainly seemed to benefit from the move, piling up 165 tackles in 1980, 180 in '81, and 162 in '83.

"I made a lot of big plays and a lot of hits behind the line," said Douglass, who was named an All-Pro by *Pro Football Weekly* in 1982 and *Sports Illustrated* in '83. "I thought of myself as a playmaker on that defense."

But Forrest Gregg didn't see things the same way. Gregg replaced Starr as head coach in 1984 and decided he wanted bigger linebackers. So after the 1985 season, Douglass was out—as were many of his teammates that played for Starr.

"Bart was an exceptional person, someone I really enjoyed," Douglass said. "I really respected how he went about things and I thought we were getting to the point where we could start having some success. So when they fired him, I didn't approve of it.

"Then along comes Forrest Gregg and he destroys the whole team. If you played for Bart, Forrest didn't want you. He killed a team that was on the rise."

But Douglass' rise to the level of an elite player was never forgotten by Green Bay. And in July 2003 he was inducted into the Packer Hall of Fame.

Making the night even better was the fact that Douglass' wife, Olga, and daughter, Marisa, were on hand.

"Going into the [Packer] Hall of Fame was one of the greatest things that ever happened to me," Douglass said. "And for my daughter to experience it, that was something else.

"For me to tell her about my career was one thing. For her to have someone else tell it was another. That was an unbelievable night."

These days, Douglass puts in at least 12-hour days helping others get in shape.

And he keeps himself in tip-top condition, too. Today, Douglass weighs 215 pounds, has just 7 percent body fat and works out daily.

Douglass, who was one of the strongest Packer players of his generation, once did 32 repetitions of 225 pounds and won several prizes in a strength and fitness competition that Starr was holding. He hasn't lost a bit of that power today and has found the perfect post-football career.

"I'm as dedicated to fitness now as I was as a player," Douglass said. "I made myself more fit because it gave me a chance to compete at a higher level. And I've just stayed with it. It's been good to me."

Just like his days in Green Bay were.

"I don't think anybody could have predicted I'd get nine years in the NFL and eight in Green Bay," said Douglass, who played his final season in San Diego. "That's something I'm still proud of today and why I still think so fondly of my time in Green Bay."

KABEER GBAJA-BIAMILA

During the course of his surprisingly sensational career in Green
Bay, Kabeer Gbaja-Biamila sacked quarterbacks a total of 74.5
times. That's more than any Packer since sacks became an official statistic in 1982.

But the sack that always meant the most to KGB came on December
8, 2002.

One week earlier, Gbaja-Biamila's mother, Bola, had died. KGB
returned to his hometown of Los Angeles for the funeral, then came
back to record a huge sack in Green Bay's 26–22 win over Minnesota
that Sunday.

On Minnesota's final drive of the night, KGB beat Vikings highly
touted rookie left tackle Bryant McKinnie. Gbaja-Biamila sacked
Daunte Culpepper and forced a fumble that sealed a huge Packers win.

"That one was big," Gbaja-Biamila said. "I bull rushed [McKinnie].
He fell and I jumped over him, got Culpepper, and knocked the ball
out of his hands. That one meant a lot."

Gbaja-Biamila had several sacks that meant a lot. And few could
have ever predicted the type of success he'd have.

Gbaja-Biamila was taken in the fifth round of the 2000 draft and
released that August. He was resigned to the practice squad, wasn't
active until October and played in just seven games as a rookie.

But through it all, KGB insists his goal never changed.

"When I got here, my goal was to break the sack record," Gbaja-
Biamila said. "It wasn't going to make or break who I am. But I just
had a goal and I did it. It didn't matter whose name was on it, but I
wanted the record."

By his second season, Gbaja-Biamila began making his move toward that record.

KGB had a breakout 2001 campaign, when he had 13 ½ sacks as a part-time player. He moved into the starting lineup the following season and continued to excel, posting 12 sacks that year.

"When you look at [KGB], you think he's more of a one-dimensional player," said former Packers defensive line coach Carl Hairston. "But that one dimension is something he does very well."

KGB continued to do that extremely well.

Then–Packers general manager Mike Sherman signed Gbaja-Biamila to a seven-year, $37.3 million contract after the 2002 season and felt compelled to play him virtually every down. While KGB often struggled against the run, he continued to develop into one of the premier pass rushers in football.

In fact between 2001 and 2004, KGB had 49 sacks, the most by any player in team history over a four-year stretch. KGB also had 10 games in which he posted multiple sacks.

"Kabeer's a guy who I don't think people had a lot of expectations for coming out of college, but he worked his way up to become a prominent pass rusher," former Packers linebacker Brady Poppinga said. "I think that's a great testament to his work ethic and his persistence. Kudos to him man. Kudos."

Gbaja-Biamila's struggles against the run only intensified, though. Finally, late in the 2006 season, first-year coach Mike McCarthy shifted KGB back to his pass-rush specialist role and inserted Cullen Jenkins at right defensive end.

"I didn't like it at first. Not at all," said Gbaja-Biamila, an extremely religious man. "When it happened I just said, 'God, you're in control.' I left it up to him.

"But I could have easily went the other way. I could have been prideful. I could have said I wanted a trade. I could have been a problem.

"But because of my faith, I said this is not [general manager] Ted Thompson's decision. This is not [coach] Mike McCarthy's decision. I said, 'God is in control of everything. If this is your will for me, so be it. I will do it.'"

The move seemed to jumpstart Gbaja-Biamila's career. Through the first 11 games of 2007, KGB had $9^1/_2$ sacks, which ranked third in the NFC and fourth in football.

Gbaja-Biamila also stormed past White that season and set the franchise's new sack mark.

"I'm humbled," Gbaja-Biamila said of breaking White's record. "It took teamwork, it took coaching, it took other teammates, it took DBs. Like I said, I'm just grateful."

While Gbaja-Biamila and White never played together, KGB said they developed a friendship before White's passing in 2004. At the heart of their relationship was religion, something extremely important to both men.

"That was big," Gbaja-Biamila said. "But then I would also call him if I had questions, or when he'd come to the game, sometimes he'd coach me up. So that was pretty cool. He was an inspiration."

Late in the 2007 season, though, KGB suffered knee and ankle injuries, then struggled down the stretch. When Gbaja-Biamila failed to regain his form during the 2008 campaign, the Packers opted to go with younger, cheaper options.

Still, KGB accomplished more than anyone could have ever imagined from a fifth-round draft pick. Gbaja-Biamila had four sacks against Chicago in January 2005. And on five occasions he had three-sack games.

Perhaps the only one not surprised by Gbaja-Biamila's success was KGB himself.

"I always believed I could do great things," Gbaja-Biamila said. "What's so funny about the brain is the brain can't tell the difference between reality and fake. You tell the brain, 'I'm going to succeed' and you start believing it."

Eventually, the rest of the NFL believed it, too.

TIM HARRIS

Tim Harris loved to talk on the football field.

He spun his imaginary six-shooters. He riled up crowds and opponents alike.

Harris drove some people nuts. Others simply laughed off his verbal exploits.

But the one thing Harris always did was back it up.

Harris played just five years in Green Bay. But in that time, the right outside linebacker compiled 55 sacks, which ranks third in team history behind only Kabeer Gbaja-Biamila (74.5) and Reggie White (68.5).

Harris' 19.5 sacks in 1989 remains a team record and his 13.5 sacks in 1988 ranks fifth in team history.

"I take a lot of pride in that," Harris said. "Every time I got a sack, that was a good moment."

Harris had plenty of good moments in a Packer uniform.

When Harris entered the 1986 NFL Draft, scouts were torn on him. Harris ran the 40-yard dash in a mediocre 4.80 seconds, leaving questions about his ability to run well enough to play linebacker. But Harris weighed just 235 pounds, making him too small to play defensive end.

Harris was still on the board in the fourth round. And Green Bay was thrilled to select him at that spot.

Harris fit perfectly at outside linebacker in Forrest Gregg's 3-4 defense. Harris had a unique ability to get to the quarterback, so the Packers could turn him loose on passing downs.

"I wasn't that fast," Harris said. "But I played a lot faster than I timed. You get out of bed at 9:00 AM and have to run a 40? That's hard to do. But I fit right into what Green Bay wanted to do on defense."

That's for sure.

Harris led the Packers with eight sacks as a rookie, and led the team his other four seasons, as well. Harris was downright dominant in the late 1980s, notching 33 sacks during the 1988–89 seasons. Harris was named to the Pro Bowl in 1989 and was named All-Pro by several outlets after both the '88 and '89 seasons.

"They taught me how to play football in Green Bay," Harris said. "I liked it there. We didn't win enough, but I liked it."

It showed.

Harris was as vocal and demonstrative as any Packer player during his era.

He told offensive players he was coming for them, then delivered. He celebrated big plays by turning his hands into imaginary guns. He played with the youthful exuberance that escapes many players when they reach the sport's highest level.

"I wasn't a hot dog at all," Harris said. "But it was also my time to express myself and have a little fun when things went well. That probably didn't always sit the best with some of the teams we played against. But there was never any disrespect. I was just having fun."

Unfortunately for the Packers, Harris' fun in Green Bay was short-lived.

After the 1990 season, Harris' contract was up and he and then-general manager Tom Braatz couldn't come to an agreement. Harris said he was asking for $900,000 a season, while Braatz wouldn't budge from $600,000.

"He was paying all these offensive linemen that much, the same guys I was whipping in practice every day," Harris said. "I thought I deserved that much."

So Harris held out at the start of the 1991 campaign. Finally after four games, Braatz had enough and dealt Harris to San Francisco for a pair of second-round picks.

Ironically, one of those second rounders was later dealt back to the 49ers for head coach Mike Holmgren. The other was used to move up and draft safety George Teague in 1993.

"Tom Braatz and I never could get along," Harris said. "I really didn't want to leave. But San Francisco wasn't a bad place. There wasn't any snow and I got my Super Bowl ring."

That he did. Harris played the 1991 and '92 seasons with San Francisco, then one year in Philadelphia before returning to the 49ers for two more years. That final trip back west proved a wise one, when San Francisco captured the 1994 Super Bowl with a 49–26 rout of San Diego.

"I liked how they approached things," Harris said of the 49ers. "We never practiced in pads. We didn't hit each other during the week. We saved that for the other team on Sundays and we beat up everybody else on weekends."

Harris certainly beat up his share of offensive tackles. And any Packer fan that remembers Harris in his prime can't help but smile.

"Those were good days, man," Harris said of his time in Green Bay. "They really were. I liked Green Bay, I really did. But I just had to move on if I was going to get what I thought was fair money.

"I wish it didn't have to be that way, but what can you do? At the end of the day, it's still a business."

JOHN MARTINKOVIC

John Martinkovic was a wide-eyed rookie, drafted by the Washington Redskins and thrilled to be playing in the nation's capitol.

The young defensive end was in Mobile, Alabama, getting ready to play in an exhibition contest. Before the game, though, someone in the organization came to Martinkovic and told him he'd been traded to Green Bay.

"The first thing I said was, 'Where the hell is Green Bay?'" Martinkovic said.

That was in the summer of 1951. Now, more than six decades later, Martinkovic still lives in the city he couldn't even identify on a map all those years ago.

In fact, Martinkovic and his wife, Clare, are in the same home they bought in 1955 and raised their four daughters in.

"There hasn't been a big reason to move," said the 86-year-old Martinkovic, who's one of the oldest living Packers. "I guess it's just been good to us here."

Martinkovic was pretty good to the Packers, too.

He played in Green Bay for six years, where he was a standout defensive end and played on the offensive line, too. He earned Pro Bowl berths each year from 1953 to 1955 and was inducted into the Packers Hall of Fame in 1974.

"I was pretty good," Martinkovic said. "I could rush the passer a little bit and we'd get $5 a sack back then, which wasn't too bad.

"There was quite a bit of holding back then and one time I hit a guy in the stomach and he keeled over. There weren't enough officials back then to see everything."

In the Box | 163

There were two major drawbacks, though. First, the money wasn't very good. Second, neither were the Packers.

In the six seasons Martinkovic played in Green Bay, the Packers went 25–46–1 and never finished above .500.

"I don't know what happened. Maybe the other teams were just better than us," Martinkovic said. "It wasn't that guys weren't trying. We just didn't win a lot of games."

Which led to unhappy fans and coaching changes.

Gene Ronzani, the man who replaced "Curly" Lambeau, resigned late in the 1953 season, one in which the Packers went 2–9–1. And even though the Packers went just 14–31–1 in Ronzani's four years, Martinkovic said he was popular with the players.

"He was pretty good. Most of us liked him," Martinkovic said. "We would always practice at a baseball park [Joannes] near City Stadium. And Ronzani would always walk around that stadium and look to see if anyone was peeking and trying to watch our practice. It was pretty funny."

Martinkovic didn't think the hiring of Lisle Blackbourn as Green Bay's next head coach was a laughing matter, though. The two never saw eye-to-eye, which was common between Blackbourn and many of his players.

"The Lizard," Martinkovic said when Blackbourn's name was brought up. "He was slimy. He talked with a forked tongue.

"He'd tell you something, then a half-hour later he'd say, 'Why'd you do it that way?' He was not well liked. Consequently if you told him off, he'd get rid of you. And I told him off a few times."

Which is one of the reasons Martinkovic was dealt away himself.

Martinkovic was making $9,800 a year in 1956 and asked the Packers for a $1,200 raise. Instead, he was shipped to the New York Giants for a third-round draft choice.

The move worked out pretty well for Green Bay, as it used the pick on linebacker Ray Nitschke in 1958. Martinkovic played one year with the Giants, then called it a career.

"I asked for a small raise," Martinkovic said. "It's not like I was trying to pick their pockets.

"But the money back then was nothing like today. And we weren't like these players nowadays. We were a little bit conservative. We couldn't go and spend any money because we didn't have anything to spend."

When Martinkovic's playing days ended, he took a job as a car salesman, something he did until 1992 when he retired.

Martinkovic says he remains a Packers fan. But probably not to the degree you'd expect from someone who played for the organization, then remained in town nearly five decades after his playing career ended.

"For the most part, they forgot about us," Martinkovic said of players from his era. "I go back once a year because I'm in the Hall of Fame, so I go over there for that every year. But guys like me that played all those years ago, they don't remember us anymore. And that's all I'm going to say."

MIKE P. McCOY

When you hear professional athletes exclaim, "It's not about the money," it almost always is. But if those words ever came from Mike P. McCoy, you'd have to believe him.

McCoy, a Packer defensive tackle from 1970 to 1976, played at a time when he could have made more money pursuing a law degree at Notre Dame than he could have playing football. Instead, after mulling a return to law school following the 1973 season, he chose the game he truly loved.

"I'm really satisfied with it," McCoy said of his playing days. "I thought I played really well.

"I can't control what the media or the fans think. But I walked away feeling satisfied and had a good time doing it."

It's easy to see why.

Before the 1970 draft, the Packers sent tailback Elijah Pitts, linebacker Lee Roy Caffey, and offensive lineman Bob Hyland to the Chicago Bears for the No. 2 overall pick in the draft. Green Bay then used that selection on McCoy.

The much ballyhooed McCoy became a permanent fixture on the Packer defensive line from Day 1. And while he never became the perennial All-Pro that many envisioned he would, McCoy had a solid career that also included two years with Oakland, a little more than a year with the New York Giants, and a brief stop in Detroit.

"I played 11 years and felt I did fairly well," said McCoy, who made just $18,000 as a rookie and never made more than $55,000 as a Packer. "The expectations were enormous where people thought I'd get 30 sacks a year.

"There were years where I'd have seven, eight, nine, 10 sacks, which would be great today. But it wasn't enough back then.

"But I got double-teamed a lot on the run and I was never pan-caked in my life, so I'm proud of that. And our defense was always pretty good. The offense just wasn't there."

Nor were the victories, as the Packers had just one winning season in McCoy's seven years in Green Bay. But it certainly wasn't McCoy's fault.

At 6'5" and 280 pounds, McCoy was a mountain of a man in his day and a true force in the middle. The Wisconsin Pro Football Writers voted him the team's Most Valuable Rookie in 1970, when he won a starting job up front.

McCoy led the Packers with six sacks in 1973, a time when that statistic wasn't officially kept by the league. And by 1974, many began recognizing him as one of the league's elite defensive tackles.

Between 1972 and 1974, Green Bay allowed just 16.5 points per game with players such as McCoy, linebackers Fred Carr and Ted Hendricks, and cornerback Willie Buchanon making life difficult for opposing offenses.

"I always thought we had a heck of a defense," said McCoy, who was a consensus All-American while at Notre Dame. "But there was always a lot of turmoil."

Primarily under Dan Devine, who came from the University of Missouri and coached the Packers from 1971 to 1974, the Packers could have easily been labeled "Team Turmoil." Devine lost the respect of the players through coaching gimmicks and awful player personnel moves.

"When he put in the Missouri highlight film, that didn't go over real big," McCoy said of Devine. "It was interesting to go in that locker room every day and see what was going to happen.

"I always thought we had a good nucleus and if things gelled, we could have been pretty good. But it never happened and I think a big reason is we didn't have good team unity. It was a very difficult time."

McCoy said most players felt Devine was simply overmatched and eventually tuned him out.

"He was probably best suited for the college game," McCoy said. "It was just a bad fit with him in the NFL."

By the end of the 1976 season, McCoy and the Packers no longer fit.

Bart Starr, who replaced Devine in 1975, was left with a largely empty cupboard.

The Packers were already short on talent, and Devine had traded five draft picks—including a pair of No. 1 selections—to the Los Angeles Rams for over-the-hill quarterback John Hadl.

So Starr traded McCoy to Oakland for a first-round draft choice that eventually became John Anderson, a fourth-round pick, and defensive lineman Herb McMath.

"I just really thought Bart had no shot when he took over because he didn't have all those draft picks," said McCoy, who was a teammate of Starr's his first two years in the league. "He had to try and get something back and the pieces of the puzzle weren't all there anyhow. So he was able to get a first for me and he did it."

McCoy certainly experienced more success with the Raiders than he would have in Green Bay, competing in the AFC Championship Game in 1977. After going to the Giants and the Lions, his career ended in the 1980 season when he suffered a devastating injury to his thigh muscle.

When McCoy's career ended, he returned to Erie, Pennsylvania, and was finding success running his own business. But he gave that up to work for an organization called Champions For Life, in which he spoke to junior high school students throughout the world and tried to steer them in the right direction.

From there, McCoy started Mike McCoy Ministries, and today he speaks primarily in Catholic schools across America and abroad about the importance of good decision making, fighting drug addiction, and empowering youth.

"My daughter came home one day and told me all the problems at her school and everything that was going on in our small community," McCoy said. "And I just thought to myself, 'What can I do to make the world better?'

"Basically, it's about choices and it's an inspirational type of thing. And it's been very rewarding. I get a lot of letters back and a lot of feedback. And it's just nice to be making a difference."

McCoy certainly did that in Green Bay.

BILL QUINLAN

Bill Quinlan is in his early eighties now.

But the former Green Bay Packers defensive end says he feels like he's 15 and acts like he's 12.

What's new?

Quinlan, who played with the Packers from 1959 to 1962, was one of the hardest partiers the organization has ever had. He ran with Paul Hornung, Max McGee, Fuzzy Thurston, and Green Bay's other wild men. Quinlan loved his liquor and his cigarettes. But more than anything, he may have loved his gambling.

And until Vince Lombardi decided Quinlan's off-the-field wildness outweighed his on-field contributions, he left an indelible mark on the NFL's smallest city.

"We were all drinkers, No. 1," Quinlan said of the fun bunch he was part of. "If someone said raise your hand to see who's the biggest drunk, all hands would go up at the same time.

"We were all animals. We were all drunks. Fuzzy was the craziest, and I was the mouthiest S.O.B. We dodged a lot of bullets."

Quinlan has dodged his share of bullets since.

Retired today and living in Lawrence, Massachusetts, Quinlan has survived cancer of the throat and of the bladder. He's stopped drinking and smoking, but he gambles as much as ever and Quinlan says he's never really grown up.

And he's in no real hurry to do so.

"I haven't slowed one bit," said Quinlan, whose primary occupation after his football days ended in 1966 was running bar rooms.

"I've gambled all my life and I love it. I used to book and all that [expletive]. But I love it and it's been very good to me."

It was also one of the biggest reasons Lombardi sent Quinlan packing after the 1962 season.

Ironically, Lombardi traded Billy Howton—one of the team's most rebellious players—to Cleveland for Quinlan and halfback Lew Carpenter in 1959. Although Lombardi knew Quinlan came with the reputation of being somewhat unruly, Lombardi's belief was in building a winner through a dominant defense.

So he was willing to take the bad with the good. Combined with Henry Jordan and Willie Davis—two other former Browns that Lombardi traded for—as well as Dave Hanner, the Packers began developing a dominant front.

"Lombardi was tough. He worked on your mind and your mental toughness," Quinlan said. "His belief was that if you thought positive, you were going to make it. Outside of that, he was a son of a bitch."

You can see why Quinlan feels so strongly.

He was in Green Bay for the start of the Lombardi era. And he reaped the rewards of Lombardi's rebuilding project, playing on championship teams in both 1961 and '62.

"There were so many great games, so many great memories," Quinlan said. "You don't even know where to start."

Because Lombardi loved much of what Quinlan provided on Sundays, he tolerated some of the chaos the other six days offered. But following the 1962 season, Lombardi decided enough was enough.

The NFL had investigated Quinlan for gambling on league games, a probe Quinlan was eventually cleared of. But that investigation led to a one-year suspension of star running back Paul Hornung for the 1963 season.

Hornung had gone to his mother's home in Louisville the summer before the 1963 season, and Lombardi forbid Quinlan to visit him. Quinlan ignored his coach's words, and paid the price as Lombardi traded him shortly thereafter.

"He was one of my good friends. Of course I was going to go visit him," said Quinlan, who still frequently goes to horse races with

Hornung. "Vince told me not to go to Louisville and see him and I did anyhow.

"That pissed him off and he got rid of me. It might have been more than that, but that was a big part of it. I would have loved to stay in Green Bay, because we had some wild times."

Like the time Nitschke's brothers came after Quinlan because he was in a fight with the legendary linebacker. Or the non-stop partying that, according to Quinlan, "really pissed Vince off."

But as wild as Quinlan was, he says there are two things he never did. The first was bet on football and the second was cheat on his wife, Betty.

"After the season was over, I gambled," Quinlan said. "I gambled all my life. But I never bet on the team or football games during the year.

"And as a group, we were reckless and wild men who lived hard. But I can truthfully say they were the nicest bunch of men you'd ever meet on and off the field.

"I never saw one fellow punch another. And you couldn't talk to broads or go with women or you'd need a lawyer because the town was too small. Everybody always knew what you were doing, so that helped keep us in line a little bit."

B.J. Raji

The giant man had unique power, surprisingly good hands, and nifty feet. That much we knew.

But few knew just how well B.J. Raji could dance.

During the 2010 NFC Championship Game in Chicago, Raji had the play of the game when he intercepted Bears quarterback Caleb Hanie and returned it for an 18-yard touchdown. Raji's score gave Green Bay a 21–7 lead midway through the fourth quarter, and the Packers went on to a 21–14 win.

As thrilling as Raji's touchdown was, his antics afterward might have been even more entertaining.

After reaching the end zone, Raji broke out the "Championship Belt" that quarterback Aaron Rodgers made famous. Raji then put his hands on his hips and shook his midsection like he was Michael Jackson.

As memorable as the touchdown was, the dance might have garnered even more buzz.

"Oh man, I've gotten so much stuff, from 'Great dance,' to 'Need a new teacher?' to 'Need some lessons?'," Raji said of the dance. "I got a whole slew of things."

Raji also etched a permanent spot in Packer history with the most important touchdown that day.

The Packers and Bears were meeting for the 182nd time in a rivalry that began in 1921. Amazingly, these bitter adversaries had met just once in the postseason, though. That came in 1941, when George Halas' Bears defeated Curly Lambeau's Packers 33–14 in a Western Division playoff game played at Wrigley Field in Chicago.

The Packers were in control of the second meeting most of the day. But the Bears closed within 14–7 early in the fourth quarter after a Chester Taylor touchdown run, and Chicago had the ball back with hopes of tying the game.

That's when Raji made a play that Packers coach Mike McCarthy would later classify as a "game-winner."

The Bears had a third-and-5 from their own 15-yard line. Raji lined up over center Olin Kreutz, showed rush, then dropped into the middle of the field, where Hanie was trying to get the ball to running back Matt Forte.

Hanie never saw Raji and threw the ball right into his enormous mitts. Raji caught the ball naturally, then waltzed to the right corner of the end zone to make it 21–7. Raji didn't have an interception in the NFL or college, so his timing was ideal for Packer Nation.

"It's just a great feeling," Raji said. "It was a great call. I was behind the back and obviously he wasn't expecting that. I just caught it and ran it back."

Packers defensive coordinator Dom Capers was the mastermind behind the timely zone-blitz call.

On the critical play, Green Bay rushed linebacker Clay Matthews and cornerback Sam Shields off the edges. Defensive tackle Cullen Jenkins and linebacker Desmond Bishop rushed inside.

Raji took one step toward Hanie, dropped three yards off the line of scrimmage, then picked Hanie off and scored.

"I'm only in my second year in the league, but I've been around some good coaches," Raji said the day after his memorable touchdown. "I've never seen a guy [like Capers] that can just create such great defenses in a short period of time.

"We'll practice on Wednesday, and Dom will have something to look at. And we'll come back on Thursday in meetings, and Dom will have three or four new defenses that are completely different. I mean, he's a great defensive mind. I'm just happy to have him on our team."

The Packers were awfully happy to have Raji on board during that 2010 season.

A first-round draft pick in 2009, the 338-pound Raji had a break-out season. The tireless Raji held together a defensive line that was ravaged by injury. He played virtually every snap and was third on the Packers with 6.5 sacks, had 12 quarterback hits, and 12 quarterback pressures. Raji was largely unblockable with just one player, so he constantly took on double teams.

Raji even mixed in a little time at fullback in the 2010 postseason.

First, Raji helped clear a hole for fullback John Kuhn to score a one-yard touchdown in a playoff win that season against Atlanta. Raji then was lined up at fullback in the NFC Championship Game and used as a decoy on a one-yard TD run by Rodgers.

Chicago defensive lineman William Perry was dubbed "the Fridge" back in the 1980s. Now, 25 years later, Raji became known as "the Freezer."

"I was mic'd up for the Atlanta game, and one of the trainers came to me and said you look like the Fridge out there," Raji said. "And I was just playing around and said, 'I'm the Freezer.' I was making a joke, just making light of the situation and having a good time with it. So I guess, in retrospect, I came up with the name."

Raji also came up with the biggest play of the NFC Championship Game—and helped Green Bay eventually claim its fourth Super Bowl title. For that, Raji's place in Packer history is safe and secure.

"He is a special athlete," Packers coach Mike McCarthy said of Raji. "He has a unique body type, and…quickness. His instincts too. That was a huge play in the game for us."

DAVE ROLLER

Maybe it was the "Dancing Bear" that he made famous. Or the jokes he and his teammates used to play on defensive tackle Mike McCoy.

It could have been the Thanksgiving Day gags he played on rookies. Or the "King Ugly" contest he later started in Minnesota.

Each and every one brought big-time laughs. And that was arguably the greatest legacy left behind by former Green Bay Packers defensive tackle Dave Roller. Roller's demonstrative ways earned him the nickname "the Imperial Lizard" from teammates.

"Life's too short to be conservative," said Roller, who played for the Packers from 1975 to 1978.

Lord knows, Roller was anything but conservative. During his football days, things were always hopping when Roller was around.

Long before Mark Gastineau popularized the sack dance, Roller had his own version. There was nothing artistic to it, but each time he notched a sack, he danced like a bear.

"I caught a lot of hell for that from [Dave] Hawg Hanner," Roller said of the Packers' defensive coordinator at the time. "But that's who I was and it was really exciting to get back there."

Things off the field were awfully exciting with Roller, as well.

Each Monday when the Packers were reviewing film of the previous day's game, Roller and teammate Jim Carter would jot down everything the coaches said McCoy had done wrong. The two would then gather that night, write McCoy a letter pointing out those exact flaws and sign it "A Fan."

Tuesday is the traditional off day for players, so when McCoy returned to work each Wednesday, the letter would be waiting for him. McCoy would read it and be stunned that a random fan could point out the same mistakes the coaches saw two days earlier.

"He would say, 'These people must be zooming in on me with a telescope,'" said Roller, who told McCoy of the prank years later. "He couldn't believe it. And J.C. and I would be sitting there just cracking up."

Roller also claims to have started a Thanksgiving tradition that still exists today.

Veteran players send the rookies to a local grocery story each year to pick up turkeys. The rookies are told they're free, but the joke's on them when they actually have to foot the bill.

Roller and the Packers film man at the time actually videotaped the stunt nearly 40 years ago. Today, local television stations record the exact same gag.

"I remember the manager not giving some of the rookies the turkeys way back then," Roller laughed. "I helped start all that."

Roller also started what he called a "King Ugly" contest in Minnesota, where he played during the 1979–80 seasons. To break up the monotony of training camp, Roller set up a box and had everyone vote for who they felt was the ugliest player on the team.

One of the times, Roller had everybody vote for Ron Yary. And the gigantic offensive tackle didn't like the results one bit.

"Oh, he was so pissed," Roller said. "He grabbed that damn box and just tore it up. But I wanted to do something to break things up, otherwise camp is so dull."

Roller's playing career was almost as lively as his off-the-field antics.

He was taken by the New York Giants in the 13th round of the 1971 draft, and spent a year there. He then played a year with Hamilton in the Canadian Football League and another year in the World Football League where he had a league-high 18 sacks.

When the WFL folded in 1975, Roller signed with Green Bay and joined the Packers late that season. By 1977, he had earned a starting spot and his eight sacks that season tied for the team lead with Dave Pureifory.

Roller developed a bond with fans thanks to his outgoing ways. And following a 10–9 win over Detroit near the end of that season, Roller was carried off the field.

"I was very gregarious and outgoing with the public," he said. "And I'll never forget them carrying me off. Those things are pretty rare."

While Roller loved his time in Green Bay, the Packers were going nowhere fast, posting a 13–29 record during those three seasons.

"We didn't have enough talent across the board," Roller said. "We had a few good players, but that was it.

"And I don't think back then [coach] Bart [Starr] and his coaches could relate very well to us. They really didn't understand us."

Or maybe they just didn't understand Roller. He started again throughout the 1978 season, but wasn't re-signed when his contract expired.

"I think Hawg was instrumental in letting me go," Roller said of Hanner. "I don't think it was Bart because we were in the playoffs one year when I was in Minnesota and I got a letter from him wishing me luck."

Roller spent most of his post-football days in sales, and considering his outgoing and demonstrative personality, it was the perfect line of work.

"You've got to keep life interesting," Roller said. "I've always lived that way and won't stop now."

REGGIE WHITE

When Reggie White got there, our culture was losing. We had no idea how to win. And I remember Reggie saying he wanted guys to go to Bible study. It was on Fridays at 6:00 in the morning and no one wanted to go, of course. Then he wanted to do it an hour before games at 7:00 in the morning on Sundays.

Now Reggie and I were very close and I was kind of a clown and Reggie was pretty serious. And I said, "Reggie, if you want these guys who go to the clubs or hang out—the younger generation—to come to Bible study, you have to come down to their level."

You see, I was still a young guy and my generation went "Bible study? Nah, I'll get some extra sleep." Most guys didn't even know how to open the Bible.

But Reggie thought if he could get on their level, then maybe. Now, every Thursday night, pretty much everybody in the league goes out, drinks, has some wings. Just being a guy. So Reggie went to a watering hole that we would always go to, which he never did. Hell no. Reggie was in bed at 7:00 o'clock.

But he got to that establishment early, one of the first guys there at like 6:00 or 7:00 that night and he stayed until like 9:00. And the guys, they saw that and now there was an incredible connection. Well, the next morning, there were like 40, 50 guys at Bible study. Before that, he maybe had three to five guys there.

And that's when I knew we were a team. We couldn't win until we were together. He was being one of the guys that night, but you also realized that if he was making a sacrifice by being somewhere he really didn't want to be, you should probably get to Bible study. He

Reggie White waves to the crowd as he leaves the field after his last game at Lambeau Field.

just wanted to show the connection that if we can have camaraderie here, in the bar, we can have camaraderie there at Bible study.

And it's not about praying and shouting and all that. It's about the camaraderie of doing something new. And I think that was very intelligent for a leader to do that. He said, "How do I get these guys on the same page?" and that was a great way to do it. Once that happened, the culture seemed to change as far as trusting one another. It was like a different team. You had all these guys, free agents, draft picks, all these personalities, and Reggie seemed to channel all these personalities toward one collective goal—winning a championship.

We were lucky to get him. The whole time, I saw him going to San Francisco. I went in there one day and saw him sitting at the table and I thought he was lost. I said, "What the heck are you doing in Green Bay?" Then I wanted to get his autograph, which was kind of funny. I mean, I was shocked.

He was the No. 1 free agent and at the time nobody—and I want to stress nobody—talked about free agency. It was all Plan B. But Reggie really started free agency. If it wasn't for Reggie, I don't think we'd have free agency like we do today. So to have the historical guy in Green Bay was pretty amazing.

Now, Ron Wolf told Reggie that no matter where he went he'd be a great player, but if he came here he'd be a legend. And I told Reggie, "This is the difference—the other teams want you. We need you."

I just said, "When you're here, we're going to take our game to another level." Now, if he had gone to San Francisco, I don't think they would have ever lost again. They would have been phenomenal because they were getting Deion Sanders, Charles Haley, that offense, George Seifert was at the height of his career. Oh my God.

But again, the want and the need was the big thing. That was the difference. And I remember Reggie standing up saying it was about the quarterback. We had to embrace Brett Favre.

No player ever did that, to just hand it off like that. But back then, not everybody on the team had embraced Brett. There were some guys that really liked Don Majkowski. They didn't know what to expect out of Brett. They knew he had a strong arm, but they thought he threw too many picks. But I told guys, "Let's just go get it back. Let Brett be Brett."

But getting Reggie was the key. Without him, we would have been just a vanilla defense because we had no pass rush. Later on, we got Sean Jones, but he came because of Reggie. Santana Dotson came because of Reggie. We were trying to build a front four that was smart and compatible with some of the other teams in the league. So we had to have Gilbert Brown on the strong side, Santana Dotson on the weak side, Sean Jones and Reggie.

And that front four, I don't think I've ever seen a front four like that. They were as good at stopping the run—like when we held Barry Sanders to negative yards in the 1994 playoffs—and they got a bunch of sacks and we got a bunch of picks. And because of those guys, I could run wild. They were tying guys up and it let me do some fun things. People don't know how good that defense was. We were No. 1 across the board. We believed in each other and we trusted each other. Those were good old days, and Reggie was a huge reason it all happened.

5

THE SECONDARY

TOM BROWN

Dallas was on the rise.

The Cowboys were threatening to pass the Green Bay Packers as the NFL's dominant outfit during the 1966 season. And when the two powers met for the NFL championship that year, Dallas was in position to slow down the Packers' dynasty.

Green Bay led the Cowboys 34–20 in the fourth quarter that day, when Dallas quarterback Don Meredith tried playing hero. First, Meredith hit Frank Clarke for a 68-yard touchdown with five minutes left to pull the Cowboys within 34–27. Then after Dallas stopped the Packers offense, Meredith went back to work.

Meredith and the Cowboys drove deep into Green Bay territory in the final minute. Meredith then threw into the end zone for Bob "Bullet" Hayes, hoping to tie the game.

But Tom Brown played spoiler—and stole the hero title from Meredith and Hayes in the process. Brown, a Packers cornerback, intercepted Meredith with just 28 seconds left to preserve Green Bay's win.

Two weeks later, the Packers routed Kansas City 35–10 to win the first Super Bowl. And one year later, Green Bay defeated Oakland in Super Bowl II to claim its third straight NFL championship.

Brown became the first man to play major league baseball and participate in two Super Bowls. And without Brown's heroics in Dallas, Green Bay's magical run of five titles in seven years probably wouldn't have happened.

"That's probably the play I'll always be best known for…and that's great," Brown said. "We had so many big plays and so many great players. But that was probably my shining moment."

For quite some time, it appeared Brown's shining moments would come on a baseball field.

A two-sport star, Brown was chosen by the Packers in the second round of the 1963 draft and was also signed by the Washington Senators. After little debate, Brown decided to try his hand at baseball.

"Baseball was always my first love," said Brown, who played both sports at the University of Maryland. "I played it every day from the time I was 14. I tolerated football and I thought I was decent at it. But baseball's where my heart was."

But it wasn't how Brown would eventually make his living. Brown had a solid spring training with the Senators in 1963 and began the year as Washington's starting first baseman. But after three months, he was sent down to the minor leagues.

That off-season, Packers coach and general manager Vince Lombardi called Brown to see if he was ready to give up on baseball.

"He said, 'Brown, are you still interested in football?'" Brown recalled. "And I'd had a frustrating year in baseball and wasn't sure what to do. And he said, 'We're still interested in you, but you can't miss another year of football.' So I told him I would start one more season [1964] of baseball, then make up my mind July 1."

After another frustrating baseball campaign, Brown showed up in Green Bay that summer. And over the next five years, he became a solid cog on a team that produced NFL championships from 1965 to 1967.

Brown played very little in 1964, but won a starting cornerback job in 1965 and held it through 1968. Brown was never flashy, just solid, which Lombardi seemed to appreciate.

"I wasn't a great tackler, but I got 'em down," Brown said. "And that's all that mattered. I think Lombardi really liked me and the things I could do."

Brown also thought the world of Lombardi, and said he appreciates his genius even more today. "The one thing that really stands out is when we were going for three straight championships; that was something that had never been done before," Brown said. "And he told us we wouldn't appreciate it until we were 50 years old.

"And the Old Man—we always used to call him 'the Old Man'—was right. But he was over and above a coach. What he stood for and to be on those teams was incredible."

Brown has had some pretty incredible experiences since his football career ended, as well. The highlight has been the success and growth of Tom Brown's Rookie League.

Brown owns 7 1/2 acres of land in Salisbury, Maryland. There, he's built two baseball diamonds, a pair of soccer fields, and enough room for four football fields.

It's there that Brown runs a recreational program for kids ages six to 12 that gives them the opportunity to play baseball, football, basketball, and soccer. It's his field of dreams.

"God gives people a certain ability," Brown said. "And if you can find what that is, do it well and enjoy it, that's a great thing."

Brown established the program in 1974, and has watched it grow into an incredibly popular arena for young athletes to get their feet wet.

Brown runs almost everything himself, and doesn't allow parents to coach. Instead, students from local Salisbury College receive credits for pitching in.

The main premise is to teach kids basic fundamentals without the pressures of winning that many parents place on today's youth. Brown focuses on improvement and educating the youngsters, and he pays little attention to wins and losses.

"This is something that the parents and the kids all seem to like," Brown said. No one is criticized or yelled at. The kids improve and they feel good about themselves.

"We teach them the basic fundamentals and try to keep it as fun as possible. And I think the kids have a lot of fun."

Much like the fun Brown had during his time in Green Bay.

Three titles. Five great seasons. And of course, an unforgettable interception against Dallas that Packer Nation will never forget.

"I think if I had stayed with baseball, I could have played 15 years as a utility player or something," Brown said. "But I don't have any regrets how things worked out.

"I played on some incredible teams in Green Bay and have found something that made me happy ever since. I was extremely lucky the way everything worked out."

WILLIE BUCHANON

It will go down as one of the greatest games a Green Bay Packers defensive back has played. Heck, it will be remembered as one of the best games an NFL cornerback has ever had.

During the 1978 season, Green Bay cornerback Willie Buchanon and the Packers were at an impasse. The two sides couldn't agree on contract terms, so Buchanon was in the process of playing out his option and auditioning himself around the league.

And what an audition it was.

On September 24 of that season, Buchanon had four interceptions and returned one for a touchdown as the Packers routed the San Diego Chargers 24–3. The four picks in a single game tied Buchanon for a NFL record that still stands. Ironically, his interceptions came against the team Buchanon would eventually be traded to.

"I didn't want to leave Green Bay," Buchanon said. "I just wanted them to pay me the salary I deserved. And it was too bad, because the difference ended up being $25,000."

That is too bad, because Buchanon was one of the NFL's elite defensive backs during a terrific 11-year career.

The 6′, 190-pound Buchanon came to the Packers with the seventh overall pick of the 1972 draft and left his mark immediately. Buchanon won the starting left cornerback job in training camp and tied for the team lead with four interceptions.

Buchanon was named the NFL's Defensive Rookie of the Year by the Associated Press and the NFC Defensive Rookie of the Year by Newspaper Enterprise Association. But more importantly, the Packers were winning.

Little did Buchanon know Green Bay's NFC Central Division championship that year would be its last until 1995. And the playoff appearance—which ended in a 16–3 loss to Washington—would be the Packers' last until 1982.

"That was the year," Buchanon said of 1972. "We had a good combination of players that came in and we really shored up the secondary.

"It was also a year where I learned a lot about football. [Running back] MacArthur Lane was my mentor and he taught me a lot about the politics of football, how to adjust and always be ready that someone could be waiting to take your job."

Buchanon didn't have to worry about that much. Although the Packers went in the tank under Dan Devine and later Bart Starr, Buchanon was always one of their elite players.

Despite missing eight games in 1973 after breaking his leg, then missing 12 more in 1975 with a similar fracture, Buchanon and Green Bay's secondary were excelling.

The group of Buchanon, Mike P. McCoy, Steve Luke, and Johnny Gray—which started together in 1977–78—nicknamed themselves S.W.A.T.

Luke was the S, Buchanon the W, Gray the A for his nickname "Abdul," and McCoy the T for his nickname of "Tasmanian Devil."

"Steve Luke came up with the acronym and we had fun with it," Buchanon said. "Our safeties were big hitters and we were pretty good corners. And anytime we needed a big play or to make something happen, we'd yell 'S.W.A.T!'"

Buchanon, who had a terrific combination of size and speed during his era, was always making something happen. He was named to the Pro Bowl in 1973 and '74, but his best season in Green Bay was his last.

Buchanon finished the 1978 season with nine interceptions, which remains tied for second all-time in Packers single-season history. Buchanon was also voted to the Pro Bowl again and was named All-Pro by most media outlets.

Instead of paying Buchanon, though, Packers coach and general manager Bart Starr traded him to San Diego that off-season. In return, Green Bay received a first-round draft choice that later became George Cumby and a seventh-rounder that became Rich Wingo.

"My time in Green Bay was a lot of fun," Buchanon said. "Seven great years and a lot of great friends. I'll always be loyal to that organization."

Buchanon, meanwhile, went to the Chargers and joined one of the most prolific offensive teams in league history. That group featured Dan Fouts, Charlie Joiner, and Kellen Winslow.

Buchanon stayed with the Chargers four seasons before retiring. Before leaving, though, he participated in what many consider the greatest game ever played.

In the 1981 AFC divisional playoffs, the Chargers defeated Miami 41–38 in overtime. That contest saw the Chargers blow a 24–0 lead, score late to force overtime, then win it in the extra session.

The game, which is still shown regularly, is perhaps best remembered by a shot of a courageous Winslow—who blocked a potential game-winning field goal—being carried off the field due to fatigue.

"That was the greatest football game ever played," said Buchanon, whose team lost the following week in Cincinnati in the AFC Championship Game. "I've never been more tired in my life.

"After the game, everybody sat there for at least a half an hour. No one showered, no one moved. We couldn't. The humidity and the intensity of that game were unbelievable. I still think about that game all the time."

Buchanon also looks back on his time in Green Bay with great pride.

Although the Packers had just two winning seasons and played in only one playoff game during his seven years, Buchanon certainly did his part in trying to restore Green Bay to its 1960s Glory Years.

"I had seven great years in Green Bay and will never lose touch with that," Buchanon said. "I'm just a guy who's into palm trees and the ocean. And if it wasn't for the snow, it would have been a great place to live."

NICK COLLINS

Nick Collins was always one of the more soft-spoken members of the Green Bay Packers. But boy, did he get loud in the 45th Super Bowl.

Collins' 37-yard interception return for a touchdown gave the Packers a 14–0 lead, one they would hang on to on their way to a 31–25 win. Collins' play was undoubtedly among the game's biggest.

"Oh man, that was the highlight of my day right there," Collins said. "I was able to read Big Ben [Roethlisberger] and got a nice jump on the ball. I made a couple cuts to get into the end zone."

Green Bay had just taken a 7–0 lead late in the first quarter when Collins struck.

Pittsburgh began on its own 7-yard line after an illegal block penalty. And on the first play, Roethlisberger made the game's biggest blunder.

Green Bay rushed just four, but Roethlisberger was trying to hit a home run to Wallace, so he needed substantial time for the play to develop. That allowed beefy defensive end Howard Green—who was signed off the street in October when the Packers were ravaged by injury—to get home.

Green whipped left guard Chris Kemoeatu and drilled Roethlisberger as he let loose a bomb for Wallace. The pressure caused Roethlisberger's pass to be severely underthrown and Collins was waiting for it.

Collins, who was named to three straight Pro Bowls, took off down the right sideline and made a nifty cut to the inside. When Collins reached the 3-yard line, he jumped and reached the end zone.

In a matter of 24 seconds, Green Bay had surged to a 14–0 lead.

"There were a lot of throws I'd like to have back," Roethlisberger said afterward.

Truthfully, Collins left a lot of quarterbacks saying that exact same thing.

Collins was a little-known player from Bethune-Cookman when Packers first-year general manager Ted Thompson used a second-round draft choice on him in 2005. But it was easy to see why Thompson fell in love with Collins.

Collins ran the 40-yard dash in 4.37 seconds at the NFL Combine and had times of 4.34 and 4.44 at his campus pro day. He also posted a 40-inch vertical leap at the Combine. At Division 1-AA Bethune-Cookman, Collins had 13 interceptions in 34 career games, two of which he returned for touchdowns.

"He's a marvelous athlete," Thompson said the day he drafted Collins. "He's a small-school player, but he is athletic. He's the kind of guy that lines up at strong safety at times, at free safety at times, and in certain games he is athletic enough to go out and take away the star receiver of the opposing team."

The light didn't go on right away for Collins, though.

Collins was a starter from Day 1. But he had just four interceptions in his first three seasons and failed to give the Packers the big plays they craved.

"I don't focus too much on stats," Collins said during the 2007 season. "I can't help it. A lot of balls don't come my way. That happens. I have to deal with it. When I get the opportunity to make a play, make a play."

In 2008, Collins began making plays everywhere. That season, Collins tied teammate Charles Woodson for the NFC lead with seven interceptions. Collins also returned three of those interceptions for touchdowns, which were the most by an NFL safety since 1986.

Collins' 295 interception return yards that year were the sixth-most in NFL history and broke Bobby Dillon's franchise record of 244 set in 1956. Collins also finished second on the team with 18 passes defended and became the first Packers safety to start a Pro Bowl since Darren Sharper in 2002.

"Clearly, he's a very explosive young man," Packers defensive coordinator Dom Capers said of Collins. "He does some things back there that a lot of players can't do, some things that really excite you as a coach."

Collins continued trending upward. And as his play rose, so did the performance of Green Bay's entire secondary.

Collins had six interceptions and went to his second straight Pro Bowl in 2009. Collins then had four interceptions, 12 passes defended, and reached a third straight Pro Bowl in 2010.

"You can't say enough about his instincts and his ability to break on the football, especially when he gets his hands on the football," Packers coach Mike McCarthy said. "He's such a dangerous returner."

Unfortunately for Collins, it all came to a screeching halt during Week 2 of the 2011 season. Collins suffered a herniated disc during a game in Carolina and had cervical neck fusion surgery.

Collins never played another snap in Green Bay, and the Packers released him shortly before the 2012 NFL Draft. While Collins hasn't officially retired, it seems unlikely another team will ever risk allowing him to play.

"Nick Collins, you look at the beginning of his résumé he had a heck of a chance to go to Canton," McCarthy said. "Just the way he was starting the first half of his career. But that was not the tough part at all, because it wasn't a professional decision.

"It was clearly a personal decision specifically with Nick Collins. Just based on the information, as an organization, Ted Thompson and I sat down and the final question gets asked: if Nick was your son, would you let him play? So that's why we made the decision we did."

While it wasn't the type of ending anyone hoped for, few will ever forget what Collins meant to the Packers. And never did he mean more than during the 45th Super Bowl.

"A dream come true. It's a dream come true," Collins said of being a Super Bowl champion. "We're going back to Titletown baby! This is big. It's coming back home. The Vince Lombardi Trophy is coming back home."

Thanks in large part to Collins.

AL HARRIS

Matt Hasselbeck called heads.

Seattle's quarterback watched as his prediction was correct, then declared, "We want the ball and we're gonna score."

Al Harris had another idea.

During a 2003 NFC wild-card playoff game, Green Bay and visiting Seattle went to overtime deadlocked at 27. When the Seahawks won the coin toss, Hasselbeck made what would soon become a failed guarantee.

On Seattle's second possession of overtime, Hasselbeck threw a pass in the left flat for wideout Alex Bannister. Packers cornerback Al Harris jumped the route, intercepted Hasselbeck, and raced 52 yards for the game-winning touchdown.

Green Bay 33, Seattle 27.

"We hadn't pretty much got any work all day over there," said Harris, who was in his first year with the Packers after coming in a trade from Philadelphia. "I jumped a lot of routes. [Hasselbeck] made a lot of good reads because I jumped a lot of routes today and he would look it off and go to the guy that was open.

"I was just praying that he would throw the ball, because I knew I was going to gamble on that play. As a DB, you pray that they will run that route—a hitch or a slant—something you can jump quick and get to where you have to go."

To this day, that play ranks among the most memorable in franchise history.

In fact, a giant picture of Harris' interception hangs in a hallway outside the Packers locker room at Lambeau Field, along with other photos of great moments in franchise history.

"It was a big play, a big moment in my life, in my career," Harris recalled. "But I wouldn't define my career by that play. It rarely happens like that. You call the blitz, and what you're looking for happens. It was a lucky play."

Not entirely.

The two offenses had gone back and forth all day, combining for nearly 750 yards and 35 second-half points. So when Hasselbeck said his team was going to score, most believed him.

After the two teams traded punts, the Seahawks picked up one first down, then faced a third-and-11.

Green Bay defensive coordinator Ed Donatell, who had watched his unit get picked apart the entire second half, wanted a lot of pressure—and fast—to force Hasselbeck into a short throw. So Donatell called for a blitz package called "Thriller." And a record-setting crowd at Lambeau Field and Packer fans everywhere couldn't have picked a name more apropos.

Green Bay had three defensive linemen, two linebackers, and six defensive backs in the game. And Donatell rushed seven men.

Defensive linemen Kabeer Gbaja-Biamila, Cletidus Hunt, and Jamal Reynolds, along with linebackers Nick Barnett and Hannibal Navies came up the middle. Safety Darren Sharper blitzed off the left edge and safety Marques Anderson came off the right side, leaving only Mike McKenzie, Michael Hawthorne, Bhawoh Jue, and Harris in the back half.

Seattle lined up with four wide receivers and Hasselbeck took a three-step drop. He never took his eyes off of Bannister and let go of the ball in 1.09 seconds. Anderson came the closest to Hasselbeck, getting within about two feet of the Seahawks quarterback before the ball was out of his hand.

Green Bay anticipated Hasselbeck would have to throw something short and quick in the face of intense pressure. So Harris squatted on Bannister's route, then jumped it beautifully at the Green Bay 48-yard line.

By the time Harris hit the Seahawks' 45-yard line, he had a hand in the air knowing full well that the slow-footed Bannister wasn't going to catch him. Hasselbeck still had a shot and lunged for Harris at the 9-yard line, but he narrowly missed Harris' right foot.

That quick, Harris was in the end zone and the Seahawks' season was over.

"That's what we spend a lot of time upstairs waiting for," Donatell said of dialing up the all-out blitz. "And when the critical time comes for a player or a coach to step up and make a play or know that it's time to call that play, then it's time. It's that time.

"And our players delivered under pressure. They did what they were supposed to do when they were supposed to do it in a playoff environment. I think it's a big thing to build on."

Before the dramatic ending, Green Bay called timeout when it saw Seattle come out with a five-wide receiver package—a look that had too many pass catchers for the Thriller defense to defend. When the Seahawks returned, they went to four receivers, Green Bay stayed with its intended blitz scheme, then Hasselbeck came to the line and audibled.

"It was a play that I thought was pretty safe," Seattle coach Mike Holmgren said. "Either Al Harris made a wonderful play or we did something just a little bit wrong, the depth of the route or something like that."

Hasselbeck certainly knew he did something wrong.

"What hurts about it is I had the ball in my hand," Hasselbeck said. "I could have done something different and we don't lose the game. I could have thrown the ball away. I could have...I don't know.

"It's tough. It hurts right now. I'm not exactly sure how it all went down. But knowing Al Harris, knowing the kind of player he is, he is a smart player. He takes chances sometimes and has had big plays this year."

Harris had many big plays in his seven years with Green Bay. He reached the Pro Bowl twice, was named All-Pro once and became a lockdown corner for a short period of time.

Most importantly, though, he lifted the Packers to one of their most memorable playoff wins ever.

"I was just thinking, *Don't drop the ball*," Harris said. "'Make sure you secure the catch,' and it was a footrace from there on."

And a foot race into history.

Doug Hart

The phone call came in the summer of 1963.

Doug Hart, a rookie free agent without a home, had just been signed by the Green Bay Packers. But when Pat Peppler, Green Bay's director of player personnel, called Hart with the news, he took a pass.

"I told them I was going to law school instead," said Hart, who was home in Arlington, Texas, at the time.

Peppler wasn't ready to cave, though.

The Packers were playing a preseason game in Dallas at the time. And Peppler told Hart he'd have to resolve the matter with Packers head coach Vince Lombardi.

"I'm not sure really why I had to go and talk to Lombardi," Hart remembered. "But I'm glad I did.

"The Packers were playing in Dallas…and I went to Lombardi's room, where I woke him up from a nap. After I told him I wasn't going to play football, he said, 'We'll give you your release.' But then I changed my mind and said, 'I don't want to miss my chance.'"

Good choice. As the Packers readied to play Dallas that week, Lombardi worked Hart out and liked him enough to bring him back to Green Bay.

Hart spent the rest of that 1963 season on the "cab" team, which is similar to the practice squad today. And by 1964, Hart was the primary starter at right cornerback.

Amazingly, Hart spent the next eight seasons helping Green Bay accomplish greatness on the football field. And the funny thing is, he's about the last person anyone would have targeted to be part of the Packers' dominance in the 1960s.

Coming out of Texas-Arlington in 1963, Hart went undrafted. Hart quickly signed a free-agent deal with the St. Louis Cardinals, but was cut after just two weeks and returned home.

That's when the Packers signed Hart, liked what they saw, and he eventually chose the gridiron over the courtroom.

"For me, it was such a great surprise to go there and see just how thoroughly football can be played," Hart said. "When we watched film, the way we did things at times was so perfect and so thorough, it was incredible.

"If high school football is played at a level of 1, college is four times more difficult than that. And pro football is at least 10 times more advanced than that. But there were times we just made it all look so easy."

Much of that was due to Lombardi, of course. The ultimate taskmaster and perfectionist, the Packers coach got the best out of almost everybody.

Hart credits lessons learned from Lombardi for many of his post-football successes. And today, he remains highly active in Lombardi Legends.

"He created a profile for high performance and leadership," Hart said of Lombardi. "He told you to figure out your target, then commit yourself to that. His role was to be a highly demanding leader and he knew how to play his role."

Hart settled into his role, too. Bob Jeter won Hart's job in 1965 and he became a back-up corner. Hart remained a reserve for four years, then became Green Bay's starter at strong safety his last three seasons.

Along the way, Hart had some highly memorable moments.

He returned a fumble for a touchdown at Minnesota in 1965, at which point he was approached by Paul Hornung, who told him, "You broke your virginity now." Hart had 15 interceptions as a Packer, three of which he returned for touchdowns.

And of course, he won Super Bowl championships in both 1966 and '67.

"You try to think back and look at it sometimes and it's kind of like landing in Chicago at night," Hart said. "You know how you have all the lights and all the people, it's kind of like a fantasy.

"Well that's how Green Bay was. It was kind of like a fantasy. Sometimes I question if I was really there because it was such a great time in my life."

Hart's post-football life has been pretty good, too.

He became a vice president at Arctic Cat in Neenah, Wisconsin, then became president and chief operating officer of a portable toilet manufacturing company in Minnesota. He also ran a textile mill, before achieving his greatest satisfaction.

In 2000, Hart moved to southwestern Florida, got his Coast Guard captain's license and became a licensed fly fisherman. Hart, an avid outdoorsman while in Green Bay, then became a fly fishing guide and a fly casting instructor.

"Green Bay was wonderful for hunting and fishing," Hart said. "And Carroll Dale actually taught me how to hunt. So that was really thrilling."

Like many former Packers, Hart often reflected on his days in Green Bay and his time with Lombardi when life got dicey.

"I could never, ever not think about Green Bay and Coach Lombardi whenever I had problems to resolve," Hart said. "For so many years, we competed under the highest pressure possible and maintained our poise. That really helps you later on in life.

"My time there was unbelievable. As I think back on it, I'm just so glad things worked out the way they did. It was just a terrific, terrific time."

BOB JETER

It was the summer of 1962 and Bob Jeter had no idea where he was headed.

Jeter, a Green Bay Packers second-round draft choice in 1960, had played 2 1/2 seasons in Canada. But now, he was considering a move to the NFL.

Only Jeter wasn't thinking about becoming a Packer. He was interested in playing for the Pittsburgh Steelers and being closer to much of his family.

"I called up Coach Lombardi just to let him know I was interested in the NFL," Jeter said before his death in 2008. "And he asked me, 'What in the hell are you doing in Pittsburgh?'

"He told me to get my butt to the Pittsburgh airport and there would be a ticket waiting for me to come to Green Bay. And the rest is history."

That it is.

After sitting out one season, then making a full-time move to cornerback, Jeter became an integral part of the Packers' dominance in the mid-1960s. Jeter started at cornerback between 1965 and 1970, made two Pro Bowls, was named All-Pro twice, and was inducted into the Packers Hall of Fame in 1985.

Jeter combined with Willie Wood, Herb Adderley, and Tom Brown to give Green Bay arguably the NFL's best secondary, which helped the Packers win three straight titles between 1965 and 1967.

Jeter played in Green Bay through the 1970 season. But after the firing of Phil Bengtson in 1970, Jeter was shipped to the Chicago Bears, where he played the last three years of his career.

"You look at those guys I played with," said Jeter, who was a stand-out cornerback and running back at the University of Iowa. "The guys in the back like Wood and Adderley and Brown. Ray Nitschke, Lee Roy Caffey, Dave Robinson, Willie Davis, Lionel Aldridge, Henry Jordan. I had good players all around me. You couldn't help but be good. I was very fortunate."

Those that played with Jeter feel awfully fortunate, as well.

Jeter was the Rose Bowl MVP in 1959 after rushing for 194 yards on just nine carries.

Green Bay selected Jeter with the 17th overall pick in the 1960 draft, but when some of Jeter's close friends elected to play in Canada, he joined them. After two-plus seasons with Vancouver and then Hamilton, Jeter realized he'd made a mistake.

"I thought it was a good idea when I first went there," he said. "It wasn't."

Coming to Green Bay most certainly was, though.

Jeter practiced for one day at running back, then Lombardi decided to move him to wide receiver. But after being stuck for two seasons behind Max McGee and Boyd Dowler, Lombardi moved Jeter to cornerback at the start of the 1965 season.

Jeter felt like his chance to make an impact may never come, though. In fact, during the Packers' next-to-last exhibition game of 1965, Cleveland running back Jim Brown ran right through Jeter and broke four of his ribs in the process.

"It was such a long road to get a starting spot," Jeter said. "Because I wasn't used to ever sitting on the bench."

Jeter's patience was rewarded, though, and he made it back later that season.

Ironically, it was against that same Cleveland team where Jeter made his greatest contribution. In the NFL Championship Game that season, Jeter kept Cleveland All-Pro wideout Paul Warfield in check as the Packers cruised to a 23–12 win and their third title under Lombardi.

Over the next few years, Jeter developed into one of the NFL's top shutdown corners and the Packers added Super Bowl I and II titles to their list of achievements.

Bob Jeter brings down Gale Sayers in the Midwest Shrine exhibition game in Milwaukee in 1967.

"People didn't throw my way much," said Jeter, whose son Rob is the men's basketball coach at UW-Milwaukee. "I really do think I was one of the best.

"The passing game back in my day wasn't what it is these days. But I think I could hold my own in any era."

What Jeter always wondered was how good of a running back he could have been. Blessed with speed, size, and vision, Jeter believed he could have excelled behind one of the best offensive lines of his time.

"I wish I could have found out how I'd do running behind Jerry Kramer and Fuzzy Thurston and Bob Skoronski and Forrest Gregg," he said. "It would have been fun to see how good I could have been."

Overall, though, Jeter had few complaints.

He finished his 11-year career with 26 interceptions for 333 yards and two touchdowns. He played for arguably the greatest coach of all time. And he played on some of the most legendary teams in NFL history.

Just think if Lombardi hadn't intervened—and Jeter had wound up in Pittsburgh.

"I knew Pittsburgh was interested in me and that's why I was there in the first place," Jeter said. "I wanted to give the NFL a chance and I thought that would be my best spot because I never heard from Green Bay the whole time I was in Canada.

"But it couldn't have worked out better. I'm real glad Vince told me to get up to Green Bay."

So were the Packers.

BOB KAHLER

Bob Kahler was exiting the Rose Bowl back in 1941. His Nebraska Cornhuskers had just lost to Stanford, and Kahler thought his football days were over.

Sure, Kahler had been a nice player at Nebraska. Yes, he could run like the wind, as evidenced by his American indoor record in the 70-yard low hurdles.

But Kahler had gone undrafted by the NFL. And he figured if he was going to be drafted, it would be to serve in World War II.

As Kahler was leaving the legendary stadium in Pasadena, California, though, he encountered Green Bay Packers coach Earl "Curly" Lambeau.

"He came up to me after the game and asked me if I wanted to play pro ball," Kahler recalled of Lambeau. "I had spent two years in the ROTC and was almost sure I was going to be drafted [into the service]. But I wasn't drafted until 1944. I was surprised. I didn't think I'd ever be playing pro ball."

For the next three years, though, that's exactly what Kahler did. Kahler, who was 96 when he died in 2013, had a blast playing for Lambeau and the Packers.

"He was very interesting," Kahler said of Lambeau. "He had a great personality, very outgoing and friendly and really a players' coach.

"He was a very flamboyant guy. He was a flashy dresser and he drove a Lincoln Zephyr. But he expected you to do a job and made sure you did it. He was really a great coach."

Kahler also played with Packer legends such as Don Hutson, Tony Canadeo, Ted Fritsch, and Cecil Isbell. Kahler said as dynamic as Hutson was on the field, he was equally humble off it.

"He was a terrific person, very unassuming," Kahler said of Hutson. "Nothing like the characters of today."

In an era where rosters contained just 28 players, Kahler played both ways like many other Packers. Although he didn't start on either side of the ball, Kahler saw time at both running back and in the defensive backfield and served as the Packers' emergency punter.

Kahler's three-year statistics were extremely modest, to say the least. In that time, Kahler had nine carries for nine yards, caught two passes for 21 yards, and returned one punt for 14 yards.

"I had size, good hands, and a lot of speed," said the 6'3" Kahler, who played at 200 pounds. "I think [Lambeau] really liked my speed."

After being on teams that finished second in the Western Division in both 1942 and '43, Kahler was part of the Packers' Western Division title team in 1944. That group went 8–2 in the regular season, then faced the New York Giants in the NFL Championship Game.

Playing on a half-frozen field at the Polo Grounds in New York, fullback Fritsch scored a pair of touchdowns and Green Bay's all-purpose halfback, Joe Laws, set a playoff record with three interceptions and added 74 rushing yards on just 13 carries. That was enough to propel the Packers to a 14–7 win as they claimed the NFL championship.

It was even sweeter considering the Packers had lost to the Giants during the regular season 24–0.

"It was a big deal," Kahler remembered. "We had a fine reception at the railroad station when we returned and there were a lot of fans waiting for us. It was pretty neat."

In that day, Kahler played for $300 a game, so the $1,500 bonus that went to the winning team was big-time money. It's a far cry from today's game of $20 million players and $120 million salary caps.

Kahler, like many former players, isn't a fan of the way the NFL has evolved from its infancy to the sporting giant it is today.

"Oh jeez, it makes me ill," Kahler said. "All the dancing around after they make a tackle. Isn't that the name of the game?

"And the salaries, just like golf, have gotten crazy. When I played, we had two pairs of shoes, one for games, one for practice. It seems to have all gotten out of hand."

One of Kahler's best memories remains the Green Bay–Chicago rivalry, which seemed to get out of hand on a annual basis. Kahler remembers a particular game in 1944 that best symbolized the desire of both sides to win.

"It was always a do-or-die game, every time," he said. "And the surface that day was so hard that we were using aluminum cleats.

"Well, Ted Fritsch got stepped on and cut his buttocks pretty bad. He went into the dressing room and they were going to send him to the hospital. Well, Lambeau came in there and told the trainer to stitch him up and get him back in the game. You didn't leave a game against Chicago."

Kahler was forced to leave the game altogether following the 1944 season when he was drafted into the Second Air Force Super Bombers. He served for two years in Colorado Springs before being discharged.

He earned his Masters degree in education from the University of Nebraska and got his doctorate in sports medicine at Northern Colorado. He then worked as a professor in the athletic training field at Northern Illinois for 30 years, before retiring in 1984.

But Kahler's time in Green Bay, playing under Lambeau and having a role on a championship team, will always hold a special place in his heart.

"I had a great time there," he said. "Remember, I thought I was going into the service right after the bowl game. So to even have the chance to play pro football was a blessing. And then to do it with a great coach and some great players around me was pretty special."

AL MATTHEWS

Most members of the 1972 Green Bay Packers believe they were a team of overachievers.

A group that maximized its talent in winning the NFC Central Division with a 10–4 record, before bowing out to the Washington Redskins in the first round of the playoffs.

But Al Matthews isn't one of them.

To this day, it eats at the former Packers safety that the 1972 season ended when it did for Green Bay.

"I really felt we should have went to the Super Bowl that year," Matthews said. "We had a really good team, and if we'd have beat Washington, we would have had Dallas at home. That still bothers me."

It's easy to see why.

Matthews played in Green Bay for six years after being selected in the second round of the 1970 draft out of tiny Texas A&I. And aside from the '72 campaign, the Packers had five losing seasons in the time Matthews donned the green and gold.

But the 1972 season was different.

The defense became one of the league's best. The running game, powered by John Brockington and MacArthur Lane, was dominant.

Green Bay's Achilles' heel, though, was a subpar passing attack. And it finally caught up with them in a 16–3 loss to a Washington team that eventually reached the Super Bowl and lost to Miami.

Packers quarterback Scott Hunter had just 150 passing yards that day against the Redskins. And after that game, Green Bay went 10 years without reaching the playoffs again.

"I thought we had a great run in '72," Matthews said. "We did what we had to do on defense, but I thought we lacked direction on offense. We were a young team and we were missing one little piece."

The Packers never found that piece during Matthews' time in Green Bay. But that didn't stop him from becoming one of the NFL's more respected strong safeties.

Matthews, who played both sides of the ball at Texas A&I, began his Green Bay career as a cornerback and started on the right side in 1971.

But his lack of speed was a major liability, and late in the 1971 season, the Dan Devine–led coaching staff moved him to safety. Matthews didn't mind the switch one bit. It's just that the timing could have been better.

"It was our last game of the year and we were playing the Dolphins," Matthews said of what would become a 27–6 loss to Miami. "And they sent me in to replace Willie Wood. Well, it was Willie's last game, and having to tell him to come out wasn't much fun."

Fortunately for Matthews, things got easier. He became the permanent starter at strong safety in 1972, combining with cornerbacks Willie Buchanon and Ken Ellis and free safety Jim Hill to form a potent unit.

The 6', 190-pound Matthews was a punishing hitter and a tremendous competitor who sparkled against the run. He enjoyed perhaps his finest year in 1974, when he intercepted three passes, finished among the team leaders in tackles and was mentioned prominently for the Pro Bowl.

"Not to toot my own horn, but I really did think I got the most out of my talent," said Matthews, who was born and raised in Austin, Texas. "I didn't always get recognized, but I held my own in the secondary.

"I was glad they moved me inside, because I was better against the run than the pass. But I think I was a really good leader and a good team player."

Matthews was also something of a pioneer. During the off-season in 1974, Matthews went to the University of Texas and served as a volunteer assistant coach for his good friend, head coach Darrell Royal.

Matthews, who worked with the wide receivers, became the first African American coach ever at the University of Texas. And he also became just the second black coach in the history of the Southwestern Conference.

"I didn't feel any pressure at all," Matthews said. "Darrell and I were great friends and he had a great staff and they were all good with it. It was a good fit."

Following the 1975 season, the Packers decided Matthews was no longer a good fit for them. Coach and general manager Bart Starr left Matthews unprotected and Seattle took him in the expansion draft.

After playing the 1976 season with the Seahawks, Matthews was out of football most of the 1977 campaign. But late in the year he was picked up by San Francisco. Fittingly, the final game of that season, and of Matthews' career, came against Green Bay at Milwaukee County Stadium.

"That was a neat way to finish up," Matthews said.

Most expected Matthews to pursue a career in coaching when his playing days ended. But instead, he returned to Austin and went into real estate, something he did during his playing days as well.

After spending some time in the construction business, Matthews became a sales manager at a Ford dealership in 1988 and later moved to Lexus.

While being in the heart of Cowboy country means encountering Dallas fans at every turn, Matthews loves playing devil's advocate.

"Hey, we all know the Green Bay Packers are the real America's team," he said. "The Green Bay Packers are a household name.

"I still go to restaurants and people will say, 'That's Al Matthews of the Green Bay Packers.' I still get something in the mail every day from the people to sign.

"I cherish those days, all those great memories and all the great guys I played with, it's just incredible."

Matthews just wishes his Packers could have won a little more. During his six seasons, Green Bay was 35–45–4 and made just that one playoff appearance in 1972.

"My only wish is we could have won some more games," he said. "We didn't win like they're winning today. But Green Bay is a great place and everywhere you go, everybody knows the Green Bay Packers."

EUGENE ROBINSON

The Green Bay Packers needed something. Anything.

The George Teague experiment hadn't gone as well as planned. And as the Packers chased a Super Bowl title in the mid-1990s, general manager Ron Wolf knew he had to improve the free safety position.

"It was a problem," Wolf said years later. "We had to get better there if we were going to catch Dallas and San Francisco."

So Wolf did what the great general managers do: he fixed the problem. In June 1996, Wolf made one of his best trades ever, shipping little-used defensive end Matt LaBounty to Seattle for veteran safety Eugene Robinson.

Robinson, who played his first 11 seasons in Seattle, was entering the twilight of his career. But he proved to be a key component in the Packers getting over the hump and reaching back-to-back Super Bowls.

Robinson's smarts and leadership were a major upgrade over what Teague had brought to the position. And Robinson could still run a bit, timing at 4.58 seconds in the 40-yard dash.

"I think I gave them a little more leadership in the back where LeRoy didn't have to do everything," said Robinson, who lives in Charlotte today. "We worked pretty well back there. It was a good marriage thing.

"LeRoy was the better blitzer and had a knack for getting into gaps and stuff. And I took over the verbal stuff."

And it worked like a charm. Robinson and Butler were arguably the league's best pair of safeties in their two years together, helping Green Bay become the league's No. 1 defense during its 1996 Super Bowl championship season.

For his part, Robinson led Green Bay with six interceptions in 1996—the most by a Packer free safety since Tom Flynn in 1984—and was fourth on the team with 82 tackles. He followed that up with a pair of interceptions in Green Bay's 35–14 win over San Francisco in a divisional playoff game, then led the Packers with nine tackles in their 35–21 win over New England in the Super Bowl.

To this day, Robinson calls his two seasons in Green Bay the highlight of his 16-year career.

"Coming to Green Bay was the best thing that ever happened to my career," Robinson said. "I want to thank the people of Green Bay for two wonderful years. It's a special town and those were the best years of my career."

Eugene Robinson and me holding the Lombardi Trophy and talking to Ron Pitts after winning Super Bowl XXXI.

Robinson had just one interception the following season, but put together a brilliant postseason. Robinson had an interception against John Elway on a pass intended for Rod Smith in the end zone during Super Bowl XXII, but his interception in the NFC Championship Game may have been even bigger.

With the Packers leading 3–0 early in the second quarter and San Francisco driving, Robinson made the play of the game. The crafty veteran jumped in front of 49ers tight end Brent Jones and picked off a Steve Young pass at the Green Bay 14-yard line, then returned it 58 yards to the 49ers' 28.

Two plays later, Brett Favre found Antonio Freeman on a quick slant that the receiver turned into a brilliant 27-yard score for a 10–0 Packers lead. The 49ers never challenged again as Green Bay cruised to a 23–10 win.

"Out of all our wins, that was the best," Robinson said of the 1997 NFC Championship Game. "That was a very, very tough game and that interception was huge. And afterward, I remember going to the podium [for the trophy presentation] and thinking not many people come to San Francisco and stand at the podium. It was special."

But unfortunately for Robinson, it was also short-lived.

Although Robinson wanted to return in 1998, Wolf decided second-year player Darren Sharper was ready to take over his position, something that couldn't have been more wrong.

Robinson ripped the move at the time, saying Sharper wasn't ready. And he was right, as Sharper struggled immensely early in his career.

"It wasn't anything personal against Darren," Robinson said. "He had all the physical gifts in the world and went on to have a great career. But at the time they gave him my position, he wasn't ready for it. I could certainly see that and said so before I left."

Robinson signed with Atlanta, where he helped the Falcons reach Super Bowl XXXIII. On the way, Atlanta pulled off one of the most memorable postseason upsets ever, defeating 11-point favorite Minnesota 30–27 in overtime in the NFC Championship Game.

"Beating Minnesota was always fun because they were pretty inflated on themselves," Robinson said. "But we knew we had the offensive power to go against them if we could just withstand and make some defensive plays."

That placed Robinson in his third consecutive Super Bowl, but also set the stage for the biggest mistake of his life. The night before the game, which was being held in Miami, Robinson was arrested for soliciting an undercover police officer.

The ordeal trashed what had been a flawless image and threw his family life into chaos.

"I wish I could forget it," he said. "But I learned an incredible lesson about staying close to the Lord and that my family is more important than my own selfish needs.

"That's not something that defines me now and I refuse to be debilitated by it. I own it and it's my responsibility. But I still have a lot to go ahead and do."

Robinson has done many of those things since retiring after the 2000 campaign.

Robinson currently works as a color analyst for the Carolina Panthers Radio Network and is the varsity football coach at Charlotte (N.C.) Christian School.

"This is what I want to do. It's ideal for me," Robinson said. "I wanted to make sure I transitioned into something quickly and didn't feel displaced and I think I found the perfect thing. This is something I know, I know football. I can't stand my voice. I hate hearing myself.

"But I think I've got a lot of knowledge and enthusiasm and I try to pump it up. I live vicariously through the players and I'm squirming in my seat during games. And I think I make it fun."

Robinson certainly had his share of fun in the NFL. His 42 interceptions in the 1990s were second most of any player that decade. Robinson also was voted to three Pro Bowls.

And Robinson's arrival in Green Bay helped the Packers get over the hump and win their first super Bowl in 29 years.

"That was just an amazing time and group of guys," Robinson said. "Guys played for each other, not themselves, and that doesn't happen very much anymore. But that was just an amazing time for every one of us."

JOHN ROWSER

I

t's comical, really.

Today's NFL has players making in excess of $20 million. Salary caps are in excess of $120 million.

Back in 1970, Green Bay Packers defensive back John Rowser was making $25,000 and asked for a $5,000 raise. Despite the fact Rowser helped Green Bay win Super Bowl II and was a valuable contributor as its third corner, the Packers balked at his request.

Their response? The Packers traded Rowser to Pittsburgh for tight end John Hilton.

"They told me, 'You're not going to start in front of [Herb] Adderley and [Bob] Jeter,'" Rowser recalled of the All-Pro players he was behind. "So they sent me to Pittsburgh."

That didn't work out too bad for Rowser. He spent the next four seasons as a starting cornerback on Pittsburgh's legendary Steel Curtain defense. He then spent the final three years of his career as a starting corner and free safety with Denver's famous Orange Crush defense.

Hilton, meanwhile, played one year with Green Bay and caught 25 passes.

"I didn't necessarily want to leave," Rowser said. "I just wanted to be paid what I thought was fair. I wasn't making any money, but they didn't want to pay me because I was behind Adderley and Jeter."

Ironically, Rowser would have likely earned a starting spot in 1970. That off-season, Adderley left to play with Dallas, but by then, Rowser had already been traded.

Green Bay was a team in decline at that time, though, while Pittsburgh, and later Denver, were both teams on the rise. That gave

Rowser a chance to play on three of the more vaunted defenses in league history. Perhaps his only complaint was the Steelers and Broncos reached the Super Bowl the year after he left, although he did win a ring his rookie year with the Packers.

"I was real lucky to be on those defenses," Rowser said. "I played with a lot of All-Pros and Hall of Famers. That's something else."

Rowser thought being in Green Bay was something else when he first arrived. The Packers used a third-round draft choice on Rowser, but considering Green Bay was coming off of back-to-back world championships—including a win in Super Bowl I—Rowser was just praying he'd make the team.

"I knew with Vince [Lombardi] there, there weren't a lot of spots open and not a lot of room," said Rowser, who played collegiately at Michigan. "All I was hoping for was to make the team."

Rowser certainly proved worthy of that, as Green Bay moved backup cornerback Doug Hart to safety to make room for him. And for the next three years, Rowser excelled on special teams and was viewed almost as a fifth starter in the defensive backfield.

"The thing is with Herb and Bobby there, I had no chance to start," Rowser said. "I was a pretty good player, but they were both unbelievable players. It was a lot of fun to be part of that secondary, though."

That 1967 season—which produced the Packers' fifth title under Lombardi—was remarkably fun, as well. That was also Lombardi's final year in Green Bay, and to this day, Rowser feels privileged to have played under Lombardi.

"Playing for Vince, that was quite an experience," Rowser said. "He didn't say too much to you. He made sure the All-Pros and vets led by example.

"His time was always 10–15 minutes before something started. If you showed up on time, you were 10–15 minutes late. And the thing I remember about Vince is he'd go to church every morning, yet by 7:30 or 8:00 every morning, he'd be cursing at you."

But Rowser, and the rest of the Packers, were cursing when Lombardi left following the 1967 season. Phil Bengtson took over, and although he inherited an aging team, things went south faster than most thought possible. In Rowser's final two years with the Packers, they went a very mediocre 14–13–1.

"Bengtson was more of a defensive guy," Rowser said. "And I don't know if he got as much out of the vets as Vince did. That was all a big change, and a lot of others left after Vince did, too. Still, it was a nice experience to play there."

Rowser's post-football life was quite nice, as well.

Rowser owned a car-leasing business and a nightclub that both did well. Then he retired in 2000.

To this day, though, Rowser looks back on his Green Bay days with a touch of romanticism.

"The thing I'll always remember about Green Bay is that team was all about winning," said Rowser, who's still part of Lombardi's Legends and returns to Green Bay every fall for Alumni Weekend. "I learned a lot from those guys. It was a great experience."

Moving to Safety

Ray Rhodes was the one who convinced me. He called me up and he said, "We're going to take Buckley with the fifth pick and we're going to move you to safety."

I said, "Ray, I'm only 191 pounds. I can't play safety." Remember David Fulcher? He was 6'4", 235 pounds. Tim McDonald was 6'3". I said, "I can't play safety. I'm going to get killed."

He said, "No, no, no. I've got this thing about moving guys. You're one of my best cover guys. I want to move you on the inside on third downs, so I need to move you to safety so I can put [Terrell] Buckley at corner." And it worked. It worked. And I loved corner, but I absolutely loved safety.

Ray Rhodes saved my life. I had so much fun at safety. He convinced me you don't have to be really big. I eventually got to 205, maybe 208, because I played so much up at the line that I had to bulk up a little bit.

My shoulders were always really small. So strength and conditioning coach Kent Johnston would bulk my shoulders up. That really helped. But again, I had that deceptive speed. On third downs, I think I was the only safety in my era where on first and second down I played traditional safety, then on third down I came up and covered a wide receiver. I used to cover guys straight man-to-man and I used to play that weak side.

I remember Ray Rhodes saying, "I'm not going to get these third and fourth corners. I'm going to put you up there. You're my best guy. You're a Pro Bowler. I want you [staying] on the field, so I want you to go up and cover."

It was really flattering. It was a challenge to me because I always wanted to cover a receiver, and my cornerback skills helped me with that. That was awesome.

． ． ．

As far as the defensive backs I got to play with, there were some special ones:

Doug Evans was smart. Man, he was smart.

Craig Newsome was a tough guy. We needed an enforcer because we didn't have one. We were a finesse team. We didn't feel like we had a guy who would hit you in the mouth, but Craig would. Craig would mess you up.

I'd go tell him, "You know that guy just cracked me, No. 81." And he'd say, "I'll take care of him." He was like that. We didn't care about his coverage skills, we cared about bump-and-run, get-up-in-a-guy's-face skills.

Eugene [Robinson] is someone I needed to be compatible, so the coaches could trust me to do some of the things I wanted to do—the eight-man front, the blitzing, things of that nature. I still don't know how we got him. It was a blessing. But we needed a guy like that. He was the best center fielder in the league.

There were so many people that wanted Eugene and I still don't know how he chose Green Bay. I know we traded for him, but he wanted to come and play with me and Reggie. And he was such a great guy. He was probably the smartest player I've ever played with. By far. We were so compatible. I mean, we were interchangeable; we really respected each other, and he made me elevate my game.

I used to call him Magic Johnson, because he could facilitate. He knew formations, he knew tendencies. I would study quarterbacks and he would study formations. He would say, "LeRoy, this is a weak formation. You know they love to do these top 10 plays." So we would study those plays and we'd see that formation. And offenses were too arrogant to break their tendencies, so we would just do some great things.

He was a joy to work with. He really was. Eugene is one of my favorites.

When they went to Darren Sharper (after the 1997 season), it was like most teams. Green Bay thought they had gotten the most out of the player. But Eugene still had something left. Even if he didn't have the foot speed, his study habits and his anticipation and knowing what to do were incredible. And that's the biggest problem I had was working with guys that didn't know what the hell to do. That's why Sharper was refreshing. Now I was Eugene and Sharper was me. You go make the plays and I'll play center field.

Now Sharper wasn't ready in 1998, but in his defense, they didn't have a role for him because he wasn't a hitter. He was too tall to be a safety and he wasn't physical enough. So they just said go be a playmaker.

I went to him at one point and said, "You need to anticipate if you want to be a great safety. You've got to read your keys, believe in yourself, and go. Pull the trigger." And he didn't know what I meant.

I said, "Go look up the word 'anticipation' and write it down for me." I told him that that was the kind of player he needed to be. Anticipate. The ball's going where you want it to go. It's like a funnel. They can't throw away from you because you're going to anticipate where the ball's going to go. And he got more interceptions than a lot of people, and for touchdowns, because he trusted himself. Some of our guys said, "I can't pull the trigger." Well he pulled the trigger.

HAROLD VAN EVERY

arold Van Every called himself lucky—and he wasn't being the least bit sarcastic.

"Lucky" to have come around at the time when $4,000 a year was the salary an NFL first-round draft choice commanded. And "lucky" to be drafted into World War II, which essentially ended his playing days.

But before Van Every's passing in 2007 at the age of 89, Van Every knew just how lucky he had been.

"Oh, it's been a good life," Van Every said during an interview shortly before his death. "A really good life."

And a wild one, to say the least.

Van Every enjoyed a stellar career at the University of Minnesota, where he was a standout running back and led the country in 1939 with nine interceptions. The Packers then selected Van Every with the ninth overall pick in the 1940 draft, making him just the fifth first-round draft choice in Green Bay history.

"I was very proud to be chosen with the No. 1 draft pick," Van Every said. "They were good people and they had good ownership in Green Bay. They were just the tops."

Van Every's days in Green Bay were a lot of fun, too.

He was primarily a backup in both the offensive and defensive backfield in 1940–41, a stretch in which Green Bay went 16–5–1 and tied for the Western Division championship in 1941.

Van Every also had a chance to play for the legendary Curly Lambeau, an experience he says he'll always treasure.

"He was a pretty tough individual, but that's okay because he knew what he was doing," said Van Every, who was a two-time letterman in basketball at Minnesota, too. "He'd walk into a buffet and if he'd see you eating stuff you shouldn't be, he'd fine you $50. That was a lot in those days. He was tough."

Van Every also played with some awfully tough former Packers, such as wideout Don Hutson, quarterback Arnie Herber, and running back Cecil Isbell.

"Don Hutson was as good as it got," Van Every said. "Fast, shifty, just an amazing player.

"Arnie Herber could throw the ball 80 yards. Greatest arm I've ever seen. And Cecil Isbell was the left halfback star. I wasn't any great player. But I was a good substitute and had a good time."

Even though the pay left something to be desired.

Football players in the 1940s made table scraps compared to today's players, and Van Every was a perfect example of that. Despite being Green Bay's No. 1 draft choice, he received just $4,000 per season and no signing bonuses.

"Twenty years later, Donnie Anderson was the Packers' No. 1 draft pick and he made $400,000. Thirty years after that, Darrell Thompson was the Packers' first-round draft pick and he made $1,000,000," Van Every said. "I certainly came around a little too early."

And he wasn't allowed to stay long enough.

Van Every was drafted into the service following the 1941 season and began flying with the Air Force in 1942. In 1945, his plane was shot down by the Germans and he was forced to eject from 22,000 feet.

Van Every was captured and spent a year in a prison camp in Poland. Once a month, he'd receive a package from the Red Cross that measured 15 inches wide and six inches high that contained canned meat, chocolate, and some other staples.

But that was barely enough to stay alive, and Van Every lost 50 pounds during his year in the prison camp.

"You want to really punish a man, you starve him," said Van Every, who went from 200 pounds to 150 during his time in the prison camp. "That's how you can get a man to crack."

Van Every got out of the service in 1946 after the war ended and wanted to resume his football career. But during his plane crash, he had suffered back injuries and the pain from football would have been too great.

So he went to work for Principal Life Insurance as a chartered life underwriter. Amazingly, he worked there until his late eighties.

"Every day he was at the office," Van Every's wife, Drexel, said. "He was really driven."

Even in his later years, Van Every never slowed down.

An avid golfer, Van Every shot an 86 when he was 89. During a celebration for his 65th wedding anniversary, Van Every entertained guests on the piano. And he and Drexel were passionate Minnesota Gophers sports fans and rarely missed a football or basketball game.

Through it all, Van Every always kept tabs on the Packers—and considered himself lucky for kicking off his career in Green Bay.

"Occasionally, I still cheer for the Packers," he noted. "I liked my time in Green Bay. I stayed busy and took piano lessons and learned how to type when I was there. So I'll always have really good memories of Green Bay."

TRAMON WILLIAMS

It didn't seem like the time to gamble.

Green Bay led Atlanta 21–14 in the final seconds of the first half during an NFC divisional playoff game in 2010.

The Falcons were driving into scoring range. And the safe play would be giving up a field goal attempt, not risking a touchdown.

But Tramon Williams wasn't in the mood to play it safe.

With just 10 seconds left in the half, Falcons quarterback Matt Ryan took a snap at his own 35-yard line. Ryan rolled left and threw back against his body for wideout Roddy White.

Williams jumped the route, though, made a nifty cut past Ryan at midfield, then sailed to the end zone as the half expired. That 70-yard interception return gave Green Bay a 28–14 halftime lead, propelled it to an eventual 48–21 win, and was one of the biggest moments in the Packers' eventual march to the Super Bowl title.

"I had watched so much film of those guys, I had a feeling that's what was coming next," Williams said. "They were just trying to get into field goal range. They didn't have enough time to do much else. I guess it just shows what can happen when you're prepared."

And boy, was Williams prepared throughout the 2010 postseason.

In a wild-card game at Philadelphia that year, Williams had a game-saving interception. Eagles quarterback Michael Vick lobbed a jump ball to the end zone for 6′4″ wideout Riley Cooper. But the 5′11″ Williams went up higher than Cooper, snatched the ball away, and preserved a 21–16 Packers win.

The following week, Green Bay and Atlanta were deadlocked at 14 late in the second quarter. Ryan took a shot to the end zone for 6′4″

wideout Michael Jenkins, but Williams played the ball better. And when Jenkins lost his footing, Williams went up and intercepted Ryan's pass.

It was all part of a breakout postseason for Williams. He had three interceptions in Green Bay's first two playoff games, then had blanket coverage against Chicago in the NFC Championship Game and Pittsburgh in Super Bowl XLV.

"I think we have lots of guys on the defense that can make those plays," Williams said. "I think I've just been put in that position and made those plays from my teammates. I don't see it as a big deal."

But Williams' emergence was a huge deal. And the fact Williams became one of the NFL's elite cornerbacks was one of the league's great surprise stories.

Back in the fall of 2002, Williams was spending his Saturday afternoons at Joe Aillet Stadium, home of the Louisiana Tech football team.

Williams, a 19-year-old freshman, wasn't in a Bulldogs uniform, though. He was in street clothes, just another student in the crowd.

It was then that Williams realized he'd made a colossal mistake.

Earlier that same year, Williams had turned down a scholarship offer from then–Louisiana Tech head coach Jack Bicknell. Williams didn't think he wanted to play football anymore. Instead, he was planning on being strictly a student.

But all it took was a few Bulldogs home games for Williams to discover that sitting in the stands wasn't for him.

"I don't know why I stopped playing. I really don't," Williams said. "I can look back and say I should have took the scholarship from the start. But things happen for a reason.

"I was going to the games and that's when I realized I can still do this. I knew I had never lost my love for the game. Not once. I knew I had to try it again."

So in the spring of 2003, Williams went to Bicknell and asked back in.

"He was very positive about it," Williams said of Bicknell. "I went out there in the spring and impressed him, got invited back to the camp. I just keep pushing. It was a longshot for me. I came out and did what I had to do and it turned out good."

For both Williams and Green Bay.

Williams wasn't invited to the NFL Combine in 2006, ran a slow 40-yard dash time on his pro day (4.59), and went undrafted. The Houston Texans brought Williams to training camp that summer, but released him on the final cutdown.

"We were stone-cold lucky Tramon Williams was available…when we signed him," Packers general manager Ted Thompson said. "It's not an exact science. That's what makes it so compelling for those of us in the business. We don't know how it's going to turn out."

Williams joined Green Bay's practice squad later that season, and slowly began working his way up the ranks.

In 2007, Williams won a job as Green Bay's No. 3 cornerback and was a dangerous kickoff return man. Williams was a part-time starter in 2008 and '09 and had nine interceptions in those two seasons.

By 2010, Williams was entrenched at right cornerback and was named the first alternate for the Pro Bowl.

"He's a very talented young man that developed late, or whatever category you want to put him in," Packers coach Mike McCarthy said. "But he's someone that's really taken full advantage of our program here. He's someone you can point to, he's an excellent example of a young man that's here all the time.

"He doesn't miss any workouts. He's up there one-on-one with his coaches, both in special teams and the defensive back room, taking full advantage of his opportunity. We're really proud of what he's accomplished."

But Williams' greatest accomplishments came in the 2010 postseason.

Williams made arguably the play of the game against Philadelphia in the wild-card round. He made undoubtedly the biggest play of the divisional playoffs against Atlanta.

And Williams' consistent brilliance eventually helped Green Bay win its first Super Bowl in 14 years.

"I'm very proud of myself," Williams said. "I have a lot of confidence in myself, but it was a rough road. I just tried to stay positive… and it worked out."

Boy, did it ever.

WILLIE WOOD

For Willie Wood, it all started with a letter.

Amazingly, it ended with a trip to the Hall of Fame.

Wood, one of the top safeties in NFL history, was undrafted coming out of the University of Southern California in 1960. A big reason for that is Wood was a college quarterback, and at that time, there were no black quarterbacks in the NFL.

Wood had already come to the painful realization that if he was going to play at the next level, he'd have to become a safety. So he began studying which teams needed help at that position.

Wood then sent letters to the 49ers, Rams, Giants, and Packers. He made a case for himself by detailing his collegiate career and explaining why he could be an asset.

The only team he ever heard back from was Green Bay.

Packers coach Vince Lombardi wrote back to Wood, then sent his personnel man, Jack Vainisi, to USC to work Wood out. Wood was invited to training camp and was the last man to make the 34-man squad in 1960. He played that year for $6,500.

"I was just full of enthusiasm and so happy I made the team," Wood said. "There was always some doubt. But I didn't worry about the other stuff and gave it my best shot."

And what a shot it was.

Wood was tutored by veteran Emlen Tunnell during his rookie season. Then in 1961, Wood took over the free safety position and didn't let anyone else grab it until he retired following the 1971 season.

Over the next decade, Wood was named All-Pro nine straight years and went to eight Pro Bowls. Wood also had 48 interceptions, which is second in franchise history.

Wood played in six NFL Championship Games and helped the Packers win five of them.

"Coach [Lombardi] would stand up and tell us we were making history," said Wood, who roomed for most of his career with Herb Adderley. "He'd tell us people would remember us as a great football team for years. And what he said was true. He was a great philosopher because he had the ability to see things we couldn't.

"At the time you're going through it, you have no idea you're making history. But that's what we were doing. Coach understood the big picture back then, even as it was going on around us."

Wood's career was packed with one highlight after another.

Wood led the NFL with nine interceptions in 1962. He led the Packers in thefts five different seasons.

But one of Wood's biggest individual plays came during Green Bay's 35–10 win over Kansas City in Super Bowl I.

Early in the third quarter, the Packers were clinging to a 14–10 lead, when Wood intercepted Chiefs quarterback Len Dawson. The Packers blitzed six on the play, and Dawson threw behind tight end Fred Arbanas and directly to Wood.

Wood returned the ball 50 yards to the Kansas City 5-yard line, and moments later, Elijah Pitts had a five-yard TD run. The Packers were in total control from that point forward.

"I was disturbed in the first half," Packers quarterback Bart Starr said years later. "We weren't moving the ball at all. Then we settled down and did just what we were supposed to do—get out there and win the ballgame."

Wood also points to the 1967 Ice Bowl as one of the most unforgettable events in his memorable career.

When Wood went to his car that morning, his battery had died. And after just a few minutes outside, Wood was frozen himself.

That's what happens on a day when the kickoff temperature is 13-below zero and the wind chill was minus-46. Never did Wood think the NFC Championship Game between his Packers and the Dallas Cowboys would be played that day.

"I didn't think there was a chance in hell they'd make us play that day," Wood said. "It was unreal."

It sure was.

During that unforgettable contest, the referees' whistles froze. One fan died due to exposure and several others were treated for frostbite.

And in the end, Green Bay rallied for a 21–17 win in which Starr scored the game-winning touchdown with 13 seconds left.

"That was a defining game for a lot of us," Wood said. "We had gotten a little bit older and it was kind of our last hurrah. Dallas was a team on the rise, and for us to find a way to rise up and beat them that day was pretty remarkable."

Wood ranks the 1962 Packers as the most remarkable team he played on. Green Bay went 13–1 that regular season, defeated the New York Giants for the NFL championship, and outscored its foes 431–155.

"We had won a championship the year before, so we had some experience," Wood said. "And a lot of us were still really young and just hitting out prime. That was a great, great football team."

While things were utopian for Wood on the field, they weren't always golden off of it. The 1960 U.S. Census showed that there were just 128 blacks living in Brown County, .01 percent of the total population.

Several landlords were unfamiliar with blacks and refused to rent to Wood. He ended up living in a downtown YMCA, where his bill was $1.50 per night.

"I was just amazed and surprised," Wood said. "I had never been in a place where there weren't any black folks.

"But I think it was more ignorance than it was racism. People thought that if you were black, you were violent.

"I had a neighbor later on who really resented that I was leasing a townhouse across the street from her. But before the season ended, she was one of my best friends and remained that way."

Wood said that finding a place to rent became rather easy as the city of Green Bay began making some progress in the early '60s. But the real progress—for Wood and the Packers—came on the football field.

And to think, it all began with a letter to Lombardi.

"I loved playing in Green Bay, and I have no regrets about my career whatsoever," Wood said. "I got more out of it than anyone would have ever imagined."

CHARLES WOODSON

On paper, it was just another October game. It was no different than the hundreds of games that came before it for Charles Woodson.

But one play in that 2007 contest provided the perfect microcosm for the greatness Woodson brought to the field every Sunday.

Green Bay was clinging to a 26–22 lead against Kansas City with just more than a minute remaining. On a third-and-2, Chiefs quarterback Damon Huard threw over the middle for running back Priest Holmes, but Woodson jumped the route.

Woodson intercepted Huard, took off for the right sideline and raced 46 yards for a game-clinching touchdown. Amazingly, Woodson scored 10 touchdowns during his seven years in Green Bay, which is a franchise record.

Instincts. Speed. Hands. Smarts. Woodson had them all, and he showed it on this play and in this game.

"He's a Hall of Fame player," Packers cornerbacks coach Joe Whitt Jr. said of Woodson. "I tell my other guys, 'Don't look at Woodson now. He has the ability to do some things other guys just can't do.'"

And for seven years, Woodson did exactly that in Green Bay.

Woodson, the only defensive player to ever win the Heisman Trophy, played his first eight seasons and made four Pro Bowls in Oakland. But by the time the 2005 season ended, Woodson was coming off an injury-plagued season and was considered moody; both sides were eager to part ways.

Woodson, an incredibly bright and articulate man, thought the free agent offers would come pouring in. But his reputation had taken a hit and many teams considered him a declining player.

Sure-fire Hall of Famer Charles Woodson returns an interception for a touchdown against the Detroit Lions.

Two months into that free agent season, Woodson was still unsigned. The Packers were the only serious bidder, but Woodson was holding out hope of playing in a bigger city. Finally, one day while driving around Houston, Woodson realized it was Green Bay or bust.

"I wasn't happy that day," said Woodson, who signed a seven-year, $52 million contract with the Packers. "I wasn't sold on coming here, but there were really no other options. It got to a point where I just had to accept what was going on. There just wasn't a lot of interest, and I tried damn near every other team. I was amazed.

"I was talking to my agent every day and he was making phone calls to different teams. I'd call and say, 'What did this team say?' And he'd say, 'They feel they have what they need.' And I was telling people I'd play safety, whatever. And every time I called him, he'd say, 'Well, Green Bay called.' And I'd say, 'Anybody else?'"

Shockingly, Woodson and the Packers became the perfect couple. And Woodson became the second-best free agent in team history, behind only Reggie White.

It wasn't always that way. The somewhat temperamental Woodson butted heads with then–rookie head coach Mike McCarthy throughout the summer of 2006.

"Charles and I had some big-time growing pains in his initial stages here," McCarthy said. "We made it through that and the benefits definitely outweighed the negatives."

That's for sure. Somewhere during that 2006 season, the two began to peacefully co-exist and Woodson once again became one of football's elite corners.

Woodson won NFL Defensive Player of the Year honors in 2009, when he had nine interceptions (returning three of those for touchdowns), had four forced fumbles, and one fumble recovery.

Woodson had at least seven interceptions in four of his seven years with the Packers. He was named to four Pro Bowls in Green Bay and was instrumental in the Packers' run to a Super Bowl title in 2010.

Woodson scored touchdowns in six different seasons in Green Bay. And 38 of his 55 career interceptions came in Green Bay.

"It could not have worked out any better," Woodson said. "I don't know what else I could have done anywhere else that I've been able to do in Green Bay."

A huge key to Woodson's success was that Green Bay used him in a myriad of spots. Woodson lined up at cornerback, safety, linebacker, and operated from the slot. He even played on the line of scrimmage in a package the Packers call "Bear."

Woodson could match up with No. 1 wide receivers, eliminate tight ends, and do everything in between.

"He's just a fantastic football player," Packers cornerback Tramon Williams said of Woodson. "I've learned so much just watching him."

In a league packed with eye-popping athletes, Woodson's gifts stood out even more. They helped him win a Heisman Trophy at the University of Michigan in 1997, and they helped him stay a step ahead of the competition while in Green Bay.

Woodson had the soft hands typically found on Pro Bowl wide receivers or nifty running backs. That's why if a ball was even in the vicinity of Woodson, he was a good bet to haul it in.

That was only half the battle, though.

What Woodson's teammates discovered is he studied as much film as almost any defender on the roster. That's why when Woodson gambled from time to time, he almost always won.

"I think he's smart and knows things from releases to splits to what patterns a guy runs," former Packers wideout Ruvell Martin said. "He uses all those things to know what pattern a guy might run and where a quarterback is going to throw the ball. He can bait a quarterback.

"I would think there would be a lot of people that would love to have the information he has. I also think he has the talent."

Woodson's resurgence in Green Bay helped his Hall of Fame candidacy gain momentum.

There are 20 defensive backs that have made the Hall and they averaged 56.0 interceptions. The fewest picks of any defensive back in the Hall of Fame is 40.

"I don't know," Woodson said. "That's a tough deal to get into that place. That's up to you guys. If it happens, it's a great deal."

Even if that doesn't happen, Woodson's journey to Green Bay will go down as an enormous success, something few would have thought possible back in 2006.

"I guess you never know until you give something a try," Woodson said.

The Packers are thrilled he did. Amazingly, so was Woodson.

6

SPECIALISTS

DON CHANDLER

It was one of the most controversial kicks in NFL history.
One that Baltimore Colts loyalists will always say missed wide right. And one Green Bay Packers fans will always tell you was good by a mile.

In the days before his death in 2011, Packers kicker Don Chandler insisted the biggest kick of his life was good.

"It was good," Chandler said during an interview shortly before his passing. "I'm sure of it."

It was December 26, 1965, and the Packers were hosting the Colts in the Western Conference championship. Green Bay trailed 10–7, when Chandler trotted out for a 22-yard field goal with just 1 minute, 58 seconds left in regulation.

While kickers made roughly 50 percent of their attempts in that era, Chandler still called the kick "a chip shot."

The ball flew high above the right upright and Chandler's initial body language indicated he missed the kick. But field judge Jim Tunney, who was standing directly under the goal post, said the kick was good.

"The kick went down the middle, but the wind was blowing," Tunney said years later. "I was the only official standing under the goal post and it went over the crossbar, and then after it crossed, from the kicker's standpoint, the wind blew it past the right post. In those days, the posts were only 10 feet above the crossbar, so I drew an imaginary line up that side."

After that season, the NFL raised goalposts from 10 feet to 20 feet so officials could make clearer judgments on similar kicks. On this day, though, all that mattered was Tunney called it good.

And if Tunney's word wasn't good enough, Chandler also had validation from the NFL's most honest man.

"Bart [Starr] said it was good," Chandler said, referring to Packers quarterback Bart Starr. "And Bart never lied."

Chandler's kick sent the game into overtime, and shortly thereafter, Chandler drilled a 25-yard field goal to lift the Packers to a 13–10 win. Afterward, Baltimore head coach Don Shula and the Colts insisted Chandler's kick at the end of regulation missed to the right—and that the wrong team won the game.

"I saw Shula years later and we laughed about it," Chandler said. "He still didn't think it was good, but I know it was good."

One week later, Chandler had three field goals and Green Bay defeated Cleveland 23–12 to win the NFL championship. And the Packers had to feel like Chandler was their ultimate lucky charm.

Green Bay's kicking game was a mess in 1964, when Paul Hornung made just 31.6 percent of his kicks. The Packers went 8–5–1 that season, losing two games by one point and another by three. They finished second in the Western Conference.

So that off-season, Lombardi gave the New York Giants a draft pick for Chandler—who also handled the punting duties—in one of his better moves.

Chandler upgraded both positions immensely, and made 65.4 percent of his kicks in 1965. Chandler then made a combined 54.4 percent of his kicks over the next two seasons, and helped the Packers win Super Bowls I and II.

Chandler's final game remains one of his most memorable, as he drilled four field goals in Green Bay's 33–14 win over Oakland in Super Bowl II. That remains tied for the most in Super Bowl history with San Francisco's Ray Wersching.

"I was very fortunate," Chandler said. "Not many people had the luck I did. I was kind of disenchanted with the Giants and they were disenchanted with me. The Packers needed a kicker and it was the perfect place to wind up."

Chandler retired after the 1967 campaign and Green Bay's kicking went in the tank again. The Packers made just 13-of-29 field goals the next season (44.8 percent) and Green Bay lost five games that were decided by a touchdown or less.

That was a large reason the Packers went from Super Bowl champions to a 6–7–1 season under Phil Bengtson.

"It was just time for me to retire," said Chandler, who was 34 years old at the time. "I don't know exactly what happened after I left.

"I think it had a lot more to do with the big guy that left [Vince Lombardi] than it did me. You don't replace someone like him. I was just glad to get a chance to play there."

Ironically, Chandler and Lombardi had a long history, dating back to back to Lombardi's days as an assistant coach with the Giants.

In 1956, Chandler and fellow rookie Sam Huff were contemplating quitting. The two went to turn in their playbooks one afternoon and woke Lombardi from a catnap. Chandler and Huff told Lombardi they were quitting, and he went ballistic.

Chandler and Huff decided to go through with it, though, and made their way to the airport later that night. Then Lombardi showed up. He ordered them both back to camp, and Chandler was always thrilled he returned.

Chandler had a fantastic nine-year run with the Giants as a standout kicker and punter. Then Chandler became reunited with Lombardi and won three straight championships at the conclusion of his career.

"My relationship with Vince was very good," Chandler said. "His approach was very hands-off. I don't even think we had a kicking coach. He pretty much left me alone.

"Going to Green Bay was a blessing. It was a welcome to get out of New York. I wasn't big on New York and I had been kind of picking at them about everything. It was a big change, but I really welcomed it."

So did the Packers.

In addition to Chandler's marksmanship on field goals, he made 117 of 120 extra points with the Packers and was inducted into the Green Bay Hall of Fame in 1975. Chandler was also named the punter on the NFL 1960s All-Decade Team.

"I got an opportunity to play in the biggest city in the league and the littlest," Chandler said. "I got the best of both worlds."

Still, when talk of Chandler's brilliant career comes up, the topic of choice is almost always the 1965 Western Conference championship game.

"That seems to be what I'll always be remembered for," Chandler said. "And I guess that's not too bad."

DESMOND HOWARD

All it took was a sliver.

If you gave Desmond Howard the tiniest of openings, he was gone.

Howard, one of the dominant return men of his era, had a remarkable 1996 season in Green Bay, shattering the NFL record for punt return yardage in a season (875). Howard had a memorable postseason, too, highlighted by his 244 all-purpose yards in Super Bowl XXXI, which earned him MVP honors.

Howard's magical Super Bowl night included a 99-yard kickoff return for a touchdown late in the third quarter. Without Howard's heroics, Green Bay's 35–21 win over New England that night would have been far more difficult.

"He wasn't quite big enough or good enough to be a starter for us, not for our offense," former Packers general manager Ron Wolf said of Howard. "He was what he was: a great returner.

"I still think of the one year he had with us in 1996. As that season went along, he became more and more a threat to take it all the way every time he touched the ball. He's the best return guy I've ever seen. He never really made it as a wide receiver, but he put it all together that year as a returner."

And how.

Howard won the Heisman Trophy at Michigan in 1991, then the Washington Redskins traded up to take him with the fourth overall pick in the 1992 draft. After three years, though, Howard had just 66 catches and five TDs, and Washington let him go.

Jacksonville selected Howard in the 1995 expansion draft, but he lasted just one season there. Wolf, who had targeted Howard when he was coming out of Michigan, thought he'd take a chance—and it paid off in a big way.

But it almost didn't play out that way.

When Howard first arrived in Green Bay, he didn't show any of the skills that Wolf had remembered. But in the Packers' second preseason game that year, Howard probably saved himself a trip to the unemployment line. Howard brought a punt back 77 yards for a touchdown against Pittsburgh and went from long shot to big shot.

"If we'd only played [one] preseason game, I don't know if he would have made the team," Wolf said. "To be honest, he wasn't having much success in the NFL and was touted as overrated and all that. But I figured he was still an exceptional return guy."

Howard realized even then how close he was to being released. And to this day, he's somewhat amazed how things played out.

"It makes for a tremendous story, a guy who was on the cusp of being released and his final act was he walked away with the Super Bowl MVP. I don't know if it gets any better than that," Howard said. "I really don't think so.

"There were a lot of lessons to be learned. Great teammates, man. People don't understand how valuable that is to a person like myself. I'm all about the team and I'm never about any individualism. Brett Favre, the late-great Reggie White. Those were some Hall of Famers and I just wanted to do my part."

He did.

Howard had a solid kickoff return average during the 1996 season (20.9). But it was on punt returns where he really made headlines. Howard led the NFL that year in punt return yardage (875), punt return average (15.1), and punt return touchdowns (three).

In the postseason, Howard took it to another level.

First, on a muddy field in the NFC divisional playoffs against San Francisco, Howard brought a punt back 71 yards for a touchdown to give the Packers a 7–0 lead. Later in the first quarter, Howard returned a punt 46 yards to the 49ers' 7-yard line to set up another TD in what would become a 35–14 Green Bay win.

"You could tell it broke their spirit," former Packers running back Edgar Bennett said of Howard's returns.

That was nothing, though, compared to what Howard had waiting for the New England Patriots in the Super Bowl.

Interestingly, Howard had a knock on his hotel door the morning of Super Bowl XXXI. On the other side were people from Disney, explaining what would happen if Howard was the game's MVP.

"I was flattered by it, but that was the furthest thing from mind," Howard said. "I was just trying to win the game and get a ring. We are out there playing for that jewelry. I was flattered by it so it crossed somebody's mind. I'll be damned if it didn't happen."

It did—thanks largely to Howard's touchdown that remains one of the biggest moments in Packers history.

Howard was in the middle of a solid night that immediately turned spectacular late in the third quarter. The upstart Patriots had just trimmed Green Bay's lead to 27–21 when Adam Vinatieri's kickoff drove Howard back to his 1-yard line.

Howard shot up the middle, got key blocks from Keith McKenzie and Bernardo Harris, then whipped Vinatieri on a 99-yard TD that was the longest return in Super Bowl history.

"We had a lot of momentum and our defense was playing better," Patriots coach Bill Parcells said afterward. But [Howard] made the big play. That return was the game right there. He's been great all year and he was great again today."

Wolf and the Packers were surprised—albeit pleasantly—that New England even kicked the ball to Howard.

"My thought at the moment of his kickoff return was, 'They just did and they paid for it,'" Wolf said.

Amazingly, that was the only kickoff return for a touchdown of Howard's career.

"I've always had an understanding of why things happened the way that they did in my career," Howard said. "If you focus on being the best at what you can do you can't worry about the things you can't control."

Howard made so many huge plays during the 1996 season that it almost seems like he played multiple years in Green Bay. But after just one season, he was gone.

Howard signed a hefty free agent contract with Oakland that off-season, but flopped there. Howard later played eight games in Green Bay during the 1999 season and three more years with Detroit.

But Howard never came close to duplicating his remarkable 1996 season, in which he saved his career and helped the Packers break a 29-year title drought.

"It was tremendous because of the teammates I had," Howard said. "I'm on a team with some Hall of Famers—Reggie, Brett, Keith Jackson, LeRoy Butler. The list goes on and on."

With Howard right near the top.

RYAN LONGWELL

Ryan Longwell could live to be 100 and every detail of September 7, 1997 will remain burned on his brain.

Green Bay's then–rookie kicker had enjoyed a tremendous start to his professional career, making his first six kicks, including three that day at Philadelphia. With 15 seconds left that afternoon and the defending Super Bowl champion Packers trailing, 10–9, Longwell trotted out for what looked like a chip-shot 28-yard attempt.

Moments earlier, though, the football gods smiled on the host Eagles and rain began pouring down. The turf at the old Veterans Stadium then became extremely slippery.

"I was running around to try the kick, and Brett (Favre) ran over to talk to me," Longwell said. "He said, 'Watch it. It's really slick out there.'"

Longwell quickly found out just how slick. As he approached the ball, his drive step slipped out from under him. That sent his body slightly out of whack and he missed the kick to the right.

For an undrafted kicker who had made the team largely because third-round pick Brett Conway flopped, it was an extremely inauspicious beginning. And a slight part of him wondered if he'd just kicked his last ball as a Green Bay Packer.

"There were only three rookies that made that team," Longwell said. "It was (Ross) Verba, (Darren) Sharper and myself.

"It was a veteran-laden team, the defending world champs. There was talk of going 16–0 and repeating as Super Bowl champs and as a rookie, we had to fit in. And when you miss that, certainly you didn't want to make a habit of it."

Ryan Longwell celebrates after kicking a game-winning 46-yard field goal against the Texans in 2004.

Longwell certainly didn't.

Longwell played in Green Bay for nine seasons and set the franchise scoring record with 1,054 points. When Longwell became a free agent after the 2005 season, Packers general manager Ted Thompson didn't make an offer.

So Longwell continued his prolific career in Minnesota for six more seasons. When Minnesota went in a different direction after the 2011 season, Longwell had amassed a remarkable 1,687 career points, which ranked 13th in NFL history.

Not bad for a guy who thought the Packers might leave him in Philadelphia during his rookie season.

"I think he faced some adversity as a young player, which toughened his skin a little bit," said Rob Davis, who was Longwell's long snapper for all but nine of his games in Green Bay. "He played with a certain amount of fear—not fear of an opponent, but fear to fail.

"And when you go out and approach your job like that, I don't care if it's flipping burgers or whatever, if a guy doesn't want to fail most of the time he's not going to. I think it's why he became one of the better kickers in this league."

Longwell certainly became the best kicker the Packers ever had.

Longwell made 81.59 percent of his kicks in Green Bay, which remains a team record. To this day, Longwell has four of the top five seasons for field goal percentage in team history.

Longwell made 14 consecutive field goals on two occasions in Green Bay, and 13 straight two other times. His 226 field goals as a Packer are a team record, and his 33 field goals in the 2000 season remain tied for a team record.

"He's so consistent that if you watch him kick, whether it's an extra point or a 52-yard field goal, it's always the same swing," former Packers special teams coach John Bonamego once said of Longwell. "He has a really, really good understanding to how his ball's going to react to different situations, with wind and that type of thing. He knows what he has to do and he's very, very accurate."

What made Longwell's accuracy even more impressive is where he was kicking. Historically, Green Bay's Lambeau Field ranks with

Chicago's Soldier Field and Kansas City's Arrowhead Stadium as the toughest places in the NFL to kick.

Not only is the weather in Green Bay typically nightmarish the second half of the year, but Lambeau isn't pointed in one true direction, making the crosswinds brutal to deal with. The turf at Lambeau also isn't conducive to kickers because the heating coils are often turned on, making the field wet and slick.

Longwell believed that kicking in Green Bay was harder than any other place in the NFL.

"(Lambeau) is the hardest," Longwell said. "The thing is the wind, the temperature and the field. The field is really not very good and that's a big, big factor in kicking.

"Whether your foot is going to stick or slip. It gets really soft… because the heating coils always keep it moist. So it's always wet. It's never a hard, fast track. It's always slick, the field is soft and your foot sinks down and there's adjustments you have to make to kick that you don't have to make elsewhere."

Still, Longwell always fared better than most when it came to handling the elements.

Longwell made 118 of 143 kicks inside of Lambeau Field (82.5 percent) while he was a member of the Packers. Longwell also made 81.2 percent of his kicks (69-of–85) with the Packers after December 1 when the weather got nasty.

"That's so impressive because the thing with Lambeau is you don't get a lot of true wind," Bonamego said. "You get a lot of buffeting back and forth. It swirls around.

"Just look at the flags on gameday sometime. Look at the flags on top of the stadium and they're going one way, on one goal post they're going one way and on the other end they're going the other way."

One key to Longwell's success in Green Bay is he stayed extremely grounded. Many kickers are a different breed and their moods seem to vacilate. Longwell was the exact opposite, though.

"There's a lot of guys that get real high and real low," Longwell said. "I try not to get too excited after a long stretch of kicks or a game-winner and I don't get too depressed over the misses because you can't if you're going to be successful. And I think that's what you see in the successful guys is there's just a real even keel."

Longwell's steadiness helped him put that 1997 miss against Philadelphia in the rearview mirror and drill several enormous kicks with Green Bay.

Longwell made a huge 43-yard field goal just before halftime against San Francisco in the 1997 NFC Championship Game. Longwell's kick came on a rainy, muddy day and gave the Packers a 13–3 lead.

"I had to play a huge hook," Longwell said. "And it was at a point of the game right before halftime where it gave us a ton of momentum. That was a big kick."

Longwell had four game-winning field goals in the 2004 season alone, and 10 total during his Green Bay career. And for the time being, Longwell is the runaway winner as the top kicker in Packers history.

"I'm really proud of my accomplishments," Longwell said. "The odds of doing some of the things I did weren't great. But I just always tried to stay the course and be consistent, and things certainly worked out."

CHESTER MARCOL

The smallest man on the field had two choices.

Run left and run fast or be hammered into next week.

Chester Marcol chose option No. 1. And the Green Bay Packers had one of the most improbable victories in franchise history.

During the 1980 regular season opener at Lambeau Field, the Packers and Chicago Bears were tied, 6–6, in overtime. Green Bay drove deep into Bears territory and Marcol lined up for a potential game-winning 35-yard field goal.

The snap was perfect, and so was David Beverly's hold. Marcol's kick was low, though, and hit defensive tackle Alan Page in the face.

But amazingly, the ball caromed straight back into Marcol's hands. And the tiny kicker from Opole, Poland, had the instincts and where-withal to race around the left edge.

"I had no choice but to go left," Marcol said. "The left side was wide open because they overloaded the middle since they were going all out to block it. I just took off."

Marcol, a former soccer goalie with nifty hands, raced for the left corner of the end zone. Marcol picked up a key block from teammate Jim Gueno, was never touched, and scored one of the more memorable touchdowns in team history.

Packers 12, Bears 6.

"I played a lot in high school and college and it gave me some football sense," Marcol said that day. "I've done these things before."

For Green Bay, it was a monumental win.

The Packers were coming off a sorry 5–11 season in 1979 and had gone winless during the exhibition season. Chicago entered the game as heavy favorites and certainly didn't expect to be challenged by its oldest rival.

When the Bears lost on one of the flukiest plays in this long and storied rivalry, it made the defeat even more nauseating.

"We bat the ball back, and that little weasel runs it in," Bears defensive end Dan Hampton said. "It was like bursting a balloon."

Amazingly, Marcol's Green Bay balloon was burst just one month later.

After a stellar nine-year career in Green Bay, Marcol was cut by Packers head coach Bart Starr following a rough game against the Cincinnati Bengals. Starr said it was because Marcol's kickoffs were too short, but it had far more to do with his personal life.

Marcol battled alcoholism much of his career. And shortly before that win over the Bears, Marcol had become addicted to cocaine, as well.

"That was the straw that broke the camel's back," Marcol said. "When I started using cocaine, everything just crashed. Just crashed. I thought I could use it recreationally, but I'm the kind of person that after a while, I wanted lots of it."

Unfortunately for Marcol—and the Packers—his off-the-field problems clouded what had been terrific production on the field.

Marcol lived in Poland until he was 14, when his father committed suicide. Marcol's mother brought the family to the United States, where a gym teacher discovered Marcol's kicking talents and introduced him to football.

Marcol eventually attended Hillsdale (Mich.) College, where he was an NAIA All-American. The Packers were impressed and took Marcol in the second round of the 1972 draft.

Marcol kicked four field goals in the first game he ever played—a 26–10 win over Cleveland in the 1972 season-opener. He led the National Football League in scoring that year with 128 points and was named both Rookie of the Year and All-Pro.

Marcol was quickly dubbed the "Polish Prince." There were Chester Marcol fan clubs popping up across the state and he became an instant hero.

"It was an incredible beginning," Marcol said. "There was no way to expect that and it was kind of overwhelming."

Marcol went on to lead the Packers in scoring six different seasons. Marcol's 33 field goals during his rookie season remain tied for the most in a single season with Ryan Longwell (2000). And Marcol's 120 career field goals still rank fourth in team history.

But the drinking and drug use eventually took a tool. And by October of 1980, Starr had seen enough.

"I believe today that everything happens the way it's supposed to happen," Marcol says. "But unfortunately, I induced several of these things. I believe I cheated myself, whatever you want to say, because I made those choices."

Marcol's choices didn't get any better immediately after his football days ended.

In 1986, Marcol attempted suicide by drinking a mixture of battery acid, rat poison, and vodka. That left his esophagus severely damaged, and he still must have his esophagus stretched as treatment.

Today, Marcol has slowly recovered from his addictions and does work as a drug and alcohol counselor.

While Marcol's post-football years have been a struggle, he remains revered by much of Packer Nation—thanks in large part to his 1980 heroics against the Bears.

"I was just thankful I played other positions in high school and had some experience," Marcol said. "I knew what to do. It was a heads-up play."

And one Packer fans will never forget.

JAN STENERUD

Jan Stenerud was on a plane to Green Bay late in the 1980 football season.

He'd already spent 13 fantastic seasons in Kansas City, revolutionizing the place kicking position and etching his name among the game's all-time greats. As Stenerud's plane crept closer and closer to Austin Straubel Airport, the legendary kicker had but one thought.

"I just kept asking myself what in the world am I doing?" he said.

It didn't take Stenerud long to find his answer. He won the kicking job the following season and held it for three years.

And while Stenerud experienced countless highs during his 19-year career—capped by him becoming the first kicker ever inducted into the Hall of Fame—his time in Green Bay ranks among the best.

"I've said many times, I had a long and wonderful career," Stenerud said. "But if I hadn't got a chance to play in Green Bay, I would have missed out.

"It's so special and so important up there. Looking back, I'm thrilled I got that opportunity. I enjoyed it so much."

Few who have ever played the game have kicked like Stenerud—something that still surprises him to this day.

Stenerud was born in Fetsund, Norway, attended Montana State on a skiing scholarship and never tried kicking until his senior year in college. He was a natural, though, and was selected by the Chiefs in the third round of the 1966 AFL redshirt draft.

Over the next 13 years, Stenerud set or tied nine Chiefs records, including field goals attempted in a career (436) and season (44), consecutive games played (186) and consecutive games scoring field goals (16). He also made three field goals, including a 48-yarder, in Kansas City's 16–7 win in Super Bowl IV.

But in 1979, then–Bills coach Marv Levy told Stenerud his kick-offs were too low and too slow and tried changing his style. Stenerud didn't adapt particularly well, and Levy later cut him.

"I should have never had to change my style," Stenerud said. "It's like you'd never ask (Lee) Trevino to try swinging like (Jack) Nicklaus."

Many teams across the league thought Stenerud's leg strength was gone, because his change in kickoff style meant shorter, higher kicks. But Bart Starr brought Stenerud to Green Bay late during the 1980 season.

The following year, Starr brought six kickers to camp, as was often the norm back then. And Stenerud, who scored 1,699 career points and made 373 field goals, still lists a kick from that preseason as one of the most important of his career.

Green Bay was playing Oakland in Milwaukee, and rookie punter Ray Stachowicz was getting booed mercilessly. Stachowicz had signed late after being taken in the third round and was struggling that night. So when Starr had the option of trying a 54-yard field goal or punting the ball late in the first half, he called on Stenerud.

"I think a big reason we kicked there was (Starr) didn't want Stachowicz to get booed anymore," Stenerud said. "But it was great for me because I made the kick.

"And the next day, all the competition was gone. That kick was worth five more years for me."

That's certainly how it turned out.

Stenerud spent the next three years in Green Bay, highlighted by a brilliant 1981 season where he made 22 of 24 kicks for the highest single-season field goal percentage (.917) in team history. Stenerud finished his Packer career making 59 of 73 attempts for a mark of 80.8 percent, second in franchise history behind Ryan Longwell (81.6 percent).

Stenerud thrived despite tough conditions that doomed many before him. Stenerud said of all the places he's kicked, Shea Stadium was the toughest, followed by Soldier Field and then Lambeau Field.

"It wasn't like kicking indoors. It was a tremendous challenge," Stenerud said of kicking in Green Bay. "It's fine early in the year, but you know that you're going to have three or four late home games every season. And that probably means you're not going to the Pro Bowl."

When the 1983 season ended, Starr was fired and replaced by Forrest Gregg. The Packers had taken Eddie Garcia in the 10th round of the 1982 draft and Gregg seemed committed to him.

"I told Forrest I wasn't interested in coming back unless he could assure me there would be equal competition," Stenerud said. "I just wanted a chance to compete."

Gregg couldn't make that promise and opted to go with Garcia, who flopped and was replaced at midseason by Al Del Greco. Stenerud was traded to Minnesota for a seventh-round draft choice and enjoyed two more stellar seasons with the Vikings before a back injury ended his career.

Stenerud was named to the NFL's 75th Anniversary All-Time Team in 1994. And he finished his 19-year career as arguably the greatest kicker of all time.

But to this day he insists it wouldn't be quite as special if it weren't for his four years in Green Bay.

"Kansas City has tremendous fans and I enjoyed Minnesota, too," Stenerud said. "But there's no question Green Bay is as special as it gets. I was very lucky to get a chance to play there."

7

SIDELINES AND FRONT OFFICE

LEW CARPENTER

Back in 1995, Lew Carpenter had just left a job with the Philadelphia Eagles and was contemplating his next career move.

Carpenter had already played the game 11 years as mostly a running back. He coached another 30—including stops in Green Bay as both a player and a coach.

Carpenter's wife of 42 years, Ann, had experienced enough of this life. She told Carpenter she was tired of moving, and if he took another job, she wanted a divorce.

When push came to shove, Carpenter chose the game over the girl.

"I lost 125 pounds in one day," Carpenter joked shortly before his death in 2010.

That story, in a nutshell, pretty much sums up Carpenter.

Football was always his true love. A three-sport standout at the University of Arkansas, Carpenter began his NFL career with Detroit in 1953 and won a world championship there.

He played two years in Cleveland, then came to Green Bay in 1959 in one of Vince Lombardi's first trades. Carpenter spent five years in Green Bay as a running back, tight end, flanker, defensive back and punt returner.

He won two championships with the Packers in 1961 and '62, then began his coaching career in 1964 with Minnesota. After three years with the Vikings, Carpenter quit, and a few days later, his phone rang.

"I picked it up and the guy on the other end said, 'Lew, do you want a job?'" Carpenter recalled. "I said, 'Who is this?'"

It was Lombardi, and Carpenter thought it was a slam dunk he'd return to Green Bay and work for his former boss. Carpenter came in for an interview, was offered the job and told Lombardi he needed to talk it over with his wife.

On his way out of town, Carpenter stopped off for a few drinks and ran into some former teammates, including Ray Nitschke. It was then Carpenter realized that coaching guys he once played with might be too tough.

The next day, he called Lombardi and turned down the job.

"That was the hardest thing I ever had to do," Carpenter said.

Their paths would cross again, though.

After Lombardi left Green Bay and was hired in Washington, he again offered Carpenter a job. This time, Carpenter didn't say no.

The two became extremely close, with Carpenter serving as Lombardi's dinner companion every Wednesday night.

"I learned a lot about how to handle the guys from him," Carpenter said of Lombardi. "And he had a great sense of humor.

"I remember one time we were leaving (Redskins headquarters) and these two good-looking gals came up to us and said, 'Coach Lombardi, can we have your autograph?' He signed it and we started walking again and he said, 'Lew, if you were as good looking as I am, they'd have asked for your autograph, too.'"

Lombardi passed away in 1970, and Carpenter left Washington. He then coached in St. Louis and Houston, before returning to Green Bay in 1975 as Bart Starr's receivers and passing game coach.

"Bart was one of the finest people you could ever work for," Carpenter said. "The only problem he had as a head coach is he listened to a lot of the wrong coaches in the organization."

Carpenter played a large role in getting Lynn Dickey to Green Bay. He also worked closely with James Lofton, who Carpenter says was the second most talented receiver he ever worked with, behind St. Louis' Bobby Moore, who later became Ahmad Rashad.

Carpenter, who became Green Bay's receivers coach in 1975, helped spearhead a rebirth of Green Bay's offense in the early 1980s. With Dickey, Lofton, Paul Coffman and John Jefferson, the Packers offense became one of the NFL's finest.

"I was just a half-ass receivers coach until I got Dickey and Lofton and Coffman," Carpenter said.

Nothing could have been further from the truth. Which is why Forrest Gregg wanted to keep Carpenter on board when he replaced Starr in 1984.

But that relationship quickly soured.

And at the end of the 1985 season, Carpenter had gone into the hospital for a hip operation. Gregg came there to tell Carpenter he was going to replace him as receivers coach, but wanted to offer him the position of assistant head coach. Carpenter saw the offer as a demotion and told Gregg as much.

"I told Forrest to take it and stick it up his [expletive]," Carpenter said. "I was not going to be his [expletive] flunky.

"Forrest tried to be like Lombardi, but he was no Lombardi. Personally, I think he's a [expletive]-head. You are what you are. You can't change that. And he's a [expletive] head."

Things worked out fine for Carpenter. He coached for two years with Detroit and five with Philadelphia, before dabbling in the college ranks for a few years.

Still, his time in Green Bay—and with Lombardi—was always tough to top.

"Those were some unbelievable times," Carpenter said. "You don't always know how good things are until they're done. That was kind of the case with my time in Green Bay and with coach Lombardi."

MIKE HOLMGREN

We were really tight. I think I was tight with everybody, though. My mom taught me to get along with everybody when I was growing up. She wanted me to be a people person and that's how I tried to be.

But Coach Holmgren was different than most coaches. Most coaches just coach, but Holmgren would call you up and ask, "How's your family?" He knew all of our wives' names. And he would protect his players like I've never seen before. I don't think I've ever seen a guy go to bat for his guys like Coach Holmgren did.

We had full protection, full, full protection. If you had a bad game, he'd blame it on himself. He wouldn't let you blame yourself because he had another game to worry about next week. He couldn't have us bitching about the one that just ended.

And he taught us to learn to deal with losses. I remember losing to Indianapolis when they were 0–10 (in 1997). How do you deal with that, getting beat by them? So he was like a therapist, a shrink and a coach.

I remember after we lost to Dallas in 1995 (in the NFC Championship Game), coming home on the plane ride. He wasn't even that upset. He was just mentally pissed off because we gave it away.

There's nothing worse than feeling like the other team didn't beat you and I still say that's what happened. Dallas didn't beat us that day. We beat ourselves. You damn right!

We had never been in that position before and Dallas was very experienced. And we crumbled in the fourth quarter. But as long as he was my coach, I felt like I was the smartest player on the field. He taught me the whole West Coast offense.

I used to go in there with him and (wide receivers coach) Gil Haskell. I'd say, "OK, everybody's going to this West Coast offense crap. What is the terminology with this?" I need the fronts, I need this, I need that and he would teach it to me.

I don't think many defensive guys studied the West Coast offense and I studied it. Oh, you damn right. But once I knew a quarterback's progression, oh [expletive]! I was all over him.

He'd come to the line and he'd have the same checks as Brett. "Two Jet All Go, Two Jet Lion." And I'd say, *Oh, Brett said that in practice. This has to be a dummy call.* Then I found out the West Coast offense, they're too arrogant to change their calls. Terminology stays the same. They may flip-flop colors. Same thing. Formations? Same thing.

Robert Brooks was one of the first guys in the backfield. So was Jerry Rice. So we're mimicking them. Come out of the backfield matchups. If they shift over, Antonio Freeman's backside by himself. And if Freeman's by himself, you've got Mark Chmura wide open on a corner route.

Then we brought in Keith Jackson and it was like, Dang. Wait a minute now. You've got two tight ends—and Chmura was one of the best guys I ever played with now—and you've got both of these tight ends going up the field and crossing and then you've got Freeman coming underneath and Robert running a post. Oh my God now! We give up now.

But people were doing that stuff to us. It's a copycat league. So I asked Holmgren, "How do I defend this [expletive]?" I knew what my coaches were telling me on defense. That side of my brain, I've got that part. But what are you trying to do to me with all this other stuff?

Once Holmgren took what George Seifert and "The Master," Bill Walsh, developed and brought that to us, they were killing us (in practice). There was a whole paragraph for every play. We didn't understand. "Two Go, All Go, X, Y, Hook." I was like, *What the heck is Brett doing?* They were taking a long time in the huddle and everything meant something and the letters meant the receivers. We used to go by numbers.

So I went to Coach and said, "What is all this terminology?" And he laughed.

Mike Sherman really sharpened my skills later on. He made them idiot proof. But Holmgren, he sat down and showed me. This is what we were going do.

He would leave it up there on the board after meetings and I'd go in there and study it. Because again, we had 30 percent of the league running this stuff. You look at the good quarterbacks, they were completing between 65–68 percent of their passes on short passes and that stuff.

And I studied. Man, did I study. Next thing I know I knew it like my own. I knew it. But the 2-minute defense, I would run the defense.

Defensive coordinator Fritz Shurmur would point to me and say, "You got it. You make the calls." And I knew what would shut down the West Coast offense. You had to have a front four that could get after the quarterback. And I knew what coverages it took. Somewhere, Coach Holmgren had taught me.

RON WOLF

We were probably too tight. It was almost embarrassing how tight we were, because you're not supposed to be that tight with the general manager. You can be tight with the coach, but not the guy that can hire and fire you. It was a little embarrassing because he was one of my favorites, and I was one of his.

And I remember him saying something and everybody took it out of context. I was really small and they wanted me to put on some weight and I didn't want to. And I remember him saying, "Once LeRoy puts on some weight and gets bigger, he's going to be a great safety." It was all over the news…and I got a contract extension that same week.

He used to call me up and say, "I'm going to put the transition tag on you." And I'd think, *He should be telling that to my agent*, because I never wanted to go anywhere. I didn't want to go play for anybody else. I loved the Packers. And this is when I was in my prime. I could have gone somewhere and got double the money. I mean I was getting six sacks, six picks a year. I was all over the place and playing 100 percent of the plays.

So I was like, if I can do all that, I could go and get paid. And he was like, "Well, yeah. I know." But I said, "Ron, I don't have to be the highest paid. Just make me one of the highest paid."

At the time it was a three-year, $5.4 million deal. And you see, I loved it here and my wife loved it here. There was one time he restructured my deal and put me in the top three just to be fair. He didn't need to do it, but I was way better than these safeties getting more money, so he just re-did it and made it fair.

That's why it was easy for me to get the phone call from (director of player finance) Andrew Brandt to restructure for less. Yeah, they already gave me money. So I restructured a couple times so we could sign (Darren) Sharper, give Brett (Favre) his $100 million deal, all that stuff.

But Ron and all those guys knew how I was. They never tried to muzzle me or challenge me. They really enjoyed the player I was. They knew I was very loquacious, spoke my mind, I had fun with it, but at that same time was never a detriment to the team. It was all in fun.

But I always knew the media had a job to do and it was my way of talking to the fans. When we lost to (0–10) Indianapolis in 1997, I stayed in that locker room and answered questions. I said, "We played terrible."

And I thought I can let them write what they want to write or I can help them write what I want them to write. And I tried to use that to my advantage. And a lot of players don't get that. It's kind of a head-scratcher.

If you're very honest and available for the media, that's key. That's the key word—available. Win, lose or draw, be available. Face the music, get the glory. You want to be "The Man," you've got to be "The Man" 24-7. And I enjoyed that. I really did.

This was all before social media, so they relied on us to get quotes. So if a fan reads the story and there's no quotes from me, it's like, "Ah, good story. But I'd rather hear it from him." So I got that. I knew fans liked that. And fans would come up to me and say they really enjoyed what I had to say after this particular win or loss.

Coach Holmgren called me up to his office one time and said, "We really, really enjoy you. You're a different guy on our team. But just try to channel all that energy into helping people around you." And I knew what he meant by that. In other words, don't let the media lead you down roads you don't want to go. If you want to go down there, go, but don't let them lead you.

He said, "Always control the interview." He used to tell me that. You control the interview and you'll be fine. I said, "Okay." That's some of the best advice I ever got.

FAVORITES

If it wasn't for Ray Rhodes, I don't think I would have made it as a player. He convinced me to move to safety after he called me and told me they were going to draft Terrell Buckley. He said I'd be an All-Pro safety. And he was right. You darn right he was.

He told me I'd come up and cover the No. 3 or 4 wide receiver on third down and I knew I could do that. He told me he'd blitz me a little bit. Ray Rhodes made me believe I could do whatever the hell I wanted to do. I love Ray Rhodes.

So I was pretty upset after he was fired after just one year (1999). Not necessarily at Ron Wolf, but more the process. I mean, we were spoiled at the time and 8–8 wasn't good enough. But when you look at that roster we had (in 1999) and Ray needed more than one year. So I appreciated him getting a shot, but he should have gotten at least three years.

With Mike Holmgren, they would police you. But with Ray Rhodes, you would police yourself. Every guy holds another guy accountable. So it's hard to tell a grown man to be in by 9:00, and guys took advantage of it.

If I had to rank my favorite coaches, Ray Rhodes would be No. 1 and Mike Sherman would be 1B. Holmgren would be third.

I love Mike Sherman. Even when he left, we stayed in touch. Even now, we stay in touch.

8

RIVALS

Chicago Bears

Our games with them were always really good, really memorable. To have a rivalry game you need two teams that are both good and we had that with those guys. When Dick Jauron was their coach (1999–2003), they were pretty good. And they were pretty good in the mid–90s, and we always wanted to kill them. We wanted to win 50–0. That's how we practiced on that Wednesday. There was a difference on "Bear Week." Absolutely.

There's a few plays from my career that I can highlight against those guys. The biggest one is probably the monsoon game where we had 50-mile-an-hour winds on a Halloween night (a 33–6 Green Bay win on Oct. 31, 1994). And I just remember talking to a bunch of those guys about how bad that turf was. Chicago always had bad turf, but I can't even stress how bad the turf was that night. We were looking at chunks of it all over the field. And every time Brett Favre would go back to throw the ball, he'd put his foot in the ground and a big old piece of turf would come out.

I just remember that particular game how focused we were on the elements. It was raining, it was cold and windy and we didn't care that night. And I think that kind of set us apart from a lot of teams. We had a quarterback that could throw it in the wind, so the wind didn't bother us. We didn't have to play the wind, like when it's downwind you throw the ball. We handled them pretty good because at halftime people were leaving.

And what I really remember was the focus we had. Because there's a lot of distractions when you're playing a rival, playing on their turf, they have home field, the wind is terrible. But to have a team that focused, the weather was not a huge factor for us. Coach Holmgren, I don't know how he did it, but he had us not even thinking about it. We just played our game.

And I remember that particular game I had a sprained knee and my knee was not 100 percent. But I felt that on that turf, I'd have a level playing field because no one was very fast. So I just remember that my knee was in bad shape and every time I went to the sideline, (trainer) Pepper Burruss would wrap it up and keep it warm.

It was just a calming effect that you weren't going to re-injure it. My focus shifted from the knee to other things. And I don't think I've ever been much more focused than that. That was one of the most focused games of my career. I just played on sheer adrenaline.

We watched the highlights after the game and said, "Did we just do that?" Even the Bears were coming up to us after the game and saying, "Man, we're shocked you played that well." That's one of my top five games of all-time because I was so focused. It was almost like watching Tiger Woods putt.

But it was always great playing Chicago. Once we knew it was the oldest rivalry, we really got up for the game each time. We would watch tapes when Jim McMahon was slammed down by Charles Martin. We watched games when Tim Harris was doing crazy stuff.

I remember there was a year (1993) when we were in the meeting room and Jim Harbaugh was the quarterback and they told us Chicago was going to play Craig "Ironhead" Heyward at fullback. And I said, "I'm only a 200-pound safety. I can't tackle this guy." I mean, he was big. He was right around 300 pounds. He was running wild for a couple games up until we played them. But that was one of the best games I ever played.

I used to go up to Reggie and Gilbert Brown and those guys and say, "Don't let him in that secondary. He's going to hurt us. He's a big guy." And Chicago was a bruising team.

But on one play, Ironhead got loose and I grabbed him on a play that would be a horse collar now and I pulled him down. And as I was spinning down, he came back and George Koonce jumped on him. And as Ironhead got up, he said, "LeRoy, I never thought a pipsqueak like you could bring me down. I'm embarrassed." And we both laughed.

I remember in that game I went to the sideline and started complaining that I wasn't blitzing enough. You know, blitzing always seemed like a good idea to me. And the one time I complained about it, I came flying through there and I stripped Jim Harbaugh and the ball was in a big pile. You had 300-pound guys fighting and I'm the smallest guy. And I came out of there with the ball and that was one of the most satisfying moments I can remember.

They were all still looking for the ball and I was over showing it to the ref and doing a dance. It was this weird dance and people were still trying to figure out where the ball was. There were guys fighting and clawing and scratching for that ball, but I had that ball. And when I showed it, the crowd erupted. I still have that ball today. It was awesome. That was one of my best games and favorite moments.

When you're playing a rival like the Bears and you're driving to the game, you start seeing jerseys all over the place. You see a Bears jersey. You see a Packers jersey and the whole experience gets your blood going.

And that drive was always fun. When you're driving to Lambeau and you see the field, it's almost like having a lottery ticket and you're going to the store to cash it in. You just can't wait to get there. And it's even better in a rivalry game like Chicago.

Once you get there and you see all the signs for the Packers-Bears rivalry, that's when it clicks. For a noon game, we could get there by 10:00. But if you wanted to do tape, treatment, you'd get there about 8:00.

We would stay at the hotel Saturday night, and the next morning you'd wake up, have breakfast, they'd have papers for you, whatever. And I'd always eat a grilled cheese and six egg whites. I did that my whole career. It was superstition and it was also some of my favorite foods. That was kind of weird. Then we'd go home, see the kids and all that.

If you were a healthy guy like me, you'd start driving over to the stadium about 9:30. You needed about 15, 20 minutes to get there.

But if you're in traffic and they realize your car and who you are, they start to move people. It was just like Moses. I mean, no one does that. It was just incredible. It was like, "Hey there's Butler. We kind of need him today."

Our people would always come on the Oneida side, not Ridge Road. Our tailgators would come in that side, so they were there already by 7:30. But the people driving in later off of 41—and that's the way I would come—you'd be pushing that limit to get there by 10:00.

And I remember one game against the Bears, there was an accident and I didn't get there until like 10:30 and warm-ups started in 30 minutes. Me and Eugene Robinson and Sean Jones were sitting there in traffic and I called Gilbert Brown and told him we were stuck in traffic. And he said, "Man, you're going to miss a rivalry game." And I said, "No. We'll leave the car and walk if we have to."

But if we needed it that day, the fans would have just drove us in. I loved the fans so much. They always made you feel like a celebrity, even though I always saw myself as just a regular guy. You'd see the Dick Butkus jerseys and Ray Nitschke jerseys and Walter Payton jerseys, then you'd see No. 36. That's when you say, "You know what. This is pretty awesome." And that whole rivalry was like that. It's just awesome.

MINNESOTA VIKINGS

When you were playing the Bears, it was a fun rivalry, playing against somebody that would be history. Everything you do against Chicago is history.

Playing against Minnesota is like the Hatfields and McCoys. You hate each other. I mean it. You really hate each other. And that was before Brett Favre even got to Minnesota.

It was to the point where you didn't even like the color purple. You would just go to your wardrobe and not even wear purple. Fans would come up to you and say, "No, no. Don't wear that." And it's still like that. They still hate the Vikings. And now that Greg Jennings is there, it's just going to keep getting worse and worse. It's like, "Oh my God."

When you're playing in Minnesota, it's always a long walk to the stadium. And then once you do all that walking, you've got to go down a bunch of stairs. When you finally come out and get onto the field, you can't hear anything. They've got these big speakers, six feet tall right behind us. They've got some weirdo running around with a horn on a motorcycle.

The fans—it was everything you could imagine. Everything terrible, that is.

On the bus, when we would drive up, people had peed in a bag, ziplocked it shut and they'd throw it at the bus. The first time I said, "Hey man, why are they throwing apple juice at the bus," and someone said, "That's not apple juice." Some guy, some weirdo would do that, zip it up and wait for the bus.

And we had security. We had a convoy with the cops. But it happened every time we went there. I was like, "Come on man. You all see these people throwing this nasty stuff." And not all the fans would do that, but even one was too many.

And in that place you could never really get your focus because of all the noise. The John Randle Dance. Then the T.J. Rubley fumble (in 1995). Then the Terrell Buckley game (in 1993), when he let Jim McMahon throw a long pass against us at the end of a game and we lost on a last-second field goal. There were some bad losses up there, even when we were a great team.

It almost seemed like the offensive line said, "We're not going to block for Brett this week." Even when Ahman Green was "The Man," we couldn't win. For the most part, they got the best of us up there.

Then, when they got Randy Moss, everything changed. When they got Moss, that made them arguably the most prolific offense of all-time. They had Cris Carter, Jake Reed. Moss, the running back Robert Smith was really good. And Randall Cunningham and then Daunte Culpepper would just launch it. They had a big offensive line. We had so much talent on our defensive front, but they'd run these stretch plays where Smith would run and pick a hole, but sometimes there would be play action off of that and they'd throw it to Moss. So it was tough.

But I'd still say the three NFC teams that dominated for a stretch in the '90s were Green Bay, San Francisco and Dallas. And even though I hated them, I was very surprised Minnesota didn't win a couple of Super Bowls. Now, they did go 15–1 and got beat by Atlanta in the 1998 NFC Championship Game. So that's a tribute to us and finding a way to beat them.

We had talent in the right spots. We had deficiencies in other areas. But pound for pound, guy for guy, Minnesota had more talent than we did. Oh yeah.

They had so much speed on that turf. But that team was very prolific. Their defense wasn't all that great. But that offense was great. And then we said we're going to fight fire with fire and we drafted the three cornerbacks one year (1999).

We felt like we had to get proper defensive backs to keep up with Randy Moss and those guys. But still, it didn't matter with Randy Moss. He was in his prime and even though we emphasized bigger guys for Randy Moss, it didn't matter.

And all those guys were so tough. Jake Reed was 6′2″. Cris Carter was 6′2″. And Randy Moss was 6′3″, 6′4″. We won some, we lost some. But it was a great matchup.

The other game against those guys that really stands out is when Antonio Freeman made that miracle catch in overtime on *Monday Night Football* in 2000. Freeman, in that slot, was so hard to cover. And on gameday, he had concentration that was just unbelievable. Everybody thought he had dropped that ball. But Brett felt, at that time, that throwing it to Freeman was like throwing it to Moss. He was going to get it.

This was before the back shoulder catch was popular. Brett and Freeman did it all the way back then, especially if Freeman was playing against a corner with top speed. Brett would throw it right there on his back hip because Freeman probably wasn't going to run by that corner.

Moss used to throw his hand up. That was his cue to let the quarterback know he was open. Even if he wasn't open, what are you going to do? It was like the Dad playing basketball with the six-year-old son. What are you going to do? You just keep it away from him.

But that play with Freeman was huge. I had told the guys that if we want some national recognition, we needed to win the games on national television. Even though people loved the Green Bay Packers, Dallas was always America's team. But when we started winning games like that, things started to change. Now we became rock stars nationally instead of just locally. And that's what a game like the Freeman game did. It helped make us stars, and that felt good.

If you go back and look at Coach Holmgren on Monday nights, other than that Randy Moss game (in 1998), we dominated games on national TV. When it was national TV and we saw those big national trucks, especially for divisional games, you really got ready for it.

But once the games ended with the Vikings or whoever, it was all good. And I don't think the fans always know that. That's because fans never turn it off. It's always turned up. And plus you play them twice a year and they're so close. You got to know those guys a little bit. But we always wanted to beat them bad, that's for sure.

DALLAS COWBOYS

There was almost like an awe of Dallas. They were my favorite team growing up. The first time I went to Dallas (1993), I saw the cutout roof. I actually saw Tom Landry on the sideline. He wasn't the coach, but he was there and that was pretty neat. I knew all about Jimmy Johnson because he coached at Miami and I grew up admiring him.

I just remember we were in awe of Dallas because they were so good. I think everybody was in awe of them, to be honest. It's America's Team and they were killing people. Emmitt Smith was running wild. Troy Aikman was a terrific quarterback. Michael Irvin was one of my best friends in the whole world, still is. And he was remarkably good. Moose Johnson was a great fullback. I mean, they were loaded.

And we could never get them at our place. It was always there. The only time we got them by us was the year after we won the Super Bowl (1997) and we killed them, 45–17. I'll never forget that. That was a ton of fun.

But in 1995, coming home after they beat us in the NFC Championship Game, Coach Holmgren got up on the plane ride coming home and said, "Next year we're winning the Super Bowl." I looked at him and thought, *Yeah. He's right. We are going to win it.* Because we had Dallas beat in 1995. And we made a commitment on the plane and we said that we weren't players away. We were plays away.

I took this all so seriously, and I looked at all the positions to see where we needed help. And every time we had a position where I thought we needed help, Ron Wolf went and got us that guy. It was unbelievable. We wanted to win it now. We weren't doing it that draft-and-develop way. We'd had 30 years of misery.

I thought to myself, get us the guys we need. And Ron went and did it. We needed a left tackle bad. I mean, the Tootie Robbinses of the world just weren't getting it done. We needed a punt returner and he got us Desmond Howard. He got us Eugene Robinson to play safety next to me and Santana Dotson up front. I mean, Ron filled all the holes.

That's why Ron should be in the Hall of Fame soon. He got a bunch of guys together and made it all work. He just said, "Come on. Let's go win." That man was terrific at what he did.

So Holmgren said that night after we lost to Dallas in 1995, "Get ready for this off-season. We're winning the Super Bowl. If you don't think we can do it, when you get off this plane, don't even come back." And that off-season, we were committed. You could just feel it. More so than ever.

And I said, I know we're going to win it. At that time, I was in such great shape, Reggie was in great shape, we were all in our primes. And the next thing you know, we have the No. 1 defense and the No. 1 offense in all of football. I don't think you'll ever see it again.

In back with me, we could put Doug Evans on any tall receiver and he'd hold his own. Then we needed somebody tough and physical and we got that with Craig Newsome. He'd hit anybody in the mouth. We needed a smart guy and that was Eugene Robinson.

Up front, we needed two unselfish guys and that was Gilbert Brown and Santana Dotson. They would tie up all these blockers so I could fly in and make the tackles. And Reggie (White) and Sean (Jones) were both great.

Then there was one thing that helped us a lot. We went to the coaches and told them we needed a specialist. They said what's that? And we said just someone where all he does is rush the passer. And that was Keith McKenzie. That's all we needed him to do was to go after the quarterback and he was just phenomenal.

I get emotional thinking about some of these players because they all had a role and they all understood their role and how they tied into that role. Nowadays, everybody wants to be the superstar. But not everybody can have that role. You need the George Koonce's and the Bernardo Harris' and the Wayne Simmons' of the world.

When we got to training camp we just knew it. We knew we were ready. I remember sticking my head into the offensive meetings and yelling, "Just get us 15 points boys." I mean, as great as our defense was, that's all we needed was 15 points.

And Dallas helped make us great like that. They made us get better because they were the gold standard. Everybody wanted to beat Dallas. And we found a way to pass those guys up, which wasn't easy.

Dallas pointed out our weaknesses in '95 and we went and fixed them. We needed to get bigger up front. We needed to play Gilbert differently. Instead of using him at 2-technique (nose to nose with a guard), we put him at a 3-technique (outside the guard) and just let him Warren Sapp it up the field. Gilbert just tore down stuff and I just followed him in there.

Dallas still had their core of players back in 1996 and people ask me if I wish we could have played them in the playoffs that year. But it didn't matter. We would have killed them anyhow. Our team was so good. I think even Dallas would tell you that. We were so good. I might have been the only publicly arrogant person who would say that, but we were so good.

And the reason why 1996 was such a great year for us was the coaches put in game plans that we had input into. You would never see that anymore. And we didn't do it up until that year.

The coaches used to think they knew everything and players thought they knew everything and that kept us kind of separate. But (defensive coordinator) Fritz Shurmur was one of the guys who really changed. He would actually meet with me and talk about ideas. I would go up there in the afternoon, once I scouted the opponent and I would give him my input. And then when we got the game plan, there would be stuff I recommended that was in there.

And Fritz put it to the military. He said I better find out what's going on by actually talking to these guys. So he said I want you guys to have some input. And guys were like, "Oh man! This is great." Even a guy like Keith McKenzie would be saying, "Their right tackle, I can beat him every play if you let me go over there." Normally he was on the other side, but we started putting him on the weakest guy. Makes sense to me because you're going to double Reggie, then you have one-on-one with McKenzie and he was killing people.

But we became a great team in '96 and passed Dallas, which was awesome. They had gotten the better of us way too many years. So that year was as much fun as I ever had.

SAN FRANCISCO 49ERS

San Francisco was the exact opposite of Dallas.

We were in awe of Dallas because of their rich tradition and all that. But with San Francisco, it was like playing your neighbor. Holmgren came from there and won a championship there. They had a team full of Hall of Famers. And that's where the West Coast offense originated from. It started over there. It was the mecca of the West Coast offense. We weren't supposed to run this offense better than them.

They were still a prolific offense and a great team. But we dominated those guys.

San Francisco always had the Florida State colors. So to me it always reminded me of playing at Florida State. The helmets, the uniforms. And most of the time it was almost like playing a mirror. They played the same type of offense and the same kind of defense we did and I remember thinking this is going to be weird. How is this going to work?

But what always amazed me is when we were on defense, we always knew what they were going to do because they never changed their calls or their audibles or anything. The West Coast offense was just so arrogant that they wouldn't change anything. They didn't think you could stop them, even if you knew what was coming.

They'd go red-over and flip-flop plays or do dummy signals or something like that. But it was still the same thing. You knew just what they were going to do, but you had to trust it. If he said, "Two Jet Lion," I knew what that meant in our offense, but you had to trust yourself that Steve Young was doing it, too. And usually he was. He called it out.

"Two Jet Sally" is a screen. So you'd know what they were doing, but what they did is he'd yell, "Two Jet Sally, Sally, Sally," and then they might run a Texas route off of it. Let's say it was (running back) Garrison Hearst. He'd run like he was going for the screen, then he'd cut back. So I said, "They have a little wrinkle there."

So to them, they'd keep their calls, but they decided to add a progression onto it. The number tree was still the same. Two was a slant. Nine is a go. So they're calling numbers out and you know what guys are running. But then there was always a second progression on it. So if he was yelling, 'Two, two, two' they're going to slant, but it's going to be a slant and go. So it was almost like a guessing game. They'd get you every now and then, but it would even out.

But we didn't change our stuff either. And then again, there's the arrogance. It's the West Coast offense. That's just the way it worked. So at halftime, we didn't draw up very much. We didn't change anything. I said this offense is the most confident, arrogant offense I've ever seen. And it worked.

I used to talk about it with (49ers safety) Merton Hanks and we'd laugh and say, "Dude. They just think they're better than us because there's always a second progression off the first."

There was this one play called Snake. The tight end would run a 7, which was a corner route. The wide receiver would run an 8, which is a post route. They'd call it. He'd give them the front and he'd yell "Snake." We know they're running the Snake. We know these first two guys are crossing, but backside maybe you weren't sure.

But I really liked playing those guys. I really did. I really enjoyed it because I went into the offensive meetings to find out about the West Coast offense. Coach Holmgren, Gil Haskell, Jon Gruden, Mike Sherman I had them all explain it to me. I had never heard of the West Coast offense early in my career and I said to those guys, "Why do you need a paragraph to call a play?"

So it was just straight arrogance if you're going to yell that play out of the no-huddle and you won't change it. And us defensive guys would all laugh. It was funny. (San Francisco's) Tim McDonald and Merton Hanks were good friends of mine and they'd hear Brett calling that stuff out.

"Two Jet Lion, Lion, Lion" or "Sally, Sally" or "Harry, Harry" or "Ringo, Ringo." They'd hear all these checks and they'd know. Then in one game Keith Jackson is five yards behind them and I said, "You just heard Brett call 'Snake.' What are you doing?"

If you're a fan, you see these guys talking and yelling. Talking and yelling. And you see Holmgren came from this system and Steve Mariucci came from this system. It was a lot of fun and it probably canceled each other out. But we thought that we knew it better, although it started from them.

We thought we knew it better because the guy that started it, Coach Holmgren was with us now. It was just awesome playing those guys. It was so much fun against them because your mind was even more important than your physical skills.

I probably liked playing San Francisco more than anybody else. Playing against Jerry Rice, that really got me going. That's the one team that was awesome to play. Beating them was so satisfying, because I knew all those guys would be in the Hall of Fame. The quarterback, the receivers, the linebackers, the coach, the owner.

And other than the Terrell Owens game (in the 1998 playoffs) we beat them every time. Every time. And that made us feel so good. Because there were a couple times where they had the better team and we found a way to beat them. And that's one reason I really, really enjoyed playing them.

TOP OPPONENTS

Barry Sanders was as good as it got. Playing against Barry Sanders was almost like playing against your big brother. He's going to always be better than you and always get the best of you. But the one time that you're going to get him is something you're always striving for.

When we played those guys on turf, we didn't have a chance. If we played them on grass, we had a chance. And Barry Sanders to me was one of the nicest guys I ever played against. By far. He never talked trash, he was a true professional. And he was so, so good. He didn't have a great offensive line, but out of everybody I ever played against, he was probably the best.

Jerry Rice, Michael Irvin were both incredible. People know all about those guys. They did things most players could never dream of. That's why they're Hall of Famers.

Herman Moore was a great player and maybe my best friend in the whole world. I didn't know Herman at all before we got to the league. But at the Pro Bowl and stuff, we were always together. I played against him a lot. But I just really liked him.

After he broke the NFL record for catches (123 in 1995), I called him up. And remember now, this is a rival. You don't call your rivals. Today, they all call each other because they work out together and have the same agent and all that. But I called Herman up and said, "Congratulations." That guy was phenomenal and there were years we had Terrell Buckley covering him, with help, of course.

Steve Young was probably the smartest guy I ever played against. There would be a timeout and he'd be pointing and he'd say, "You're blitzing right here, right?" And I'd say, "No." He'd say, "You're coming in the 'A' gap. I've seen it on film." And I'd say, "No I'm not. I'm going into the 'B' gap." But I'd really be going in the "A." And I'd think, *How did he know that?*

I got him a couple of times, but he knew coverages. He was just one of the smartest guys I ever played against. He knew what we were going to do, where the rotation was coming from. He knew when to run. He knew when the line was sliding to Reggie. I mean, he knew everything and it was difficult to play a guy like that. I mean, guys do their homework, but not to that level. He was tough.

I think (Detroit offensive lineman) Lomas Brown was one of the toughest guys to go against. Because I used to run up in there freely and he'd always see me. He knew. He knew. So I said I've got to go away from that guy. He's too smart. Some guys I could run right past and they'd be like, "What the hell?" But man, he was tough. Real, real tough.

Emmitt Smith is someone I really enjoyed playing against. People would say he's not fast and all that. But he'd outrun everybody in our secondary. And he was really underrated catching the ball out of the backfield.

Someone else that was really tough was (running back) Amp Lee, and a lot of people don't know about that. Amp Lee out of the backfield was probably the quickest guy I ever had to cover in my career. He was tough out of the backfield. Amp Lee was so quick. Oh my God was he quick.

Randy Moss was another guy, and after Minnesota drafted him, I tried to tell the guys what we were in for. I told the guys he ran a 4.2 (40-yard dash) when he was at Florida State and he's got a 40-inch vertical and he's 6'4". Guys would say, "He's not a true 4.2 is he?" And I'd tell them he's as good as advertised. And I remember we'd have a couple of guys on him and it wouldn't matter. It wouldn't matter. I mean, when he was in his prime, other than Jerry Rice, he was the toughest guy to game plan for.

I mean, what are you going to do? You can't line a safety up 25 yards deep. Even if you do, they're just going to launch it up there and he'll run under it. So we felt like we had to have a guy hit him in the chest, throw his timing off a little bit and beat him up a little bit. We had to throw the timing off and get the quarterback on the ground quickly.

And it's too bad the Packers never got him. They could have drafted him (1998). But what comes up most is that Ted (Thompson) could have had him (in 2007). Brett really wanted him. Instead, he goes to New England and sets all kind of records. Who knew? He came out and scored 23 touchdowns that year. I mean, 23 touchdowns! When we heard what New England gave up for him (a fourth-round draft pick), I said, are you sure about that?

To think that we should have had Randy Moss twice, that's pretty captivating. Green Bay should have definitely had him that second time, but they blew it. The guy dominated games. He was just that good and we should have had him. Brett wanted him and he let them know. That happens. But I applaud guys that make a mistake and stand up and admit it. Ron Wolf always did that and he said he made a mistake not getting Moss. Ted would never say that he made a mistake.

Then there was Shannon Sharpe and Ben Coates. Those were probably the only two tight ends in my career where I said, "Man, I have to be on top of my game this week or they're going to get the best of me." Those guys were ahead of the curve. They both were good blockers, good pass catchers and they were the favorite targets of the quarterback.

I covered some tight ends and they never got a look. So I'd tell Fritz I want to cover somebody where on third down they're going to get the ball. That's when he started letting me cover a wide receiver on third down. And I was one of the first safeties that stayed in on third down. Most of them would go back deep because they can't cover.

But Shannon Sharpe was probably my biggest threat. He was maybe my biggest threat ever. He was an excellent football player. He was so competitive, yet fun. And when it came to talking, I think I met my match. When I knew I was playing against him, I just said, "Hey, I'm focused this week boys. Everything's going to be on me," and I liked it that way.

9

GREAT MOMENTS AND MEMORIES

Getting to Green Bay

I had to wear braces on my legs and use a wheelchair when I was young. But I would say around four or five years old, I was just goofy. When you're that young, you don't know what's going on.

You just run and jump like the other kids. Now, they deal with it a little different. But back then I had those Forrest Gump braces on and was sitting around in a wheelchair. And you're in the inner city, single-parent home and you just figure you're going to be stuck there the rest of your life.

But I remember my mom asking me what I wanted to be when I grew up. I'll never forget it. I was eight years old and I told her I wanted to play professional football. I was out of the wheelchair then, but I still had the braces on.

The wheelchair was just part of the therapy because they didn't want me walking without those crutches. So if I had to go somewhere, instead of me lagging behind I had to use the wheelchair every time. The wheelchair was there if I needed it and I tried not to use it.

About eight or nine, though, I was done with that stuff. But I wasn't real coordinated. I was real skinny, always smiling and happy because I knew what I wanted to be. I was very focused. I don't think you've ever seen a more focused kid. I made an agreement with God that I'd get my mom out of the projects by playing professional football.

And I wasn't in trouble because I was scared of the police and I was scared of my mom. I didn't want to disappoint her because she was a single parent, doing the best she can. I didn't need to be out doing stupid stuff.

In the projects, you do whatever you can for money. I learned to live without money. I didn't let money rule me. I was like, "Hey man, I'm good." I'd wear the hand-me-down shirts and do whatever I needed to do. I just didn't want to disappoint my mom by getting in trouble. But she was my role model and I said, "I want to be just like her." She's a strong, strong lady.

There were five kids in the house and I was the fourth. And my mom would catch a bus at 4:00 in the morning just to catch another bus at 5:00 to carpool with another lady to get to work by 9:00. That's a real role model. We got off the bus and she'd get home about 2:45. She'd be there to cook for us, then she'd go to a night job. We lost count of how many jobs she had.

I was cooking for the family by 11, because when I stayed in the house and couldn't go outside, I learned how to cook and clean and be domestic. I just learned to value my mom. I used to ask my mom all these dumb questions like, "How do they pick uniforms?" She didn't know so she'd make stuff up or go and study football just to answer my questions.

I started playing football at about 11, almost 12. And most kids play when they're younger, but remember I couldn't. So I wasn't real coordinated. I didn't really get the gist at 11 or 12, but when I got into junior high I knew I had some special skills. Boy, I had some special skills. Just like the movie *Forrest Gump* with Tom Hanks, I could outrun everybody. That was me. I could just run, run, run.

When I was in the braces, I was watching football all the time. All the time. And when football wasn't on I'd look outside and see kids playing other sports.

I did go out for baseball, but I got hit by a pitch and I didn't want to do that anymore. Plus, they stuck me in right field and it was just so boring. Also, I sucked so bad and I was out there getting sunburned, so I didn't want to do that. That's when I found out black people can get sunburned. And I told my mom, "This is boring. I want to quit." She didn't let me quit, but as soon as the season was over I was done.

The kids used to pick on me because I didn't want to play baseball. But I told them I was going to play pro football anyway. I mean, who gives a damn about baseball? It sucks. It's too boring. But football, everything is happening—and I was good at it.

I always knew I'd play football. I kept telling the Lord, "If you get me out of these braces or you make me fast enough, I'm going to play pro football." That's all I wanted to do.

You hear stories all the time of people sleeping with footballs. I didn't even have a football. I just knew what I wanted to be. I was so focused on it and I concentrated on it.

And the Lord gave me this natural ability to make great decisions as a kid and for some reason the Lord gave me the ability to listen to my mom. Because not everybody listens to their parents. I've got kids now that don't listen. But everything she said was gospel to me. Everything out of her mouth I was like, "Oh yeah. Okay."

Most kids were robbing banks or robbing stores or selling drugs to get money. I learned to live without money because I felt like, No. 1, if I didn't have money I'd never have to worry about getting robbed. And No. 2, I didn't have to worry about wanting something I can't have.

I remember going to the Salvation Army when I was about 12, maybe 13, and they'd give the inner-city kids toys and stuff. I remember telling my mom, "I don't want any toys. Toys are for the birds."

But there were some new shoes over there and they were some Converses and I went over to the lady and said, "Can I have those?" She said, "They might not be your size. These are an eight." I said, "Well I wear a six." She said, "Well, I need to save them for some older kids." And I said, "Wait. I'll put some newspaper in the toe of them so I can wear them." And she said if I wanted to do that, then go ahead.

That was first time I had a new pair of shoes. And going to school with those new shoes was a big deal. Oh man, it was a big deal. A lot of kids went home with toys that day. I went home with two packs of T-shirts and those shoes, and that made my day.

My mom and I are still crazy close. We probably talk 36 times a day. No exaggeration. We call each other all the time. She's awesome. Just awesome.

. . .

The next big step on my journey to Green Bay was Florida State.

I have to admit, (Florida State coach) Bobby Bowden's a guy I get a little bit emotional about. There was a thing back then called Proposition 48, where you could pick like five or six guys to enroll despite substandard test scores. Once people had found out I didn't pass the SAT test, there were a lot of teams that didn't want to sign me. But Coach Bowden came down to the projects and told my mom he was going to give me a scholarship. I'll never forget that.

My high school grades were awful. I had like a 2.4 and you need something like a 3.0 if you're going to college. The kind of classes you need to have, the core classes, my school didn't have those. So I didn't have a chance to take the Algebra 2s and all that.

When I was a senior, they would transfer you to these technical schools and I couldn't make it out to those schools. I had to do it the best way possible. I didn't have a learning disability or anything. But you only had to have a 2.0 to be eligible in high school, and once I got in I just wanted to play football.

Coach Bowden gave me a scholarship despite that, and I used that first year to get my grades up. I had like a 3.3 and then had great grades throughout college. I'll never forget what Coach Bowden did for me.

I got letters from Florida, Notre Dame, USC, Texas, everywhere. And when I got that Proposition 48, everybody ran. And the quicker they ran, the quicker Coach Bowden ran toward me. If it wasn't for Coach Bowden, I would probably have had to go to a junior college.

There were other schools signing guys, and I wanted to play my freshman year, but I didn't mind going to Florida State and sitting out because it was two hours away and it was Coach Bowden. Coach Bowden was like the Pope. He was big. He did a lot of hands-on stuff. His offense was second to none. He was a guru. He was just so innovative.

. . .

When I finished at Florida State, I really thought I was going to go at the end of the first round. I did. Those were the reports I was getting. But there was one guy who always worked me out and that was Dick Jauron, who at the time was the defensive backs coach for the Packers. He came down quite a bit before the draft, and Green Bay had two first-round picks that year. But they ended up taking Darrell Thompson and Tony Bennett.

And then it got to the second round, and I thought, "Well, I better go second." And when Green Bay called, I was so excited. I really was.

Jauron came down to Florida State and worked me out a bunch. He called me a bunch, too. Houston really liked me, but I didn't get a call from them. I didn't run a great time at the combine (4.53) and my pro day was like low 4.4s, high 4.3s.

There was this guy named James Williams who was rated the best corner in the draft and he went to Buffalo. I was mad, thinking, *Give me a break, I could run circles around him. He ain't the best corner.* He only ended up lasting four or five years in the league.

But I was happy to wind up in Green Bay, a place with a rich tradition. Florida State was a place where tradition was a big word, so I was cool with everything. I was fine.

Favre vs. the Bengals

September 20, 1992, seemed like just another day when Brett Favre rolled out of bed.

Favre drove over to Lambeau Field for his third game as a Green Bay Packer. He expected to spend his afternoon watching Don Majkowski quarterback the team. And maybe, just maybe, Favre would get in for some mop-up duty in Green Bay's game with Cincinnati.

That script was tossed aside, though. Instead, the fortunes of perhaps the NFL's most downtrodden franchise changed for good.

On that day, an organization that had become loveable losers found hope. On that day, Brett Favre had his coming-out party.

"I'll never forget that day," Packers president Bob Harlan said.

Nor should he.

On that gorgeous autumn afternoon, Favre replaced an injured Majkowski and engineered one of the greatest comebacks in team history. In the final four minutes that day, Favre led scoring drives of 88 and 92 yards as Green Bay rallied past Cincinnati 24–23, for coach Mike Holmgren's first NFL victory. Favre capped the dramatics with a 35-yard bullet score to Kitrick Taylor with just 13 seconds left.

That was the first chapter in what became arguably the greatest career ever by a Green Bay Packer.

"I shudder to think where we would have been without him," said former Green Bay general manager Ron Wolf, who traded for Favre earlier that year. "Without a doubt in my mind, he was the player of the '90s."

But back on September 20, 1992, Favre was nothing but a mystery to most.

"If there's anything I remember about that day it was just like, "Wow! Where did this guy come from?'" said former Packers linebacker Brian Noble, a teammate of Favre's in 1992–93. "I hadn't seen much of him in training camp and all I knew was he was a young kid with a little bit of baggage. But after that day, people knew about Brett."

Did they ever.

Until then, all people knew about Favre was that former Atlanta head coach Jerry Glanville wanted him out of town after Favre's rookie season with the Falcons was more about bar-hopping and carousing than it was about football. Wolf, who desperately wanted to select Favre in the 1991 draft when Wolf was with the New York Jets, was happy to make a deal with Glanville.

And on February 10, 1992, Wolf sent a No. 1 draft choice to Atlanta for a player who had career passing statistics of zero completions in four attempts and two interceptions. While critics balked at the move, they'd agree today that acquiring Favre was one of the five most lopsided trades in NFL history.

"I knew right away we had something special," Wolf said. "The question was how were we going to get him to play?

"You could tell it was just a matter of time as soon as training camp started. And during camp, Holmgren and I had a long talk about how to get him on the field."

Turns out, their dilemma took care of itself. With the Packers coming off a 31–3 loss in Tampa Bay in Week 2, Holmgren had contemplated making a quarterback switch before the Cincinnati game. But Holmgren stuck with Majkowski as his starter, fearing Favre wasn't quite ready.

On Green Bay's second series of the game, though, Majkowski was sacked by Bengals defensive tackle Tim Krumrie and suffered ligament damage to his left ankle. As he was being helped off the field, NBC announcer Jim Lampley asked: "Will it ever be 1989 for the Majik Man, Don Majkowski, again? It does not appear likely."

Little did Lampley know how prophetic those words would be. And little did people know the type of magic Favre would begin creating.

The early returns in the Cincinnati game certainly weren't encouraging. It was apparent that Favre and the No. 1 offense hadn't spent a lot of time together.

On his 11th play from scrimmage, Favre fumbled a snap from center James Campen and Krumrie recovered for Cincinnati.

Favre's impatience was evident as he overshot wide-open receivers Sterling Sharpe and Sanjay Beach in the second quarter. And Favre's frustration was beginning to build after he fumbled on back-to-back plays late in the third quarter.

"It's been so long, but I can tell you this: When I became a starter, I had no clue what was going on," Favre said during a 2002 interview. "Maybe that was good. If I told you [back then] I knew what was going on, I was feeding you a line of BS."

Favre certainly looked like he knew what was going on by the end of the game, though. Green Bay headed to the fourth quarter trailing 17–3, and hadn't scored a touchdown in seven quarters.

But the light seemed to go on for Favre and the entire offense in the fourth quarter. Terrell Buckley, playing his first game as a Packer, gave the team a jump-start when he returned a punt 58 yards for a touchdown with 12:43 remaining to trim the Bengals' lead to 17–10.

After a Jim Breech field goal gave Cincinnati a 20–10 lead, Green Bay began at its own 12. That's when Favre began to look like he had been playing in Holmgren's West Coast offense for years, not weeks.

Favre guided an eight-play, 88-yard drive in which he made a handful of standout plays. On a third-and-6, he eluded the rush and ran for 19 yards. He then fired a 15-yard completion to Harry Sydney and lofted a gorgeous 33-yard pass to a wide-open Sharpe that brought Green Bay to the Bengals' 17.

After a 10-yard bullet to Ed West and an Edgar Bennett run, Favre found Sharpe for a five-yard score over the middle to make the score 20–17. The touchdown pass was the first of Favre's career and would be the first of 41 he and Sharpe would connect on.

"We knew he was going to be a good player just from watching him in training camp," running back Vince Workman said of Favre. "Most of his passes were just rocket passes.

"You noticed his arm strength right away, especially because Majkowski was more of a finesse passer. But he stepped in that day and took control right away. He had the respect of everybody right away."

If he didn't then, he certainly did by the time the game ended.

Another Breech field goal with 1:07 left made it 23–17, then rookie wide receiver Robert Brooks dug the Packers an even bigger hole when he caught the ensuing kickoff on the left sidelines and stepped out of bounds at the 8-yard line.

All Favre needed to do now was lead Green Bay 92 yards in 1:07 without the benefit of a timeout. No problem, right?

"Brett had a swagger to him, even back then," said left tackle Ken Ruettgers, who played with Favre through the 1996 season. "Even though he was 23 or whatever, it was like nothing could phase him."

And the improbable odds certainly didn't slow him down on this day.

On first down, Favre couldn't find an open man and settled on a check-down to Sydney, who was smart enough to run out of bounds after gaining four yards. On second down, Favre stepped up into the pocket to avoid the rush, then found Sharpe wide open down the right sideline.

Sharpe had run past cornerback Rod Jones, and safety Fernandus Vinson was late bringing help. Sharpe reached up high to haul in the 41-yard bullet from Favre, but in doing so, re-aggravated a rib injury.

With the clock running, Favre raced to the line of scrimmage, then dumped a 12-yard completion to Workman over the middle that brought the Packers to the Bengals' 35. Again, Favre raced to the line and spiked the ball with just 19 ticks remaining.

With Sharpe having gone to the sideline because of his rib injury, things looked dicey for Green Bay. The Packers lined up with Brooks in the slot on the left, Beach wide left, and Taylor wide right. Favre again looked right, where just three plays earlier he had found a wide-open Sharpe.

Favre pump-faked in Taylor's direction and got Jones to bite. Taylor streaked by Jones and had a good three yards of separation.

Favre then fired a laser beam to Taylor that didn't get more than 12 feet off the ground. It was a good thing, too. Vinson was closing fast, and had there been more air under the ball, the Bengals' safety would have likely broken the pass up.

Instead, Favre's bullet threaded the needle between the two Cincinnati defenders and landed right on Taylor's hands with 13 seconds showing.

The memorable touchdown pass would be the only one Favre and Taylor would ever connect on.

"On that play, I was blocking on a guy and he just kind of stopped," Ruettgers said. "That usually means he's given up because the ball is in the air.

"So I looked up and saw the ball just zipping down the field to Kitrick Taylor. I mean, it was an NFL Films moment. It was one of the few great moments that as a lineman you not only played, but got to witness at the same time. It was incredible."

In typical Favre fashion, he showed his boyish enthusiasm, ripped off his helmet, and danced around Lambeau Field. The rest of the Packers and the sellout crowd went wild, as well.

"I was standing on about the 40 when he threw it," Noble said. "And I remember thinking, *I'm glad I'm not on the field, because that ball would have hit me in the head.* There was no elevation to it. It was an incredible throw."

Workman agreed.

"I'm just really proud to say I was part of that game and proud to say I played with Brett when he was starting out," said Workman, who was Green Bay's leading rusher that game. "That day and that play really gave us an extra boost of confidence. It was our first victory and it helped us start to believe in ourselves."

That it did. Favre would lead Green Bay on a six-game winning streak later that year and to a 9–7 record for just its second winning season since 1982.

More than that, though, Favre showed the poise, leadership, and ability that made him one of the greatest to ever play the position.

Favre went on to win three MVP awards, led the Packers to two Super Bowls and an NFL championship in 1996. Favre also set the NFL career record for passing touchdowns (508), passing yards (71,838), completions (6,300)—and of course, interceptions (336).

While Favre and the Packers eventually had a messy divorce, his play on the field was second to none.

"What he accomplished in this league speaks for itself," said former Packers center Frank Winters. "What he accomplished is amazing."

Added Ruettgers, "To say I played with one of the all-time greats will be a pretty special thing."

A special thing that few would have predicted back in 1992.

"I feel fortunate that from Day 1, I knew how fortunate I was to play and get paid to play football," Favre said.

Certainly not as fortunate as Packer Nation was to watch Favre's magic.

LAMBEAU LEAP

The organic part of it was how the day started. When I got over to the stadium, I saw how cold it was and I was freaking out. I was from Florida and that was one of my coldest games. I've talked to people who went to that game and they still say that was one of their coldest games. I remember getting the turtlenecks and nylons and stuff to keep warm from the team. I said, "What are these for, our wives or something?" And one of the managers said, "No, no. Put them on and they'll keep you warm." I did, and it actually worked.

I remember when I got into the game, the quarterback for the Los Angeles Raiders was Vince Evans. He was a strong-armed quarterback and I remember this like it was yesterday. He threw a pass out to their tight end, Randy Jordan, and I hit him. And when I hit him, I felt the ball come loose. So Reggie White picked it up, though I didn't realize that Reggie had picked it up until I saw him and, I think it was Steve Wisniewski, struggling. At first, I thought they were just struggling for the ball, but Reggie was actually trying to run.

So what went through my head was that when Reggie played for Philadelphia, they pitched the ball all the time to guys like Eric Allen and Andre Waters. They always did that. I think Buddy Ryan encouraged it. And as I was running I was thinking, *Reggie's going to pitch that ball,* and we made eye contact. As he was falling he saw me running toward him, and right when he fell, he lateraled it to me.

When I caught it I thought, *Oh, this is sweet!* I remember thinking that I wanted to do something that was pretty cool when I scored. And as I was going down there, I saw this guy with this fluorescent orange on. It was deer season, although it always seems like it's deer

The Lambeau Leap—this one following an interception return for a touchdown against the Bears in 1995.

season in Wisconsin. And I just remember him having something in his hand, which I later learned was a beer. He had to make a decision to catch me or keep his beer.

Now, I was catching everybody off-guard. They didn't know what I was going to do. Normally when a guy scores, he either spikes it or goes to the referee and gives him the ball. You never interact with the fans. But me, it was like, *I'm going to jump*. So when I threw the ball down and ran over to the fans, they didn't know what I was doing. They probably thought I was going to high-five them. And as I got closer, something said, *Jump! Jump!* And as I jumped, I remember that guy having to make a decision and he threw that beer. He caught me, and I remember him yelling in my ear, "You owe me a beer!"

It hadn't dawned on me what happened until I went to the sidelines. Brett Favre and Doug Evans came out screaming. They said, "Man, what did you just do?" It was just so cool. Coach Holmgren was laughing and I just remember later, that's all people talked about. We blew the Raiders out that day and we were all talking about it in the locker room after the game.

And over the following eight to 12 months, fans started to name it. We had a contest to name what I just did and Lambeau Leap won. The media kind of wanted me to name it and I said, "No, no, no, it ain't about me. It's about the fans."

But what I loved about it was it proved that you don't need 50-yard-line seats. You don't even want 50-yard-line seats. You can't catch your favorite player at the 50-yard line. I meet people all the time who say, "I caught Donald Driver" or "I caught Ahman Green" and that's pretty awesome.

Before then, you didn't want end zone seats because when things were happening on the other end you couldn't always see what was going on. But the anticipation when your team is coming toward you and a guy may jump in your section, the adrenaline I've heard from fans is unbelievable.

I met a lady and her favorite player is Jordy Nelson and he was running toward her and he jumped up there. And she told me she thought to herself, *Thank God for LeRoy Butler. I would have never touched Jordy Nelson if it wasn't for that.*

And after it all ended, Reggie asked me how I knew to come toward him and get that ball, and I told him how I remembered seeing them in Philly and how they pitched the ball all the time. They had a middle linebacker back then named Byron Evans who did that all the time with Reggie. And Reggie said, "You're right. We used to practice that."

And that was the play, for him to lateral it to me. And to have that connection with Reggie is pretty cool, especially after he came to the Packers. That's one of his most memorable plays he ever had. He told me that. Other than the Super Bowl when he had three sacks, he said that was one of his most memorable plays. Because without him, the Lambeau Leap would have never started.

And I think I did it three more times after that. I know I did one after we beat Carolina in the 1996 NFC Championship Game and we were all jumping in. I also did it one time when we beat San Diego in 1996 after I scored a 90-yard touchdown.

But the cool thing was fans stopped caring about 50-yard-line seats. They wanted to be in the north or south end zone so they could catch a player, and it was just awesome.

1995 NFC Divisional Playoffs

We had a meeting with the coaches to get the game plan and stuff. And I remember saying to myself after that initial meeting that these are the smartest guys I've ever worked with. I always thought that I was the most brilliant guy in the world, but they took this thing to another level. Coach Holmgren was on his game that week. Oh man!

I remember coming in, and when you get the game plan, there's almost a level of excitement. It's kind of like waiting in line for the best roller coaster.

So we get the game plan about 9:30 AM. We had a team meeting about 9:00 and Fritz Shurmur came in and he had this big smile on his face. Now keep in mind, Fritz never smiled. And he said, "Guys, we're going to have fun this week. We're going to do something a little different this week."

I said, "Uh oh." Because every time we decided to do something different I was involved.

So he came and put up this defense that we had never seen. We'd heard about it, but we hadn't seen it. And he put this defense up and said, "We're going to play a little 3-4." I looked around and said, "What the hell. Is he reading my mind?" I loved that because any time you drop eight people you confuse the quarterback.

But San Francisco, they were practicing for our 4-3. We had the best front four in the world. And he drew up these plays that to me should go down in history because he confused San Francisco so much.

It was easy for us because it simplified things. Wayne Simmons, his job was to destroy the tight end. That's it. That's your job. If you get a holding call, so what! And back then, the referee wouldn't call jack. Back then, if I had to cover the tight end, I'd be out of the game plan. But this was a game plan where I didn't have to cover the tight end, so I could free up and do eight-man fronts, blitzes, and things like that.

And we caught them so off-guard. I think it had to be the third quarter before they caught up and realized what we were doing. They saw that Sean Jones or Gilbert Brown or Santana Dotson were out of the game, but it still didn't resonate what we were doing. It looked like a nickel defense.

That's why I was so excited. I still get goose bumps now. That game plan, it looks like a nickel defense. It doesn't look like a traditional 3-4 because you'd see Reggie lined up in the wide-9, and in a 3-4 he should be in the 7-technique.

So I said, "How the hell is he going to make this work?" Not only did he make it work, he made it look to a quarterback, if you were in your cadence and you want to audible and you see four guys down, you assume it's a version of 4-3. And basically, we got after their butts.

What a 3-4 does is it puts everything in front of you and now you're coming downhill, attacking. A 4-3 with only three linebackers, we always felt like we were chasing because they had so many formations.

Steve Young, who's a good friend of mine, me and him have talked about this and in the three or four times we played them, I bet they gave us 50 to 60 formations. Jerry Rice in the backfield, they had him at Y, Z, and X. And we said, "You know what, I don't care where he lines up. We set our strength and we react."

So we told Craig Newsome that Rice was his guy. If he's in the backfield, who cares? They're not going to give him the ball. So he's going to come in motion and you go with him. And Craig followed him sometimes, just to confuse them and make them think we were in man. But we were playing Cover 2—which is a hard zone—and we were running with Jerry Rice. Any guy that moved we ran with him and that really confused them.

And if you think about it, this is where the West Coast offense started. No one was really able to do that. I mean, there were other defenses that played them tough. The Giants, for instance, always played them tough. But that day, we played them out of a 3-4 and no one was doing it at the time. Then you'd see me come down in the box to make an eight-man front and sitting in the box and Steve Young would be like, "Wait a minute. This is confusing." And they'd call timeout and stuff. Soon, they started saying, "LeRoy's just disguising. He's not going to come." But I did. I was all over the place that day.

A lot of people would think it'd be hard to learn that defense in just a few days. But it wasn't. It was new, so we were energetic. It was simple. It was, "Here's what you do."

We were almost going to play like a box-and-one or a triangle-and-two. We're going to take out Jerry Rice and the tight end. The tight end and the Z, which was Jerry Rice. We're taking them out. Everybody else we defend.

They were basically the Jerry Rice Show and they weren't going to run the ball. They wanted to throw the ball, so they weren't going to beat us with J.J. Stokes and some of those other guys.

That day, we went into it saying we needed two or three turnovers and we were going to hit them in the mouth. That's all. We weren't a physical team. We were a finesse team, but we were smart.

And that's what caught them by surprise; we usually weren't that physical. Wayne Simmons, he was just an enforcer that day. Every team needs a guy like that. When I got there, we had Tim Harris and before that they had Charles Martin. You need guys like that. Like in Minnesota, they had John Randle.

You need one guy on your team to just set the tone and that was Wayne. He was unreal that day. Fritz said, "You may not have a tackle, you may not get an assist, but who cares?" We just need you take the tight end so we can do some stuff with LeRoy. And he was so unselfish.

Then on offense, we threw two tight ends at them. We ran the ball to the weak side, which we never did. We ran a lot of screens and draws at them. Basically, we were running their offense, because we had a version of it that we were going to send Antonio deep every now and then off a play-action. Usually he'd stop on a deep comeback, but this time we let him keep going and outrun those guys. Throw it up to him or Robert, next thing you know Chmura is wide open.

But that was a great game plan. I don't ever think I saw a game plan like that. It was fun. It was a great plane ride going back.

THE SAN DIEGO GAME

There was a game in 1996 against San Diego that I remember like it was yesterday.

San Diego had that kid, Terrell Fletcher that played at the University of Wisconsin. And that little guy was a nightmare to cover. I remember before the game, they told me if he ran this one particular route, I had to cover him by myself. I was like, "Okay." Because on first and second down I played safety. On third down, I would come up and cover the third or fourth receiver. But they didn't do that. He was their back out of the backfield and he ran what was called a "Texas" route. You run hard to the flat and you cut back inside. And we ran the same play, but not out of a nickel look.

And I remember trusting myself. Stan Humphries was the quarterback and I recognized that route right away. When he took off to the flat, something told me he was running the Texas route. Then it comes down to believing in yourself. Because throughout all the film study, he's never just took off to the flat. So I thought, *He ain't going to no flat. That's the old banana in the tail pipe. I ain't going for it.*

So I took steps like I was going and Humphries could see my name on my jersey. If he could see my name, then he thinks I'm going to the flat because my back was to him.

But when I opened up, I saw him releasing the ball out of the corner of my eye and I came back and it was right there. I was quick as a cat. Oh man. I was a hiccup. When I got to that ball, I was so happy that I trusted myself. And when I was running it back, Humphries started running and taking an angle. Most quarterbacks want you to cut back and the other people get you. And I remember having the speed to outrun him and the last 35 yards I was just showboating, acting like a weirdo.

I remember being so happy with my film study and my studying overall. Sometimes you just don't pull the trigger. You think you know what's coming, but you don't do it. But not only did I pull the trigger, I hit the target.

Sometimes it's like a boxer. You train and you train, then just go box and trust your instincts. You've just got to trust that your overhand right is going to work, but you've got to pull the trigger. And I just said I'm going to pull the trigger and it worked.

And to score, oh man, that was unbelievable. I never heard a crowd that loud. That was one of the loudest times I've ever heard a crowd. That was a sick game. I remember being so proud of myself, I almost broke my arm patting myself on the back.

SUPER BOWL XXXI

The thing about a Bill Parcells coached team is we knew they'd be a physical team that loved to run the ball and loved play action, and that they'd have a quarterback that doesn't make a lot of mistakes. They won't take a lot of chances, but if you can get ahead you've got them right where you want them.

They'd never seen a team like us, a team with so many things going, so many moving parts. The last time a defense was No. 1 and an offense was No. 1 at the same time was us. They were going into a buzzsaw. And not to mention, we had one of the best special teams players ever and he wound up being the MVP. So we felt like we could wear them down with all those parts.

They jumped out on us and they hurt us in the first half. But in the second half, we flip-flopped Reggie and we put a linebacker on tight end Ben Coates and I started blitzing off the weak side. It was so easy to predict when I was just following Coates around.

So they turned me loose and I got one of the most memorable plays of my life. I was coming off the offensive left, defensive right, and running back Dave Meggett came over to block me. So they were in max protection. And I remember Reggie saying, "Just because a guy blocks you doesn't mean you can't get home."

And the leverage of me picking him up and keeping my feet moving is one thing I remember. And what I did then is illegal now, it was like a horse collar. I grabbed Drew Bledsoe, who's 6′5″, and Dave Meggett was still trying to block me, holding on, and my momentum pulled Bledsoe down.

Here I am jumping up on Reggie White's shoulders after the big man sacked Bledsoe in the Super Bowl.

A lot of people don't know it but I tore my biceps on that play. But I barely even noticed. I got up and I remember thinking, *I did something in the Super Bowl, the cameras were on me, and all 40 or 50 million people were watching me at that second.* And that was one of my most memorable plays. Ever. Ever.

Reggie had a great second half, too. He had three sacks, and I was yelling at him saying, "You been loafing, man. What are you doing? We need to get some pressure. We want some picks." And he started laughing.

But Reggie started putting that club on right tackle Max Lane and boy oh boy, Bledsoe couldn't look downfield because every time he looked downfield Reggie was at his knees. Now you can't tackle a guy low like Reggie was doing that night. But I knew we had them at that point. I said, "Guys, we got 'em now."

After we won, I remember seeing the trophy and all the finger prints on it, and that was really cool. And then I was doing a press conference and it was sitting there and I was like, *Man, this is so great.*

It made me reflect on my childhood, where I came from: African American, single-parent home, from the projects, having braces on my legs and being in a wheelchair, then winning a Super Bowl. That was the pinnacle of my life. And I just remember thinking, *How do you celebrate after you've been to the mountaintop? Do you jump off or do you walk back down and start over, or what?*

And we went into the locker room and Coach Holmgren gave one of the most memorable speeches. Just paraphrasing, he said: This trophy means a lot to everybody who wins it. But it means more to you because it's named the Lombardi Trophy. You deserve it more than any other team. The trophy has come home after 30 years.

I'll never forget that. We all looked around and I remember thinking that we should do this again! This is cool. This is so cool.

After the game, most of the guys went back for the parade, which I heard was unbelievable. But I had to go to Hawaii for the Pro Bowl, and Dave Meggett was on my flight. There were four or five New England guys and four or five of our guys on the flight.

I remember getting to Hawaii and seeing the parade and how cold it was, and I was in 87 degree weather, I was like, "I think I'm good where I am." But the people that went to that parade, the fans and players, it looked awesome. What an organization.

Those people went through some tough times, the '70s, '80s, and early '90s. But I was there at the right time. And that Super Bowl experience was just awesome.

Super Bowl XXXII

We always threw it a lot and the game plan was to come out firing and use running the ball as a changeup. They were going to give up the run to stop the pass. They figured if they could stop Brett and Antonio Freeman and Mark Chmura they might have a chance.

But we did not play well that night. It may have been a combination of arrogance and some other things. We were so good, but we had some missing pieces, too.

Man, we had a stacked team, but when defensive end Gabe Wilkins got hurt, we weren't big enough up front. They just ran away from Reggie and split me out with Shannon Sharpe. I stayed with Sharpe that whole game. I don't ever remember blitzing that game, and that was the game plan.

And that was the game plan for two or three years that they'd give me five, six, seven blitzes. That's to disrupt stuff. But they didn't want to put anybody else on Sharpe.

The year before, we dealt with Ben Coates, who was like 6'5", but wasn't a real fast guy. So we could put another guy on him and go after Drew Bledsoe. But Shannon Sharpe could run and that was a good matchup for me and him. I had some good tackles in that game, but the big plays just weren't there.

And even in John Elway's book, he said the whole week their game plan was to stop LeRoy Butler. Not Reggie White. If they could eliminate LeRoy Butler, Mike Shanahan said they had a good chance of winning that game.

So they split Shannon out and got me out of the box and I had to go down with Shannon and they ran the ball into the "A" and the "B" gaps. There was one time I stayed in the box and Tyrone Williams went out there and they threw it right to Shannon for 13 yards. And we said, "Oh boy. What do we do?"

But going into the fourth quarter, we still had an opportunity. And then late in the game, it was tied at 24, and we were faced with the ultimate decision. We could let them kneel down and kick a field goal with no time left, and they would win it that way, or we could let them score with about two minutes left and give our offense a chance.

And they weren't stopping our offense. We were doing everything we wanted to do on offense. The defense lost that game. So we thought we could score on them and thought that was our best chance.

We had a timeout and went to the sidelines and talked about it. And we said, right now they can just run the ball in the middle of the field or kneel down, then kick a field goal and the game will end. So if they line up in a formation and run the ball, let them score. We even called the offensive guys down there and asked them about it. So Brett knew about it, everybody knew about it.

So I went back out to the field and I said, "We're going to let them score." And that was the right move. No question it was the right move. Terrell Davis went and scored and we got excited. All right, now we've got a chance. We didn't have a chance before, but now we do. I'll always believe that was the right move.

And we're driving down and it almost worked. We felt like if we went to overtime with these guys, we'd win the game. Momentum had switched. They were a very good football team, but the talent on our team was starting to wear them down. And boy I tell you what, when they scored, I had no doubts. I didn't even think twice that we were going to win.

After that loss in Dallas in '95 was probably the lowest locker room I've ever sat in, because we had them; we were better than them. But this was the second lowest.

It was a good game, but at the same time, we just felt like, if Gabe would have been healthy and if we would have ran the ball more and if we had a different game plan after halftime, if we would have just kept me blitzing and done some more disruptive stuff because the

West Coast is all based on timing, we could have beat them by 21 points.

I think it's human nature to get a little bit complacent. We just dominated an entire season with the No. 1 defense, the No. 1 offense, and we had the majority of our team coming back.

I remember saying before the season that we'd go 19–0. Who was going to beat us? I sat down with a reporter before the season for a joke and went through the schedule and I went "Win, win, win, win, win!" Damn right. I don't think they'll ever be another player who would do that.

And then that really got blown up. And somebody asked me after, "Were you misquoted? Was that out of context?" And I said, "I don't even know what that shit means. I told them we were going 19–0 and I told them how were going to do it."

And if you look at that year, we were close. We lost some close games and some terrible games. We lost to 0–10 Indianapolis. We lost by a point in Philadelphia. I mean it was close. The losses we had, we shouldn't have lost those games. We should have been undefeated. And then we lost to Detroit, and they weren't that good. Like I said, though, Herman Moore was my best friend in the league, so that one hurt.

Overall that was a great year, we just didn't get it done. We should have won back-to-back. That will always bother me that we didn't win two straight. We had three or four years in there, from 1995 to 1998, where I thought we were the best team in the NFL. And we should have won more than one Super Bowl.

FREEMAN: THE CATCH

Antonio Freeman ranks sixth in Green Bay Packers history with 431 receptions. Freeman's 57 touchdown catches as a Packer rank fourth in team history.

And for a four-year window in the late 1990s, Freeman was as dangerous as any receiver in the NFL not named Jerry Rice.

But when Packer Nation remembers Freeman, they all fondly reflect on November 6, 2000. That's when Freeman produced the "Monday Night Miracle," a play that will be discussed around Green Bay for generations to come.

On that night, Freeman hauled in a miraculous 43-yard touchdown that gave the Packers an improbable 26–20 overtime win over heavily favored Minnesota. On the game-winning play, Minnesota's Cris Dishman appeared to have a sure-fire interception, then the ball seemed to hit the ground, which is where Freeman was lying.

But somehow Freeman hauled it in, then raced home for one of the biggest catches of his career. ESPN later labeled the catch as the greatest play in the history of *Monday Night Football*.

"Antonio Freeman with one of the greatest catches I've ever seen," Packers quarterback Brett Favre said of the play.

That's for sure.

Minnesota entered the game with a 7–1 record, while the Packers were just 3–5. The Vikings were also $3^1/_2$-point favorites that night.

But the Packers played one of their more spirited games of the year and took the Vikings to overtime, thanks largely to a 5–0 advantage in the turnover department.

Antonio Freeman leaps in his teammates' arms after his spectacular circus catch beat the Vikings in overtime on Monday night, November 6, 2000.

Green Bay won the coin toss and drove to the Minnesota 43, where it faced a third-and-4. Minnesota blitzed six, forcing Favre to throw off his back foot and get rid of the ball in just 1.59 seconds.

Favre took a shot deep down the right sideline for Freeman, who was working one-on-one against Dishman, a better-than-average cornerback. Freeman slipped and fell to the ground on a field that had been getting pelted with rain. That gave Dishman a clear shot at an interception.

Dishman had inside position on Freeman and the ball hit his right hand first. It then caromed off his left hand and appeared to fall incomplete.

In fact, the *Monday Night Football* audience heard this call from play-by-play man Al Michaels.

"Favre puts it up for Freeman and it's incomplete," Michaels said.

Hardly.

When Dishman hit the ball the second time, it ricocheted toward Freeman, who was lying facedown on the ground. The ball hit Freeman's left shoulder, and as he spun back around, the ball bounced up and he somehow managed to get his right hand underneath it.

Dishman was certain the pass was incomplete and he jumped around, five yards behind Freeman, stewing over his failed interception. Freeman knew the ball was still alive, though, and leapt to his feet after he had secured it.

"It was a lucky, lucky play," Freeman said. "But I knew that ball never hit the ground."

After Freeman rose up, he eluded safety Robert Griffith at the 14-yard line, then raced to the end zone for one of the most improbable touchdowns you'll ever see.

"It's the craziest catch I ever made," Freeman said. "Brett [Favre] could throw that pass my way 100 times, 1,000 times, and the way that ball ended up bouncing won't happen more than once. A 'Monday Night Miracle' I guess."

The play was reviewed and upheld, marking the only time all night Green Bay held the lead. Afterward, Freeman received the hero's treatment and was carried off the field by his teammates.

"As I rolled back, I got an early Christmas gift, I guess," Freeman said. "Hey, who said football was all skill?"

While the bounce was certainly lucky, the hook-up itself was premeditated.

Freeman was supposed to run a slant route, but when he noticed Dishman didn't have any safety help, he got Favre's attention.

"I was just standing there waiting and I heard, 'Brett,'" Favre said afterward. "I knew it was Free. When I looked out he kind of gave me the signal and I kind of nodded my head.

"Your star player wants the ball, give it to him. He made the play. I don't even know if you can call it a play. That was remarkable, unbelievable."

Mike Sherman—who was in his first year as Green Bay's head coach—certainly agreed.

"The ball was thrown and it was like I saw it in slow motion," Sherman said. "The whole time I thought he was going to catch that football. I don't know why I thought that, but I did. It was certainly a play that fans will always remember, as will I."

Freeman, who spent eight of his nine NFL seasons in Green Bay, had several memorable moments as a Packer.

He caught an 81-yard touchdown pass in Super Bowl XXXI, helping the Packers topple New England 35–21. Freeman also had two touchdown catches in Green Bay's Super Bowl loss to Denver the following season.

Freeman led the NFL in receiving yards in 1998. And he topped the Packers in receptions four straight years between 1996 and 1999.

But Freeman's version of the Immaculate Reception is something that Packers fans will remember for years to come.

"If that's what you're going to be remembered for, that's not a bad thing," said Freeman, who was inducted into the Packer Hall of Fame in 2009. "I know I'll never forget that play."

Neither will Packer Nation.

The End of the Road

It ended against Atlanta in 2001 when I was trying to tackle a guy most people didn't know too much about. His name was Maurice Smith. I'd made that hit a million times before.

The first thing that stands out is Cletidus Hunt lined up wrong and that made my angle different. And when I made that hit I knew that something was wrong because it didn't feel right. But I knew my shoulder wasn't responding. It was just limp. And I remember Doc looking at it and saying how bad it was.

I immediately knew I wouldn't be able to play again. I knew that because you've got to wrap up and that's not something I could do. Once I saw the X-rays, I knew it was over. I had a great career, but I knew it was over.

Even if I was 25, that injury probably would have knocked me out. Because the only injury they found close to that was people in car crashes. That was a pretty horrific injury.

I probably had a couple of years left. I had already started talking to (head coach Mike) Sherman about it. I said I wanted to play a couple more years. He said, "Okay, as long as you're still competitive, I have no problem with it."

I wasn't playing at my 1996 level, but I was still starting and playing pretty good. I was still grading out pretty good. We had talked about my last year, me being a backup and coming in on nickel. We had already talked about it.

That's why I valued Sherman so much as a coach. We talked about retirement before it was time to retire. So when it happens, no one's shocked, no one's forcing anybody out. You just know when it hits your time, we agreed how we'd handle it.

And that's a good way to do it. You don't have the player saying, "I still want to play," and the team saying, "Well, we need to move in another direction." See, me and Mike already had that. We sat down and talked about it. And that probably doesn't happen much. Either the team gets rid of you, or you do like Ray Lewis and just retire.

But it was a great ride. At first, I had friends like Emmitt Smith and Deion Sanders winning Super Bowls and I said, "Before I leave, I've got to get me a Super Bowl." And I did that.

And, you know, I'm glad I stayed a Green Bay Packer. I'm very proud of that. Very, very proud of that. All of my football cards are green and gold. Not a lot of guys did that, and not a lot of guys play 12 years.

Guys just don't stay in one place anymore. Look at Peyton Manning and Brett Favre. I mean, Aaron Rodgers might end up playing somewhere else. That's just the nature of the beast.

Look, when they took Rodgers, Brett was still in his prime. In 2007, Brett had one of his best seasons. He showed no flashes of diminishing. So when does Green Bay take a quarterback again and start grooming him to replace Rodgers? Because Rodgers is going to have a fit when that all starts to happen.

But as for me, I'm just glad I got to play there all 12 years. It was a great place to be. The fans were unbelievable to me. I can't say enough about the fans.

And you can't get a better organization than ours. For a guy who had braces on his legs, was in a wheelchair and looked out the window watching other kids play football, it's all like a dream. It really is.

I was treated very, very well by the fans. Kind of like royalty and a rock star all in one. But my mom always taught me to be a people person and that's how I always was.

I always did my thing, but I wasn't a party guy. I didn't drink and didn't smoke. I didn't do anything weird. I was naturally a weirdo, so I didn't need any of that other stuff.

Then I always mingled with the fans. If you mingle with the fans, the fans will protect you. The only time I wouldn't do a lot of the stuff was when I was with my kids because they require a lot of attention. But if I'm by myself, hey man, we can talk. I don't have a problem with that.

Because you can't have it both ways. You can't tell someone you want them to buy your jersey and then blow them off. But you also have to draw a line and hope that fans respect your privacy. We are normal people, too.

I never had an issue when I was in Green Bay. I went everywhere. I'd go out to eat, go to Wal-Mart, just tried to be a normal person. But they all accepted me. And when I told them where I lived and I told them Wisconsin, they're shocked because I used to live in Florida.

I used to have a house in Florida, but I spent 90 percent of my time up here. I tried to be a normal guy. I always tried to be a normal guy. It's still hard for me to accept being a celebrity. It's sometimes embarrassing, because I want to be a normal guy so bad. But you can't always have it both ways.

Most guys don't understand and don't accept that. They don't really like dealing with the fans. They don't want to do that stuff. You've got to be accessible yet approachable, and relax and enjoy your success, enjoy being a Packer. That's why you've got to try and do normal stuff. Although you're a celebrity, don't work so hard at trying to be one. It better be organic for you.

You can be a guy on the practice squad, and it's, "Oh, he's a Packer." There are a lot of people that didn't see me play, but their parents and grandparents have told them about me. We're doing something a lot of people want to do and would love to do and you have to accept that and enjoy that and that's what I've always done. Just have fun with it.

THE MONDAY NIGHT
OAKLAND GAME

Javon Walker knew he could play 1,000 more football games and he'd never experience anything like it.

"It was a magical night," Walker said.

Wesley Walls was part of a Super Bowl championship team and an endless stream of enormous games. But Green Bay's trip to Oakland in 2003 will always remain among his most memorable.

"Someone was watching down on us," Walls said. "I fully believe that."

That someone may have been Irvin Favre.

And with a little help from above, Irvin's son—the courageous and indestructible Brett Favre—gave the performance of his lifetime.

On December 21, 2003, Irv had a heart attack and died. The next day, the Packers—in the middle of a fight to reach the playoffs—were playing in Oakland.

Most figured that Favre, who had played in 204 consecutive games, would sit this one out. But Favre did what he always did: he played.

And oh my, how he played.

Favre threw for four touchdowns and 399 yards and led the Packers to an unforgettable 41–7 win over Oakland on *Monday Night Football*. NFL Network recently voted this the No. 1 game of Favre's magnificent career.

"I knew that my dad would have wanted me to play," Favre said. "I love him so much, and I love this game. It's meant a great deal to me, to my dad, to my family, and I didn't expect this kind of performance. But I know he was watching tonight."

Favre played in 277 games during his 16 years in Green Bay, including the playoffs. But his passer rating of 154.9 that night was the best of his Packers career and remains No. 1 in team history.

Not only did Favre shine one day after his father's death. He did so in the "Black Hole," where Oakland's boisterous crowd did everything it could to rattle Favre.

"I've never seen a leader or a player like Brett in my career, and I'm pretty sure that nobody else in this locker room has," Walls said. "I think we wanted to make him proud. Just getting up in front of the team at such a horrible and difficult time in his life really showed he cared about us. That was something I'll never forget."

Favre gave a performance that night that was truly unforgettable. Favre was razor sharp throughout, but his receivers were equally brilliant.

"We had a meeting with the receiving corps and made a pact that whatever he put up, we were going to come down with," Packers wideout Robert Ferguson said. "We rallied around our leader."

They sure did.

On just Green Bay's fourth play from scrimmage, Ferguson held up his end of the bargain with a sensational 47-yard grab. Two plays later, Walls snared a 22-yard TD pass in the back of the end zone on a play that appeared to have little chance of success.

"He played an amazing game for us, and we all felt we had to do the same for him," Walls said. "Sometimes in special circumstances, you make special plays. I think it's fair to say we were inspired by Irv."

Favre hummed a gorgeous 23-yard touchdown pass to Walker later in the first quarter. Favre also lofted a 43-yard TD strike to Walker when the standout receiver outmuscled Raiders defensive backs Phillip Buchanon and Anthony Dorsett for the ball.

Favre later hit Walker with a 46-yard completion, then capped that drive with a six-yard TD pass to tight end David Martin shortly before halftime.

Favre completed his first nine passes and threw for a personal-best 311 yards and four TDs in the first half alone. He also finished the first half with a perfect passer rating of 158.3.

"What he had to deal with was immeasurable," wideout Antonio Freeman said. "You can't put a price on what he did. I don't know how he did it, but he did it in fine fashion."

Green Bay stayed in contention for a playoff berth that night in Oakland. And the Packers qualified for the postseason the following week when Arizona stunned Minnesota in the final seconds to give the Packers the NFC North Division title.

But that wasn't the most important thing taking place.

"We needed this win to stay in the playoff hunt," Packers coach Mike Sherman said. "But we certainly needed this win for Brett Favre. He handles adversity extremely well. His focus and concentration on this game was extraordinary."

If there was such a thing as divine intervention, Favre was becoming a believer.

"I've been around people who have lost a family member or lost someone close to them and they say that that person's there watching, or angels, or whatever," Favre said. "And I would say that two weeks ago I didn't really believe in that. But I think we'd better start believing in something."

That night in Oakland, Favre gave plenty of people something to believe in.

BELATED CHRISTMAS

It was one of the loudest roars in the history of Lambeau Field. And amazingly, the Packers' faithful weren't cheering for anything taking place in Green Bay.

It was December 28, 2003, and Green Bay was well on its way to a 31–3 destruction of Denver in its regular season finale. That gave the Packers four straight wins and a 10–6 record.

But hated rival Minnesota appeared well on its way to matching that record, which would have given the Vikings the NFC North Division title. Amazingly, though, a little-known receiver from Arizona named Nathan Poole played Santa Claus for Packer Nation.

Minnesota led Arizona 17–12, and the Cardinals had a chance for one final play. There, Arizona quarterback Josh McCown found Poole open in the back corner of the end zone and hit him for a 28-yard touchdown as time expired.

Instead of going to the playoffs, the Vikings went home. And just like that, the Packers went from being on the outside of the postseason party to division champs.

"This is like Christmas, New Years, everything combined into one, baby," safety Marques Anderson proclaimed afterward in a joyous Green Bay locker room.

Tennessee had its Music City Miracle. Pittsburgh had the Immaculate Reception.

In Green Bay, the 2003 season will always be remembered for its Belated Christmas.

"It must be Christmas on December 28th," added linebacker Hannibal Navies. "Someone's looking down on us, man."

The ending capped one of the most dramatic weekends in team history, one in which the Packers' playoff fate was in the hands of several other teams. Eventually, Arizona was Green Bay's last hope—and the Cardinals delivered.

"Our game was pretty much won, and I turned around and looked at our fans and they were going crazy," Packers quarterback Brett Favre said. "All of a sudden there was just a loud roar that just kind of continued, and I guess that was as Arizona had gotten close.

"And then it kind of quieted down. As I found out, there were a couple of sacks or something. And then the roll-out at the end. It was an unbelievable feeling to see our fans and players and everyone just kind of seize the moment."

For much of this wild weekend, it appeared the Packers' season would fall short of the playoffs.

Green Bay was hoping Seattle would lose to San Francisco, but that didn't happen. Later, when New Orleans defeated Dallas, it meant the Packers would lose a tiebreaker to the Cowboys and Seahawks.

Now, the Packers' only hope to reach the playoffs was to win and have Minnesota—a $7\frac{1}{2}$ point favorite—lose to Arizona.

"All the playoff scenarios and everything, I really didn't pay too much attention to those," right tackle Mark Tauscher said. "I just knew coming in we needed to win."

Sherman wanted his team completely focused, so he didn't allow the Vikings score to be posted on any of the scoreboards inside the stadium. But many fans inside Lambeau switched their radios to the Vikings game, which was being carried locally. Others tried watching on televisions inside the club seats. Remember, this was during the pre-smartphone era.

"We didn't really know what was going on," Green Bay wide receiver Antonio Freeman said. "We just figured something good was happening when the crowd was cheering."

Down the stretch, there was plenty to cheer about.

Green Bay running back Ahman Green broke off a 98-yard touchdown run ensuring a Packers win. And in Arizona, the Cardinals were rallying from a 17–6 deficit.

On a fourth-and-goal play with just two minutes remaining, McCown hit tight end Steve Bush for a two-yard touchdown to pull the Cardinals within five at 17–12. Then the ensuing onside kick was recovered by Arizona's Damien Anderson.

McCown was sacked on back-to-back plays, though, and Arizona had just one play left from Minnesota's 28-yard line. McCown took the final snap with just four seconds left on the clock, then avoided trouble by rolling to his right.

McCown found the little-used Poole in the right corner of the end-zone and he made a spectacular grab. Poole got one foot down, then was pushed out of bounds by Minnesota's Denard Walker and Brian Russell.

Green Bay radio announcers Wayne Larrivee and Larry McCarren had started broadcasting the Vikings game, as well. And although Sherman had done all he could to prevent the score from being known, the Lambeau Field crowd erupted at precisely the same time Poole made his game-winning catch.

"We knew he took it off the board," running back Tony Fisher said of Sherman. "But basically you just paid attention to the crowd. And when you saw the crowd erupting, you knew something good was happening."

Poole's touchdown was under review. And after much deliberation, it was ruled he was forced out of bounds while making the catch and the play stood.

The Vikings had officially lost. The Packers had won the NFC North and were in the postseason.

"I had no idea what was going on and it was mad confusion," right guard Marco Rivera said. "Then I saw the crowd react and I thought, *What the hell's wrong with the crowd? The game's not going on. Is there a fight over there?*

"Then I finally asked [director of football administration] Bruce Warwick and he said, 'Oh my God! Arizona just scored.' It was unbelievable. We were in the playoffs."

Favre raised his arms into the sky, then teared up. Sherman was doused with a bucket of water. And Lambeau Field became bedlam.

Green Bay's locker room was also mass hysteria. Players whooped it up, exchanged hugs, and signed memorabilia for each other.

"It was mass hysteria, man," Packers linebacker Hannibal Navies said. "There were people running around with hats and dancing. It was something you can't even describe. It was such an exciting experience and I've never been part of anything like that."

Poole became a folk hero in Green Bay and was invited to the Packers' wild-card game with Seattle the following weekend. He was also given a grand tour of the city by Green Bay's mayor.

"Oh, we've got to get him something," wideout Donald Driver said of Poole. "As a receiving corps, we got to take care of him. That cat saved our season."

And capped one of the more incredible afternoons in team history.

Trash Talking

I could talk.

We were playing the Broncos in 1996 and I told their backup quarterback Bill Musgrave, "I dare you to throw the ball to Shannon Sharpe. I double dare you." He looked at me like, *I'm not Elway.* And I said, "You better not throw it there." I told him that the whole game.

There was one year we were playing the Rams and they had a young quarterback named Tony Banks. I wasn't miked up. They didn't start miking me up until later in my career. I told him, "I'm going to throw your ass down, pick the ball up, and step on your damn chest." And he looked at me like, *Why are saying all this to me? I'm just a kid.*

The offensive linemen would always be yelling at me, telling me to shut up or they'd find me. And I'd just run behind Gilbert Brown and say, "Yeah, come on over here and say that." And Gilbert would say, "What are you doing making these guys all mad?"

And I remember the San Diego game in 1996. I intercepted a ball and I told Stan Humphries, "You going to end your career, son, if you keep throwing it in my direction. Now stop doing that now." I was offended he was even throwing in my direction. And like four plays later I picked him off and he came over and called me an A-hole. I said, "The damage is done." I actually really liked Humphries, but I told him not to throw it my way.

I remember when we went to San Diego in '93 and I picked off a pass from Humphries over my shoulder. I was talking so much trash I was actually tired. But I never ran out steam. That was just me, especially after a big win. You talk, talk, talk, and eventually you go to sleep. But not me. I was still up talking.

I'd tell our own guys, "Man, if you guys could tie up a few more blockers, I'd have a lot more sacks. You guys are holding me back. What the hell are you guys doing?" It was just so much fun.

Coach Holmgren thought I was very entertaining. When they put him in the Packer Hall of Fame he talked about how I was one of his favorite players. I used to always talk a lot. Florida State, growing up, even back to high school, I always talked, but I could back it up.

I used to take a lot of crap coming back, too. One time (Minnesota's) Cris Carter, who talked a lot, came back and cracked me and said, "I bet you'll be quiet now." And I yelled at him and said, "I'll find a way to get you back. Don't worry. I'll get you back." I started yelling, "I'll get you when you cross the middle when you're not looking. You better have your head on a swivel."

So then I started waving my hand in front of my face and I was yelling, "I'm going to get you." He was in the huddle looking back the whole game. He was laughing. It was funny. Just part of the game.

Running Mates

My best friend was Edgar Bennett. We played high school ball together, then college, and were always really tight. Edgar was almost like being with your brother. His family and my family knew each other. And when the Packers selected him, I think I was happier than he was. I really was. I told him, "You're following me wherever I go."

He was such a breath of fresh air. Real smart guy. And we were always together. Off the field we'd always get together. And even when we weren't together and I'd go places with my family, I'd see him. It was almost like we were always thinking the same thing.

But if I wanted to go out, hang out, go to the club, Gilbert Brown was my guy. Gilbert Brown, not only was he protective of you, he was the one guy that wouldn't let you do something stupid. I didn't drink, smoke, any of that stuff. So I didn't fit in with some of those guys. But everybody thought I was funny so they'd want me around.

But Gilbert would always make sure that if we were out, no one would do anything stupid. There were no bar fights. No scandals. And this is before social media. But even today, in the world of social media, I'd still go out because I knew how to behave. I knew how to act. I'm not going to be there with two blondes sitting on my lap, kissing them, taking my shirt off and swinging it around like a fool. I always just sat down, minded my own business, and relaxed.

There are too many guys when they get that alcohol in them, they change. A lot of guys do. Now you're the big man on campus. Now they're going to go fight the bouncer. Now they're going to jump in their car and go 100 miles an hour. So I was never like that and Gilbert was there and he made sure nothing too crazy ever happened. We'd just have fun, relax; just kind of be out with the boys. If Gilbert even saw something that was goofy, he'd go squash it. And I really enjoyed that because not everyone has the sense to do that.

But if we're going to go and have some fun now, just lay back, laugh all night, eat a lot of food, come in like 3:30, 4:00 in the morning—which I really enjoyed—attract a lot of women and have a lot of fun, then I'm going to hang out with Brett Favre, Dorsey Levens, Mark Chmura and Frank Winters. That's the group I'm calling and I called them quite a bit.

I said, "We're going to Milwaukee," and I begged their wives to let them go. Dorsey was single and we had us some fun. So if I wanted to have a really good time, that's my group. And when it was time to go, Frank would whistle and we'd go. We're not getting in any trouble. Let's go home. But to feel like you're the man, that's my group.

Because every girl in the world would chase Dorsey Levens. Oh man, if you wanted to feel like a star, these were the guys. And we weren't ever doing anything illegal, we weren't getting in trouble. Actually, it was surprising that kind of stuff wasn't going on because there were so many people that used to be around us.

Being with Brett, you never had to wait in line. That's why we always had to get Favre to come out with us. That's the one thing we got him for. If there was a line around the corner at a place, some of those bouncers would be on a big power trip. Oh, you're the big-time Packers, I ain't letting you in.

But the quarterback, we needed him to get in these clubs. Brett was fun all the time. And then when we had him along, there was never any standing in line. Sometimes he wouldn't even want to go and I'd say, "Man, you've got to come and get us in, dog." So we'd make him come.

I remember there was a time we got somewhere and they wouldn't let us in with tennis shoes. And I told the guy, "I don't think Brett even has a pair of hard shoes." And the guy said, "You got Favre with you?" I said, "Yeah man, we got the quarterback. Two-time MVP," and this guy's asking me about tennis shoes. Let us in the damn club.

Then there was Chewy, who was the best-looking guy on our team for five years. You darn right he was. Chewy wouldn't even talk most of the time. We could never get him to do anything. He was one of the most reserved guys on our team. He'd laugh most of the time, but Chewy was just very reserved.

Me and Frank, we'd go back and serve drinks to people, high-five the fans; fun stuff, you know. And we'd keep the people off of Brett, like we were his bodyguards. Then Dorsey had like 55, 60 women around him, just waiting in line for a chance to say hello.

And we always went to Milwaukee. We'd go downtown. There was a lot going on. Today I go there and a lot of those places we used to go are gone now. But back in the day it was something. I get emotional just thinking about it and how much fun we had.

My thing was that I wanted to have some fun, get out, and party. Monday was the big night because we had Tuesday off, and me and Brett had a TV show in Milwaukee on Monday nights. My big thing was that I didn't want to go with anybody that was going to get in trouble.

I didn't want to go with anybody that was grabbing girls. I didn't want to be with anybody that was smoking or getting out of control from their drinking. I want *men* to go with me. So I hand-chose those guys. That was the group I wanted to hang with.

Now back then, we never brought any bodyguards and it wouldn't be like that today. If you're going to roll with that level now, you'd need them. If you were by yourself, you could probably sneak in and sneak out okay. But if you'd have four, five guys like we did, you'd have to have bodyguards. There's no way around it, because there's always going to be some guy to challenge you.

But we didn't have to go through that because people were so much in awe of us that they would never challenge us. They just wanted to hang out with us. In the mid-'90s we were the Beatles here. You darn right. And if you didn't know it we made you aware of it.

And we never had to pay. Brett was frugal anyhow. He never carried any money. Smart guy. But when Brett was around, we never paid for anything. Free drinks. Whatever we wanted. Whatever we needed.

But you don't understand how many people hated that, too. Guys at these clubs knew that all the girls would be coming toward us and they all hated that. There were some that didn't want to give us free anything. Bartenders would charge you double. I'd order a Shirley Temple and the guy would charge me $10 just because he was jealous. He was mad and just hating on us.

But when Brett was around, it changed everything. Guys would be like, "We're not worthy."

Now, there's a huge misconception about Brett getting crazy and doing wild things. I've never seen that man act like a fool. I've seen guys jump on bars. I've seen guys get like 10 shots in a row, set them all on fire and throw them all back. I've seen guys rip girls' tops off or go in the bathroom with them or go take a girl back to their room or out to their car.

But Brett never did any of that dumb stuff. He realized who he was. That stuff about him was all reputation, but it wasn't true. If one person said that, it seemed to spread. Every time I was with him, he never got out of hand. It was a real head-scratcher wondering where all that stuff about Brett came from. I was with him a lot of times, almost all the time, and I never saw him act like a fool. Never.

I had heard this stuff about Brett and Chewy and Frank womanizing. That's so far away from the truth. These were very respectable guys, because I wouldn't be with them if it was true; I'm scared of the police. These guys were stars and they acted like stars. And this is the reason I really liked those guys: when the club closed, we'd leave. We didn't hang around and get arrested like some other fools. We're grown men. And we also knew we had practice in a couple days.

These guys were great for this community, and to be honest with you, they helped the economy. Because if people knew we weren't coming, they weren't going to go to some of those places. We'd let the club owner know we were coming down, then word of mouth would spread and people would know. And sometimes we'd take a risk and just go to Milwaukee and hope we'd see a guy. But if there was a party or something, we'd tell the promoter we're coming down and they'd sell it out. We'd go there, have some fun, and go home.

This is not L.A. This is not New York. If this were L.A. or New York, maybe things would have been different because there would be five times as many women, five times as many clubs, five times as many guys to challenge you. Everything would be intensified. But this was Milwaukee. It was our L.A., but it was nothing like the real L.A.

And it's good that none of the guys ever got into any scandals or anything like that. It was always just rumored stuff. I think some of the guys got a bad rap about some stuff that was going on. I used to come back and scratch my head.

I would hear people say, "Oh, I saw Brett out and he was drunk," and I'd say, "Brett was with me. He was at my kids' softball game." So some of this stuff gets crazy. It's all rumor and once those get going, you can't stop them.

But Brett and those guys understood all that. Brett would be like, "Whatever." But I loved that group. We were so close. We took care of each other and had ourselves a lot of fun. Great group.

The Future

I have four daughters, and there's two things I've always said: I wish I had a son, and I wish I had a chance to coach. Well I got my son recently, but I still haven't got a chance to coach.

What's disappointing about it is I know so many people in the football industry and I still haven't had an opportunity to coach. And I think a lot of it is things like doing books and being on the radio, they think I'm too close to the media. But I don't think there are many guys coaching right now, especially defense, that have more knowledge than me. I just haven't gotten the opportunity.

There may also be a perception that I wouldn't start from the bottom and work my way up. Not only would I do that, I would take any opportunity I could. I just wish somebody would talk to me about it. They would see my passion for it.

The only guy I feel that fully valued my career as a possible coach was Mike Sherman. And when he got fired, that slammed that door. He understood me. He knew I'd only talk to the media when they told me to talk to the media, just like all the other coaches.

I look at some of these teams like New Orleans. They had the worst secondary in NFL history in 2012, giving up 300 yards a game. I know I can do a lot better than any of those guys.

I'd be willing to start at quality control, watching tape and working my way up. I just want the opportunity, and right now, that's been disappointing. It really is. Guys that I thought were friends of mine that are in a position to hire, especially at the GM level, haven't gotten back to me. And that's disappointing.

I always wanted to coach in Green Bay, but I know I'm not Ted Thompson's kind of guy. He wants more quiet, stay-out-of-the-media guys. He wants one voice. But it's disappointing that he thinks that about me without ever even talking to me about it. Some guys don't even want to be bothered with Green Bay, just because of where it is. Then you've got a guy like me trying to get in because I love the organization so much.

But with somebody like Ted Thompson, he doesn't care about that stuff. And to be honest, what really bothers me is when I see other organizations do stuff for their former players and Green Bay doesn't really do that. Some guys might see that as being sour grapes or bitter. But it's not like that at all.

All Ted, or somebody else, would have to do is tell me how they want me to be inside their organization. Give me the task and I'll do it. Just let me know what it is you want.

Up until recently, Green Bay was the only team I'd work for. But now, I'd move in a heartbeat. I just hope I get the chance to coach someday because I'd really like to share all the knowledge I have of football. I have such a passion for football and would love to share it with other people.

I see a lot of guys with no experience get an opportunity, guys that have never coached before. But coaches take care of coaches.

When I was a player, I took things to another level. I worked it. I wanted to learn things, like the West Coast offense, that other people didn't want to learn. And on top of that, I know how to communicate with players to help get them to that next level.

Right now, it's just almost like looking in the window at a shiny new bike and you think you're never going to get it. That's how you feel, like you're never going to get that bike.

I'm never going to give up my passion for football and for coaching. Just talking with guys and breaking down plays. Forget about the media and all that stuff. Just the coaching part of it is so exciting.

My dream of coaching in Green Bay is probably over. That would be a dream, but that dream is over. I know that ain't going to happen with Ted around. So I don't know what the best scenario would be.

I'd go and do scouting in a heartbeat. You dang right. But they don't associate me with being a scout. They say we need an underground guy to go and do that. But man, I'm just looking for a way back into an organization and get back into it again. It's my passion. That's what I want to do. And I think a team would be delighted once I get into it again.

A lot of players who want to coach eventually give up if they don't have any luck breaking in. But I'm not going to give up. If I could have my pick, I'd always pick Green Bay. That's where I'd love to be. I doubt that it would happen, but you never know. There were days when I was a kid I didn't think I'd ever walk. So you just hope for the best, I guess.

ABOUT THE AUTHORS

LeRoy Butler played defensive back for 12 seasons with the Green Bay Packers between 1990 and 2001. He was named to four Pro Bowls, as well as the NFL's 1990s All-Decade Team. He was a member of the Packers' Super Bowl XXXI squad, and is credited with inventing the Lambeau Leap after scoring a touchdown in 1993. He co-hosts *The Big Show* on WSSP-AM in Milwaukee.

Rob Reischel has covered the Green Bay Packers for the *Milwaukee Journal Sentinel*'s "Packer Plus" since 2001. He has received 12 awards from the Wisconsin Newspaper Association for his writing and editing, and he is the author of *100 Things Packers Fans Should Know & Do Before They Die, Aaron Rodgers: Leader of the Pack,* and *Packers Essential.*